CRITIQUE OF HEAVEN

Books by Arend Theodoor van Leeuwen

Development Through Revolution
Prophecy in a Technocratic Era
Christianity in World History

CRITIQUE OF HEAVEN

The first series of the Gifford Lectures entitled
"Critique of Heaven and Earth"

by

AREND Th. VAN LEEUWEN

*Associate Professor of Christian Social Ethics in the Catholic
University of Nijmegen, (Holland)*

CHARLES SCRIBNER'S SONS *New York*

Contents

		Page
	PREFACE	7
I	THE GENESIS OF KARL MARX'S CRITIQUE AS TRANSFORMATION OF THEOLOGY	9
II	ENTRANCE CARD INTO THE COMMUNITY OF EUROPEAN CULTURE	25
III	NEW GODS IN THE CENTRE OF THE EARTH	44
IV	HUMAN SELF-CONSCIOUSNESS AS THE HIGHEST DIVINITY	67
V	THE NATURAL SCIENCE OF SELF-CONSCIOUSNESS	87
VI	FROM PLATONISM TO CHRISTIANITY	108
VII	FROM THE VISIBLE HEAVEN TO THE UNSEALED WORD	126
VIII	CRITIQUE AS THE CONFESSOR OF HISTORY	145
IX	THE REALIZATION OF PHILOSOPHY	163
X	FROM THE CRITIQUE OF RELIGION TO THE CRITIQUE OF LAW	184

Preface

THIS book contains the first of the two series of Gifford Lectures which I have been invited to give at the University of Aberdeen, Scotland. This first series was given in the year, 1970. The second series, entitled "Critique of Earth", is to be given in the year, 1972.

Critique of Heaven and Earth is the over-all title of this Series of Lectures. My title may seem on first encounter slightly enigmatic, but it should be clear from the outset that my first series of Lectures will at any rate focus on a theological subject. "Heaven" has traditionally been held to be the main and, as has sometimes been falsely supposed, even the sole concern of theology. Conversely, many people have appeared to claim the earth for the non-theologians. My Lectures start from a different premise, namely, that the "critique of heaven" is a central task for theology, and that a "critique of earth" is its necessary corollary. On both levels theology can and should accomplish its essentially critical task.

I would be more inclined to call this kind of theology "critical theology" than "natural theology", but I am convinced that there is no essential contradiction between those terms. If the development of modern natural science is based on critical research and critical knowledge, then a theology similarly qualified as "natural" must present the same critical features. The interpretation given by Lord Gifford to the conditions laid down when the Lectureship was founded has impressed me by its profoundly critical implications. He directed that the Lecturers appointed should be subject "to no test of any kind and shall not be required to take any oath, or to subscribe any

6

declaration of belief, or to make any promise of any kind; they may be of any denomination whatever, or of no denomination at all (and many earnest and high-minded men prefer to belong to no ecclesiastical denomination); they may be of any religion or way of thinking, or as is sometimes said, they may be of no religion, or they be so-called sceptics or agnostics or freethinkers, provided only that the patrons will use diligence to secure that they be able reverent men, true thinkers, sincere lovers of and earnest inquirers after truth".

This description seems to have a remarkable relevance to the subject of my lectures. Though I am myself a convinced member of the Church and a committed theologian, I shall invite you in the following lectures to listen attentively to the voice of a man who belongs without any doubt to that group of thinkers whom Lord Gifford referred to as being of no religion or as being so-called sceptics or agnostics or freethinkers. It is my conviction that this man has a crucial contribution to make to what might be called a "natural theology" or as I would prefer to say, a "critical theology".

I hope in this way also to meet the expectation expressed in the letter with which I was invited to become a Gifford Lecturer: "We should certainly very much like to have as our lecturer a scholar from Holland, a country with which, in the past, Scotland has had close links." Only once before, in the years 1896–1898, has a Dutch scholar been elected a Gifford Lecturer. He was Cornelius Petrus Tiele, Professor of the History of Religions at Leyden University. The title of his lectures, delivered in Edinburgh, was "Elements of the science of religion". It has been my privilege to study at Leyden University myself and to have received my education in the history of religions there. However, although it is my intention to continue the tradition of which Professor Tiele has been such an eminent representative, there is a gap of more than seventy years, in other words, a gap of two generations between his age and ours. And what is even more important, the fateful occurrence of the Two World Wars, separating the end of the nineteenth century from the second half of the twentieth. It is to my way of thinking no longer feasible to pursue the science of religion without understanding the gulf which separates that pre-world war period from our own. As I shall hope to show, the revolutionary

7

break in the religious tradition was already there, in the middle of the nineteenth century; only we have tried, without success, to ignore or belittle its importance.

In conclusion I wish to express my sincere gratitude to the Senatus Academicus of the University of Aberdeen and especially Professor Edward M. Wright, Principal at that time, for inviting me to become a Gifford Lecturer. The privilege accorded to me was equalled by the generous hospitality I enjoyed during the weeks spent at the University. I cannot imagine my first steps to becoming an Aberdonian without the guidance of Professor John M. Graham, Dean of the Theological Faculty at that time, and of Professor David Cairns, of Christ's College. I would like to thank all those, especially the staff and the students of Crombie Hall, who made my life in Aberdeen a great pleasure.

Driebergen, February, 1972
A. TH. VAN LEEUWEN

Second Preface

A GENEROUS invitation of Union Theological Seminary, Richmond (Va.), gave me an opportunity to present and discuss part of the material contained in this volume for the James Sprunt Lectures of the year 1971. A glance at the list of lecturers over the past sixty years seems to suggest some special relationship between Richmond and Scotland, notably with the Universities of Aberdeen and Edinburgh. As one of the rare lecturers from the continent of Europe it was my privilege to confirm that tradition. I remember with warm gratitude the hospitality offered by the Seminary, President Fred R. Stair, Jr., and several members of the faculty. It is my sincere hope and expectation that the present volume may be accepted by Union Theological Seminary of Virginia as a presentation of the James Sprunt Lectures of the year 1971.

8

I

The genesis of Karl Marx's critique as transformation of theology

THERE is an age-old dilemma, almost as old as biblical theology and doubtless prior to the origins of Christian dogmatics. The dilemma concerns the question who is accountable for the fall of man. If the creation was subjected to futility, not of its own will but by the will of him who subjected it, by whose will has it been subjected? Was it the will of the serpent, the will of the woman, the will of her husband, or was it the will of the Creator?

It may reassure you to learn that this series of lectures will not deal with that desperate dilemma, let alone try to resolve it. The task I have set myself is an incomparably less pretentious one, though, to my way of thinking, still immodest enough. None the less, my main theme will recall the famous or notorious subject of theological dispute. We shall see that this affinity is more than just a question of accidental terminology, that it touches the heart of the matter.

The main theme, running through the lectures as a whole, I describe as a "Critique of heaven and earth". While the first series will be devoted to the "Critique of heaven", the "Critique of earth" I am reserving for the second series which is to follow, if not within a matter of days, at any rate within a measurable space of time. Those who infer from this interval that my theme is remote enough from Genesis, Chapter One, should at once be reassured when I say that it is still less my intention to bring the succession of the two series in line with that evolutionary

9

exegesis of the Creation story which interprets each of the creation-days as equivalent to a million years or so. But my belief in a more human measure of the creation-days may warrant a more human interval between my treatment of the "Critique of heaven" and the "Critique of earth".

Although these terms are not derived from any biblical phraseology, at least not directly, a tantalizing affinity here can hardly be denied. I am wondering whether some among my audience may not have shared with me this puzzling impression when comparing the following two texts. *The first is this:* "For the creation waits with eager longing for the revealing of the sons of God; for the creation was subjected to futility, not of its own will but by the will of him who subjected it; in hope, because the creation itself will be set free from its bondage to decay and obtain the glorious liberty of the children of God. We know that the whole creation has been groaning in travail together until now; and not only the creation, but we ourselves, who have the first fruits of the Spirit, groan inwardly as we wait for adoption as sons, the redemption of our bodies." *And the second:* "Religious distress is at the same time the expression of real distress and a protest against real distress. Religion is the sigh of the oppressed creature, the heart of a heartless world, just as it is the spirit of a spiritless situation. It is the opium of the people. The abolition of religion as the illusory happiness of the people is required for their real happiness. The demand to give up the illusions about its condition is the demand to give up a condition which needs illusions. The criticism of religion is therefore in embryo the criticism of the vale of woe, the halo of which is religion."

I will not try, at this moment, to analyse the strange mixture of resemblance and contradiction which is concealed in the relationship between the first text and the second one; nor is it the purpose of these lectures as a whole to attempt a solution of that particular riddle. The ambiguous nature of their affinity may be understood, however, as symptomatic of an underlying problem, which, indeed, has weighed with me in choosing the main theme, just as it will continue to be present in the background of my approach. It is surely unnecessary for me to point out that Paul's letter to the Romans, chapter 8, is the source of my first quotation. Identifying the second quotation seems no less superfluous, though for less sound reasons. For while the biblical source is in almost everybody's hands, and at least some phrases of Romans 8 as well as some general notion of Christian dogmatics in many people's heads, the only phrase in the second text that shares with the term "original sin" the ambiguous honour of an almost universal fame is the slogan "opium of the people". Along with the notion of "original sin", it is also subject to a ridiculous as well as tragic and dangerous misunderstanding, which often goes so far as to distort the phrase "opium of the people" into "opium for the people".

Familiarity with this slogan is apparently in inverse proportion to ignorance of its origin; and the drawback that this presents should not be overlooked. I, for one, have taken it as a challenge to devote a good part of this first series of lectures to a careful study of the sources, as it has likewise forced me to follow the texts in question literally and, when and where it seemed requisite, to introduce more or less extensive quotations in an English translation. In some circumstances this sort of procedure might seem cumbersome and heavy-handed; but where the phrase in question enjoys greater currency even than Hamlet's "To be, or not to be: that is the question", it is no less a simple matter of conscience to go back to the sources than it would be to analyse the literal wording of Shakespeare's tragedy.

I hope I may be allowed, therefore, to continue quoting from the source in question, up to the point where the main theme of these lectures makes its entry.

"Criticism has plucked the imaginary flowers from the chain not so that man will continue to wear the chain devoid of both illusion and consolation, but so that he will shake the chain off and cull the living flower. The criticism of religion disenchants man in order to make him think and act and shape his reality like one who has been disenchanted and has come to reason, so that he will revolve around himself and therefore around his true sun. Religion is the illusory sun which revolves around man only so long as he does not revolve around himself.

The task of history, therefore, once the world beyond the truth has disappeared, is to establish the truth of this world. The immediate task of philosophy, which is at the service of history, once the saintly form of human self-alienation has been unmasked, is to unmask self-alienation in its unholy forms. Thus the criticism of heaven is transmuted into the criticism of earth, the criticism of religion into the criticism of right and the criticism of theology into the criticism of politics."

The last sentence of this quotation is, indeed, the source from which the title of both series of lectures has been taken. The text which is generally considered to be the Magna Carta of the Marxist critique of religion forms part of Marx's *Introduction to a critique of Hegel's Philosophy of Law.* The article was published in 1844 in the *Deutsch-Französische Jahrbücher* (German-French Annals), a short-lived review edited in Paris, where Marx was living at that time. My quotation made use of the familiar English translation of the German original, which reads: *Die Kritik des Himmels verwandelt sich damit in die Kritik der Erde, die Kritik der Religion in die Kritik des Rechts, die Kritik der Theologie in die Kritik der Politik.* The term "criticism" used in the familiar English translation differs from the term "critique" used by the same translators in connection with the title *Critique of Hegel's Philosophy of Law.* This difference, probably to be explained as a peculiar feature of English idiom, might be inconsiderable, if it had not done vital harm to the German original. Apart from the fact that the German language does not know of such a difference, the identity of the term *Kritik* in each of these contexts is a premise of their adequate interpretation. An idiom which uses the term "critique" with reference to the philosophy of right and the term "criticism" with reference to right tends to obliterate the riddle which lies at the root of Marx's critique of religion. The full import of this must wait until I can explain it in my later lectures. At the moment, suffice it to refer to the sentence, immediately following the passage just quoted, in which Marx declares that the article *Contribution to the critique of Hegel's Philosophy of Law,* to which his present article serves only as an "Introduction", bears immediately not on the original but on a copy. In other words, he has to recognize that his critique of Hegel's philosophy of right is not the same as the critique of right, the necessity of which he has just been trying to demonstrate. The riddle concealed in this admission can be rightly understood only if and when we hold consistently to the German term *Kritik.*

There is yet another reason to prefer a consistent use, in English, of the term "critique". In nineteenth-century Germany the much favoured term *Kritik* could not possibly be used in philosophical writings without some account being taken of its basic function in Kant's critical philosophy. The meaning of Marx's critique has to be understood as arising out of this philosophical tradition. There is a certain parallelism between the succession of Kant's *Critique of Pure Reason*, followed by his *Critique of Practical Reason* and Marx's transition from theory to practice. The critique of religion and philosophy which pre-occupied Marx's mind during his earlier period and the critique of political economy which absorbed the rest of his life are rooted in a joint apperception of the essence and meaning of critique. In an article written during the period when he was conceiving his critique of Hegel's philosophy of right, Marx had recognized Kant's philosophy as the German theory of the French Revolution, as contrasted with the historical school of right, which he characterized as the German theory of the French *Ancien Régime*. Though Kant's name is not mentioned in Marx's *Introduction to a critique of Hegel's Philosophy of Law,* this remark, committed to writing a year before, can serve as a key to its interpretation. The article is, basically, a devastating critique of the anachronism of the German state of affairs in 1843, which had not yet arrived at a stage equivalent to that of French history in the year 1789. It ends by looking forward expectantly to the German day of resurrection, which will be proclaimed by the crowing of the Cock of Gaul. On closer analysis we can see, under the surface, two fundamental principles which Kant had formulated in the years before the French Revolution. Kant's famous "Copernican revolution", formulated in 1787 in the Preface to the second edition of his *Critique of Pure Reason,* is taken up in the passage, quoted above, which describes religion as the illusory sun which revolves around man until he learns to revolve around himself, having been disillusioned and brought to a sense of reality by the critique of religion. Subsequently, the transition of the theoretical critique into praxis pivots round the basic principle of Kant's critique of practical reason, the equally famous "categorical imperative". "The critique of religion ends with the teaching that man is the highest essence for man, hence with the categorical imperative to overthrow all relations in which man is a debased, enslaved, abandoned, despicable essence."

13

All this will, I hope, be taken as sufficient defence of my preference for the term "critique" in the title of these lectures. Without expressing any prejudgment on the question of a material relationship between the philosophies of Kant and Marx, it is my sole intention here to stress a formal parallelism where the key-function of the term "critique" is concerned.

The immediate scope of this first series is limited to a relatively narrow field of interest. Rather than take my title from something that Marx wrote, and then use it for my own purposes, I have taken Marx's pronouncement quite seriously and have set myself the task of investigating its meaning and genesis with all the care I can muster. The difference here might be compared to that between a sermon and an exegesis based on textual criticism. Without denying the useful function of the sermon, I share the judgment of those theologians who stress the necessity for biblical exegesis as a prerequisite for trustworthy evangelism. The principle is fundamentally the same when applied to the work of an outstanding thinker or artist. One century of Marxism has already deluged mankind with Marxist, pseudo-Marxist or anti-Marxist sermons that have one feature in common, in that they have exempted themselves from the duty to study the text and to undertake exegesis of the context.

Marx's article entitled *Introduction to a critique of Hegel's Philosophy of Law* could be regarded as a turning-point in his life and thought. Written in the year 1844, it was, in a sense, the confession of an emigrant who had just left his fatherland, his familiar social and cultural milieu, and was on his way to a new world of which he expected Paris to be the new capital. In the evolution of his thinking the article represented a transition from a critical philosophy to a critique of political economy. It was an attempt to reap the harvest of his formative years and at the same time contained the seed of his maturity. Therefore, adopting the main theme of my lectures from this article, I have deliberately taken up my position at a key-point from which a wider outlook on Marx's life and thought as a whole may be expected. As observed from that vantage-point, the present series of lectures on the "critique of heaven" will, so to speak, proffer a retrospective view, whilst the prospective view will be reserved for the second series. And whilst the latter, as a matter of course, will range beyond the limits of Marx's career as far as our own time, the *terminus a quo* for our retrospective view can be exactly defined.

Marx's formative period can be said, roughly speaking, to cover ten years. The beginning of that decade coincides with the start of his academic studies in Bonn and Berlin, 1835/36, whereas *The German Ideology*, written in 1845/46, is to be regarded as a definitive attempt to settle his account with the philosophical milieu to which he owed the formation of his ideas. Subsequent lectures will give priority to the beginnings of this formative period and devote particular attention to the first writings, dating between 1835 and 1841.

The earliest writings of Marx still extant are the compositions he was obliged to present for the finals of the Gymnasium in Trier. Three of these papers, dealing with subjects related to his personal prospects, to his religious and his classical education, afford us an insight into the thought of his adolescence. The first academic years are represented by a collection of poems and fragments of other literary essays; and the well-known letter to his father is rightly considered to be a biographical document of crucial importance. The doctoral dissertation, completed in March 1841, is the mature fruit of his later academic years in Berlin; it laid the foundation for his philosophical development as that was to take shape in the years to follow.

There are good reasons why this group of very early writings deserve special attention. To begin with an external consideration, these writings may be safely assumed to belong to the least known part of Marx's *œuvre*. This is even the case in Germany, where these sources have been an object of special study for several decades past. To mention only one product of recent research, the study by Gunther Hillmann (1966) attempts an interpretation of these earliest compositions by means of a detailed comparison with parallel parts of Hegel's writings. While the subject is difficult enough in itself, this comparative procedure is an additional handicap for reaching a wider circle of interested readers. However, this limited familiarity as far as the German language area is concerned, is far ahead of anything the English language area can boast. A good part of these sources, as far as my knowledge goes, is only accessible through selective quotations in English studies on Marx. The least incomplete English translation of the doctoral dissertation has been undertaken by Norman Livergood, who published it as an Appendix to his study on *Activity in Marx's Philosophy* (1967). Apart from a few misinterpretations of the German text, this translation is trustworthy: but the Notes, as well as the Appendix on Plutarch's polemic against Epicurus' theology, have been omitted. A much graver omission concerns the manuscript of Marx's preparatory studies, the importance of which as a source of interpretation of the dissertation proper could hardly be overrated. What is announced by the author as the first complete English translation of the dissertation represents in reality, therefore, only part of the work. These considerations have induced me to give considerable attention to these sources. Thanks to Livergood, I have been able to rely on an existing translation, at least as far as the actual dissertation is concerned.

These external considerations may serve to account for the amount of attention I have felt obliged to give to the verbatim text of these earliest writings; but the intensity of my interest is due to more essential reasons. While studying the sources, I became increasingly aware of just how crucial they are for the proper interpretation of our main theme. They reveal an underlying consistency in the evolution of Marx's thinking which, like the initial theme of a symphony, continues to run through the whole course of his life, thinking and career, from his youth on. Still more important, these earliest writings allow us to trace the genesis of Marx's inner struggle, which he was afterwards to present as the necessity for a critique of heaven.

It is often supposed that Marx received the decisive stimulus for his critique of religion from Feuerbach. Another widespread prejudice has to do with his relationship to the Christian faith. Unlike his later friend, Friedrich Engels, who grew up in a pietistic milieu and passed through a genuine counter-conversion, Marx is traditionally believed to have been devoid from the very outset of anything like deep emotions regarding Christianity. This impression has doubtless been corroborated by Franz Mehring's almost classical biography, which tones down or neglects any features in the earlier writings that might point in this direction. As will become clear enough as these lectures proceed, a study of the sources has intensified my scepticism about this traditional image. I would even be inclined to suggest that Marx's early development conceals a deep-rooted dilemma very close to the heart of the Christian dilemma in a post-Christian civilization. While a relatively extrovert character and simplicity of mind enabled Friedrich Engels to settle his account with Christianity, the genesis of Karl Marx's critique of religion suggests a depth of penetration which forces the Christian faith to an unprecedented confrontation with its own situation. Marx's writings dating from the period before his friendship with Engels and before the publication of Feuerbach's *The Essence of Christianity* reveal a genuine sensitivity to this crucial dilemma.

The doctoral dissertation, then, is not only a prerequisite for the interpretation of Marx's subsequent philosophical development, but contains his first and most purely philosophical definition of the inner contradictions inherent in the critique of heaven. This academic work shows the author patiently at work in the laboratory of European civilization, peering through his microscope, so to speak, in the hope of discovering the key to the history of Greek philosophy. In order to unravel the enigma of his own position in the contemporary historical situation, he begins to delve into an apparently remote past, and is naturally bound to strike the roots of European culture.

I have called Marx's essay *Introduction to a critique of Hegel's Philosophy of Law* a turning-point in his life and thought. It is, indeed, also against the background of this essay that the wider perspective of this series on the "critique of heaven" can be outlined. The fact that this is Marx's first writing to introduce the term "proletariat" and deal with its unique place in universal history, is in itself an indication of its key-function in his development. Indeed, the subsequent lectures will focus on the period leading up to this key-point and will deal with Marx's writings of the following two years only in so far as they belong to this formative period. In other words, I shall be dealing exclusively with the so-called "young Marx", leaving aside the "mature and older Marx" for examination in my second series of lectures.

The fact that I have divided my main theme into two subthemes and that this distinction coincides more or less with a chronological distinction in Marx's career, will perhaps be taken to indicate that I recognize the truth and rightness of distinguishing between the "young Marx" on one hand and the "mature Marx" on the other. But at the same time by setting this distinction under the comprehensive approach of the main theme, which brings the sub-themes together in the indivisible "critique of heaven and earth", I have from the very outset made it plain that I do *not* believe it right to transform that distinction into some kind of contrast. The essential point of Marx's critique lies in the unbreakable interconnection between his critique of heaven and his critique of earth. To be sure, the problem is not one peculiar to Marx, but has a fairly general significance. I will mention, in passing, two historical examples comparable in more than one respect with the problem presented by Marx's career: the final word has certainly not been said either about the distinction between the "young Muhammad" and the "mature Muhammad" or about that between the "young Luther" and the "mature Luther". In a sense, the problem could be extended to include the evaluation of historical movements. One might well wonder whether the crucial problem of Church history, arising out of the evolution of a "primitive Christianity" into a "mature Christianity", is essentially different.

As far as the study of Marx is concerned, a variety of circumstances have endowed the issue with some very peculiar features. One such circumstance is connected with the relatively late publication, partly even with the rather late discovery, of some of Marx's most important early writings. I simply mention the fact that the complete texts of his dissertation and his *Critique of Hegel's Philosophy of Law* were not published in German until 1927, and his *Economic and Philosophical Manuscripts* not until 1932. The publication of the original texts had been preceded by publication in a Russian translation.

It is part of the irony or tragedy of history that free discussion of these early writings became impossible during the thirties, in both Stalin's Russia and Hitler's Germany. It was during this period that in France the discovery of the "young Marx" became so intense and widespread a leaven in philosophical reflection that French philosophy since that time is hardly imaginable without some element of Marxist reflection in it. In a quite different form from that which Marx intended or could foretell, his prophecy has come true—that the day of German resurrection would be proclaimed by the crowing of the cock of Gaul. In one sense, such reflection and discussion in France have continued their pioneering rôle up to the present day. I need only mention, on one hand, the cross-fertilization between Marxism and Existentialism and, on the other hand, the increasing importance of Structuralism for the interpretation of Marx's philosophy. It is no accident that the discussions which have been carried on, for instance, between two prominent Marxist philosophers, Roger Garaudy and Louis Althusser, on the validity of the socialist humanism, are closely related to their evaluation of the young Marx.

France was also the country where already before the second world war a communist political leader, Maurice Thorez, had invited Roman Catholic Christians to enter into dialogue. The initiative has been renewed in the course of the sixties by the *Centre d'Études et de Recherches marxistes*. This Marxist study-centre used the celebration of the fourth centenary of John Calvin's death (1964) as occasion for inviting the Protestant Christians to engage in discussion based on one of Marx's pronouncements: "Luther shattered faith in authority because he restored the authority of faith." Once again, it was no accident that the text was derived from Marx's *Introduction to a critique of Hegel's Philosophy of Law*; for this essay could be regarded as in a sense the Magna Carta of the Marxist renaissance as well as of the Marxist-Christian dialogue.

It is impossible, within the framework of this first series of lectures, to describe the development of the Marxist renaissance and of the Marxist-Christian dialogue during the last two decades. I must content myself with a few remarks. My first one concerns the range, geographically speaking, of these developments. The Marxist renaissance and the Marxist-Christian dialogue have assumed international dimensions which not only embrace both sides of a divided Europe but reach as far as the two Americas and Japan. A second feature is the critical attitude which may be regarded as the backbone of these developments. It is a critical Marxism, on the one side, that embarks upon a dialogue with, on the other, a critical Catholicism and a critical Protestantism and, let it be added, with a critical Eastern Orthodoxy. "Critique" might well be thought to epitomize the style and aims of the discussions and arguments. It is the critics on the various sides who meet one another; and it all depends on the situation to what extent the critics of today may prove to be the "heretics" of tomorrow.

A third feature is closely connected with the two above-mentioned, namely, the emergence of what might be described as "the coming ecumenism". What I have in mind is the prospect of a secular *oikoumene* which sees the reconciliation and renewal of a divided Christianity within the wider perspective of overcoming the antagonism between Christian dogmatism and atheist dogmatism and within the broader framework of the unity and renewal of humanity. I, for one, do not believe in any kind of "new reformation" which, to mention only one example, does not take Ernst Bloch's *Das Prinzip Hoffnung* as seriously as Jürgen Moltmann's *Theologie der Hoffnung*; nor do I see any real prospects of a radical renewal of theology except in the direction of what is sometimes defined as *Politische Theologie*.

I have deliberately quoted these terms in German. Since a broader discussion of Marx's *Introduction to a critique of Hegel's Philosophy of Law* is to follow in my second series of lectures on the "critique of earth", I must content myself with stressing the fact that this essay focuses on Germany. It could rightly be described as a paramount example of "Germanocentrism"; it is obsessed with the German question. Its last utterance is the almost eschatological promise of "the German day of resurrection". Written in 1844 by a German exile living in Paris, "the new capital of a new world", as a contribution to the *German-French Annals*, the document centres on Marx's obsession with Germany's deficiency which, so to speak, has accumulated all the sins of all state forms. Exactly one century after these words were written, the Germans' Holy Empire, embodied in Hitler's Third Reich, had with a devilish precision fulfilled Karl Marx's prophecy in the hell of Auschwitz and of the many other concentration camps scattered across Europe. Indeed, Germany will not be able "to overthrow the specific German limitations without overthrowing the general limitation of the political present".

But "the German day of resurrection" is still ahead. It is no accident, therefore, that Ernst Bloch, a German Marxist philosopher who as a Jew was first exiled from Hitler's Germany and would be exiled again from Walter Ulbricht's Germany of the sixties, wrote during his war-time sojourn in the United States that great work *Das Prinzip Hoffnung*. Nor is it accidental that its Christian counterpart, which tries to transpose Ernst Bloch's principle into the terms of a "theology of hope", has been conceived by a German Protestant theologian, Moltmann, just as its translation into terms of a "political theology" is being attempted by a German Roman Catholic theologian, Johann Baptist Metz. Another symptomatic pointer is the fact that, as early as the beginning of the fifties, in Germany the Marxist-Christian dialogue was already being prepared by the *Marxismus-Kommission der Evangelische Studiengemeinschaft*, which has continued its series of *Marxismus-Studien* up to the present day. Again, one should notice that a number of other initiatives of international importance, such as the Marxist-Christian encounters under the auspices of the *"Paulus-Gesellschaft"* and the reviews *"Neues Forum"* and *"Internationale Dialog Zeitschrift"*, were also born in Germany or in Austria.

The Marxist-Christian dialogue has not simply fallen out of the blue, but is emerging at a particular juncture of modern history. If the dialogue has any meaning at all, it is the historical encounter of a Christian "theology after Auschwitz" with a Marxist "philosophy after Stalin". For as Christian theology faces a radical break at the point where it is confronted with the abysmal riddle of how Germany's Holy Roman Empire and Germany's Reformation could finally bring forth Adolf Hitler, so Marxist philosophy faces its doomsday in the abysmal riddle of how it was that Karl Marx's humanism could finally produce Joseph Stalin. Theology today is theology after the death of the God of the Emperor Charles the Fifth and of Martin Luther, just as Marxism today is philosophy after the death of the atheist "god that failed".

What we are facing today is the manifestation of a judgment which in the middle of the nineteenth century was only visible to the *clairvoyant* insight of a few prophetic minds. Karl Löwith, in his book *From Hegel to Nietzsche*, has described this judgment as the revolutionary break in nineteenth-century thinking. It was the break between an age-old Christian and a coming post-Christian civilization. Karl Marx was one of the few thinkers who had the radicality of insight and the merciless courage to discover that still concealed revolutionary break and to draw the necessary consequences. His contemporary, Sören Kierkegaard, drew consequences that were different but no less radical. Just as both thinkers have played a prophetic rôle in the history of modern philosophy, so both can be regarded as theologians. The difference is only that, while Kierkegaard's place in philosophy is generally recognized, conversely, Marx is rarely acknowledged to be a theologian.

To give just one outstanding example, the reader of Karl Barth's *Die protestantische Theologie im 19. Jahrhundert* (from Rousseau to Ritschl) will look in vain for the name of Karl Marx, not only in the table of contents but in the index of that book. His name is simply not there—despite the prominent place given to Hegel in the "prehistory" and in spite of the attention paid in the "history" of nineteenth-century theology to Strauss and Feuerbach. In the chapter on Feuerbach, Karl Barth has not omitted the names of Bruno Bauer and Max Stirner, that is, of the two Young Hegelian philosophers with whom Marx was most closely connected and who became his fiercest antagonists. Therefore, the omission of Karl Marx's name cannot be explained as accident or neglect; there must have been a deeper reason for it. If Feuerbach, Strauss, Bauer and Stirner have a place in the history of theology, then it is unreasonable to deny a place to Karl Marx.

The reason why Karl Barth did so has to be sought, I suppose, in his being faced with an insoluble dilemma. Or, to put it better, the dilemma is insoluble within the traditional framework of "theology" and of the "history of theology" which, for all his radicality, was still maintained and, in a sense, even reinforced, by the greatest theologian of our century. Inserting Karl Marx in the history of modern theology would, in fact, have revolutionized the whole notion of theology. I have the impression that Karl Barth sensed that dilemma and did not know how to resolve it. He cut the Gordian knot and followed the familiar Christian tack by simply leaving Marx out altogether.

A name which he could not and did not want to omit was

22

that of Hegel, although he obscures Hegel's function somewhat by making him the last significant figure in the "prehistory" of nineteenth-century theology. The root of the dilemma lies, in fact, in Hegel's own philosophy; for it was Hegel who not only claimed to fulfil the history of Christian theology but who finally transformed theology into philosophy, and vice versa.

That transformation exhibits an extremely ambivalent character, in both directions. From a theological point of view, it can be interpreted as the culmination of a *theologia gloriae*; and it is particularly in the writings of the mature Hegel that this tendency is embodied. Marx had been the pupil of the mature Hegel; and his critical relationship to the master hinges on his radical critique of this tendency. There is a strange parallelism between the fate of Hegel's writings and those of Marx. Just as the discovery of the "young Marx" has had to wait for our century, so has that of the "young Hegel" too. It is of great importance that a tendency which has more and more diminished in Hegel's mature writings is to be found in the young Hegel: on the one hand, it is the tendency to carry on philosophy as a very concrete reflection on contemporary socio-political history. On the other hand, it is the peculiar feature of his theological reflection as reflection on the Old Testament, particularly on the "Abrahamite" structure of Israel's history, and, as far as the New Testament is concerned, the character of his reflection as a *theologia crucis*. Both features together are to be found in a famous passage, written by the young Hegel in 1802, when he was living in Jena. The passage describes the feeling that God Himself is dead *(das Gefühl; Gott selbst ist tot)* as the feeling of infinite grief that underlies the religion of modern times. The absolute Passion or the speculative Good Friday which was once historical *(den spekulativen Charfreitag, der sonst historisch war)* must be restored in the stone-hard truth of its godlessness. It is only out of this stone-hard truth that the philosophical idea of absolute freedom, the supreme totality, can and will arise.

Marx did not know this passage, but he had a thorough knowledge of Hegel's *The Phenomenology of Mind*. The last chapter of his *Economic and Philosophical Manuscripts* of 1844 contains Marx's *Critique of Hegel's Dialectic and Philosophy as a Whole*, which is devoted to the last chapter of Hegel's *The*

Phenomenology of Mind, entitled "Absolute Knowledge". The preceding chapter of *The Phenomenology of Mind* is entitled "Religion"; its last paragraph, entitled "Revealed Religion", contains a passage closely akin to the passage above-mentioned, which Hegel had written five years earlier. This passage also relates "the grievous feeling of the contrite consciousness, that God Himself has died" to "the death of the Mediator". Hegel takes up this thought in the last chapter on "Absolute Knowledge". The final sentence of this chapter understands history as "the Golgotha (place of a skull) of absolute Mind, the reality, truth and certainty of its throne". With this reference *The Phenomenology of Mind* closes. It reads like a final affirmation of the christological structure of Hegel's philosophy.

Marx's vehement protest against Hegel's concept of "absolute knowledge" is not directed against the dialectical method of his philosophy, but against its speculative character. In Hegel's terminology, the feeling that God Himself is dead, the feeling which underlies the religion of modern times, is present in the inner recesses of Marx's thinking. Marx's protest is directed against Hegel's concept of resurrection, which is only a speculative resurrection, a spiritual victory over death, a throne erected in the mind. If God Himself has died, then His death is an earthly reality, just as resurrection is an earthly reality.

It is this thoroughly earthy character of Marx's philosophy which it is difficult for traditional theology to absorb. Nevertheless, not only in its origin but in its very structure Marx's philosophy has a profoundly theological character. Theology will not recognize, let alone accept, Marx as a theologian, until it has recognized theology in the presentation of a critique of theology. And it will not acknowledge Marx's critique of heaven until it has acknowledged this critique as a necessary critique of earth. If the confession of the Creator of heaven and earth is the first article of the primitive Christian Creed, then the "critique of heaven and earth" might be added as its "thirteenth article". We might do well to ask ourselves whether this "thirteenth article" which has, so to speak, been untimely born, is not destined to become the first article and cornerstone of a critical theology yet to come.

2

Entrance card into the community of European culture

THE earliest extant writings of Karl Marx are a number of essays which he wrote in August 1835, at the age of seventeen, as obligatory papers for his finals at the high school in Trier. Three of them are of lasting interest, in that they give us an insight into his state of mind at the end of his schooldays. The school is, in a sense, a concentrated course in civilization. Within the narrow limits of a dozen years, the child and adolescent are introduced to the accumulated experience of the civilization into which they have been born. The school system incorporates received ideas about the past and present of a particular civilization. The school selects those values which that civilization wants to hand on to the next generation; thus it reflects the expectations of a society, as well as its prospects for the immediate future.

The fact that Marx was educated at a German Gymnasium (or "high school") left an indelible mark on his thinking, not only in adolescence but for the remainder of his life. To that circumstance he owed an intimate relationship to the tradition of ancient Greece, especially to the heritage of classical Greek philosophy, of Greek political life and thought of Greek mythology and the art of the great tragedians. The Gymnasium of his day was patterned on a neo-humanistic type of education, focused upon the classical Greek view of man and world. A central feature of Marx's thinking, his deep longing for totality, is characteristic of the humanist idealism which he absorbed during his adolescent years. Neo-humanist idealism projected on to classical Greek culture and society the notion of an organic unity of body and soul, nature and spirit, sensory perception and abstract thought. Its educational ideal was the universal, harmonious development of all human capacities, as over against the philistinism that had emerged from a popularized Enlightenment and in contrast with the increasing differentiation and specialization of modern civilization.

The papers which Marx had to produce for those final examinations are as typical of the style of education he had enjoyed as of the way he had absorbed it. One such paper is the so-called German essay, entitled "Reflections of a youth before choosing a profession". Another is the essay on a religious subject, dealing with a passage from the Gospel according to John. The Latin essay, which was the third paper, deals with the Roman principate of Augustus. I shall first describe and try to interpret these papers: and then we shall consider them in their reciprocal relationship.

Despite its obligatory character, the German essay, which deals with problems regarding the choice of a profession, has a remarkable depth and maturity. Its reflections are developed within a broad philosophical framework. It takes up a theme which in subsequent years was to loom large in the background of Marx's thinking: the theme of man's uniqueness *vis-à-vis* the animal kingdom. Nature has assigned to the animal a special domain of activity in which it is content to live, undisturbed by any yearning for, or any notion of, a beyond. The general goal allocated to man by the Godhead is the purpose of working for the ennoblement of mankind and for his own perfection. But the Godhead left it to man's own ingenuity to seek the means by which to achieve this goal and to choose the adequate social standpoint for his own benefit and for the benefit of society as a whole.

These opening sentences contain, of course, certain familiar ideas inherited from the Enlightenment—so familiar that they could have been written in the eighteenth century. But Marx elaborates this general theme in a special way, so that the germs of his personal philosophy are already detectable in these reflections. The contrast between man and animal turns out to depend upon a theological distinction, the distinction between "the Godhead" and "nature". In opposition to the animal species, which is part of the realm of nature, man is related to the Godhead. The distinction is described more fully as the contrast between a linear and a circular movement. The animal species has a natural *Wirkungskreis,* a "circle of activity". Its life moves within the limitations of a hermetically sealed world which embraces the totality of its consciousness and its strivings.

Man is quite different, since his existence is not determined by nature but by the Godhead. His realm is not closed, his activity is not imprisoned within a circular movement: man has a goal, received as a gift from the Godhead, a goal which, to his mind's eye, lies beyond the horizons of a linear and unretraceable road, the road to his final destiny. That goal is his ennoblement, his perfection: the perfection of mankind and the perfection of man "himself". In this respect, too, man and animal are basically different. The animal is only a species: any distinction between the animal "itself" and the animal as a species would be pointless, since self-consciousness is a peculiar quality of man.

The term "Godhead" has a deistic background; significant in this respect is the close relationship between the Godhead and the ultimate goal of history, the goal of mankind as a whole and of every individual human being. The "Godhead" is the gentle leader and paternal guide of man towards his perfection. Whereas the life of the animal species is blindly determined by its natural instinct, man has received his free will. The Godhead has only determined a goal in general: but it is up to man himself to achieve it and to discover the adequate ways and means. What meaning has the term "mankind"? Evidently, it is not used as an abstract definition of the human species: its connotation is concrete: mankind is equivalent to "society". It is by means of his actual standpoint within society that man is enabled to work for the perfection of society and for his own perfection. Man's place in society is, so to speak, the runway from which his endeavour takes off.

This introductory description of man's essential condition is followed by a closer investigation of man's free will, which he has received as a peculiar gift from the Godhead. The train of Marx's argument is at variance with the belief in the power of human reason which he could have derived from a popularized Enlightenment-tradition. Far from glorifying man's freedom, he begins by stressing the dramatic consequences of that freedom. It follows from his free will, which he has received from the Godhead, that man is called to choose his own way to the general goal which the Godhead has provided. Certainly, this free choice is man's great advantage over the rest of nature. But it is at the same time a risk which may destroy his life, may frustrate all his endeavours, may ruin his happiness. Before choosing a profession, therefore, an adolescent must take this choice into serious consideration: he cannot allow chance to decide his most important affairs.

Thus the greatness of man's freedom to choose his own way of life is on the other hand his agony, since it includes the risk of his downfall. No less grave than this is a second dilemma, which follows from man's need of a criterion for making the right choice and saving himself from catastrophe. Where is such a criterion to be found? At first sight, the answer appears to be simple. In the heart of every individual there is an indwelling voice, a most intimate conviction which reveals to him a tremendous and alluring goal. It is the voice of the Godhead, who never leaves us earthly beings without a guide, a voice, though scarcely audible, which speaks with certainty.

Yet how can we know with absolute certainty that this inner voice is truly the voice of the Godhead? How easily it is stifled! What was thought to be enthusiasm may in reality have been a momentary impression. Our fanciful vision may have been enkindled, our feelings stirred. Apparitions may well play their tricks upon our imagination; and we may rush towards a goal which we suppose to be a revelation of the Godhead itself; however, we are soon repelled by the very thing we have embraced with such burning desire; and, lo, our very being is annihilated.

Again and again Marx stresses the enormous risks entailed by man's freedom to choose his own way of life. The most dangerous of source self-deceit, leading a man to identify a private enthusiasm with the call of the Godhead, is ambition. As soon as a man is seized with the fury of ambition, reason is powerless to restrain him, and he is carried away by his passion.

No, our own reason is unable to guide us; bereft of the support of experience and profound reflection, reason is deceived by emotion and blinded by fantasies.

Thus Marx's analysis of the true criterion for a right choice ends up with his exclaiming: "When our reason fails us, to whom shall we look: who will support us!" As a matter of fact, he fails to give an answer, at least the expected answer. Since the paper started with the proposition that the Godhead guides us through an inner voice, we might expect Marx to find the saving answer in that kind of conviction. Such a solution would, however, be immediately invalidated, if this inner voice were to prove the merest illusion. The religious answer, the way of the mystics, the solution of Augustine or Luther, all this is baseless, it is the product of circular reasoning, defenceless against the risk of self-delusion.

However—and this is an indication of his depth of mind— the method of Descartes who found the ultimate criterion of certainty in axiomatic evidence, the solution of the Enlightenment which put its faith in the clarity of reason these answers are also rejected by Marx on the same grounds, namely, that they are not safeguarded against self-deception.

There is another weakness inherent in reason, too: it lacks the support of experience and of profound reflection. This consideration leads Marx to an answer which seems appallingly naïve after the rehearsal of such a variety of serious doubts: our heart, unable to find certainty either in the voice of the Godhead or in the guidance of reason, turns to our parents, since they possess those very assets which reason lacks: experience and profound reflection. Our parents have already travelled the path of life, they have already tested the hardness of fate.

In order to understand this seemingly superficial and inadequate answer, we have to turn back to the theme of the paper: "Reflections of a youth before choosing a profession". The German word for "profession" is *Beruf*, a term closely akin to the word *Ruf*, which means "calling". The problem which Marx seeks to cope with, is the relationship between *Beruf* (profession) and *Ruf* (calling). We may enthusiastically choose a profession, convinced that it is a calling of the Godhead: but this conviction may turn out to be a mere delusion.

It is noteworthy that, involuntarily and unconsciously, Marx levels a radical criticism at the traditional propensity of Protestant ethics. The German terminology of *Beruf* and *Ruf* stems from a Christian social ethic which sees the secular career of the layman as a realization of God's own calling within the realm of His creation. The connection between *Beruf* (profession) and *Ruf* (calling) had already been adumbrated by the German "lay mysticism" of the fourteenth century. Tauler's use of the word *Ruf* with reference to *Beruf* had paved the way for Luther's theological interpretation of the secular avocation. Its principal significance lies in the application of the term *vocatio* to the common avocation of the laity, as distinguished from its traditional restriction to the monastic vocation.

In Marx's paper, the connection between *Beruf* and *Ruf* is still apparent: it is the starting-point of his analysis and of his questions. But the direction given to his analysis is different. The Lutheran problem—how to arrive at a gracious God?— is beyond his horizon: his problem focuses on the question of the right choice and of its criterion of certainty. His analysis leads to a negative conclusion, i.e. that any subjective criterion of certainty is non-existent.

At this point, another term makes its appearance: the term *Stand*. Whereas, from an internal viewpoint, the main question concerns the identity between *Ruf* and *Beruf*, the major external problem turns on the identity between *Beruf* and *Stand*. The point at issue is the proposition that for everybody there is an appropriate "estate", a specific *Stand*. In the social ethics of traditional Lutheranism the term *Stand* had acquired a static meaning, denoting everybody's fixed social position within an hierarchical, semi-feudal social system. Marx's paper introduces a more dynamic interpretation of the word *Stand*: within the framework of divine governance, directing the history of mankind, every person is called upon to play his proper rôle. The right choice of occupation is a choice of the adequate *Stand*, status, position, estate, which enables us to subserve the divine goal of history.

This *Stand* however is hard to know. The adolescent who is just beginning his career should therefore seek advice of the older generation, which has borne the full brunt of life and has experienced the vagaries of fate. The experience of our parents is, for that reason, the only trustworthy basis for a responsible choice of profession. When we have listened to them and have soberly weighed all the demands of the career ahead of us, if our enthusiasm has withstood this painful testing and we still cherish the *Stand* to which we believe we have been called, then at last we are really entitled to make a choice and to adopt our *Stand*, our proper profession. For now we may be sure that we are neither deceived by enthusiasm, nor carried away by excessive haste.

No sooner has the first problem—the criterion for the right choice—been solved, than a new problem arises; the possibility of its realization. We cannot always take up the *Stand* which we believe to be our calling. Our social circumstances begin to crystallize more or less before we are in a position to affect them.

What does Marx mean by the term "social circumstances", literally: "relations in society" (*Verhältnisse in der Gesellschaft*)? He might, in accordance with certain ideas of the French Enlightenment, have had in mind the limitations of one's social milieu, which influence the choice of one's profession so as to reduce its scope to a relatively small number of concrete opportunities. But no considerations of that kind are advanced. "Relations in society" in this paper has the concrete meaning of our physical and psychic "nature". The tension between our being called to follow a particular profession and the actual predisposition of our nature presents a new problem, to the solution of which the second part of the essay is now devoted. As far as our physical nature is concerned, this is more often than not an obstacle to our calling, Marx is evidently thinking of the whole of our physical and sensual constitution as providing the foundation of our profession. For a moment we may fancy ourselves able to overcome the weakness of our physical nature, but the next moment we find ourselves wallowing, as it were, in a morass. Our life then becomes a tragic struggle of the spiritual versus the bodily element. But great and noble deeds can only come to fruition in the soil of an inner peace. If we fail to resolve within ourselves the struggle between the spiritual and the physical, how can we expect to cope with the unruly urges of our being?

However that may be, the physical element is not the main challenge. Though joy and perseverance in our work may be hard to achieve in a poor physical condition, it could still be a lofty ideal to sacrifice our physical health on the altar of duty. The real menace to the realization of our calling consists therefore in our psychical nature. Should we be insufficiently talented for the *Stand* which we have chosen, we may ruin ourselves. Such a failure breeds self-contempt, which like a snake sucks the very life-blood from our heart, mixed with the venom of misanthropy and desperation. The inner ache of despair is more terrible than any criticism we may have to suffer from our fellowmen.

Once these risks—the failure of our physical nature and of our mental gifts—have been considered in all seriousness, we are allowed to take up our *Stand*, our occupation, our calling. But still the devious journey of Marx's analysis is not at an end. New dangers loom ahead—dangers that spring from the very greatness of our calling. An adequate *Stand* is that profession which guarantees the greatest dignity; which is based upon ideas we believe to be true; which grants us the widest opportunity to work for the benefit of mankind and to achieve the general goal of perfection to which any profession can only be a means.

The German word for dignity, used by Marx, is *Würde*: his elaboration of this term brings it very close to the Latin idea of *virtus*: virtue, dignity, honest, nobility. Virtue, he says, is that which elevates man (just as the Latin word *virtus* is derived from *vir*, male, he uses the German word *Mann*, which means "male"), which ennobles all his activities and allows him to take his stand above the crowd and unaffected by its admiration. Virtue can only be confessed by that profession which does not make of us slavish instruments but allows us to carry out original, creative work. Though such a profession may not be the highest one, it will at all events be excellent.

Marx has now apparently reached the topmost point, where his journey ends in a lofty panorama of the noblest and most perfect ideas. But, yet a third time, the very greatness of the promise makes him aware of the inherent risks. Whilst a profession which lacks virtue is humiliating, the burden of a profession based upon ideas which afterwards turn out to be false will doubtless prove intolerable. In that case self-deception will be the sole and desperate remedy.

It is as if Marx, at seventeen years of age, is measuring with his mind's eye the distance that separates him from the mountain-top which he is about to climb. Is he really prepared? Or is it safer to rest content with a less hazardous adventure, even though it may not reach the highest peaks nor yield the loftiest view? The loftiest profession is surely one more concerned with abstract truths than with the common interests of life. If his assurance is unshakable, there is no greater promise for a man than to sacrifice his life in the service of the highest ideas. But if his choice should be the result of rashness or haste, it is likely to prove most dangerous for the adolescent who, if he fails, will be ruined by that failure.

Obviously, Marx has already decided to take the risk and to engage in the adventure of a profession which would lead him to the highest ideas. But what are they? In its concluding part his paper takes up the argument of the beginning. If the general goal which the Godhead has given to a man is the perfection of humanity in general and himself in particular, then the main criterion for the choice of a profession is the well-being of mankind and our own perfection. There is no contradiction between the public good and our personal perfection, for human nature has been so arranged that only by working with an eye to the perfection and well-being of his fellows is man able to achieve his own perfection. Anyone who works for his own benefit alone may be a fine scholar, a sage, an excellent poet, but he will never be a perfect, never be a really great man.

The great men of history are those who have ennobled themselves in working for the common weal. We know by experience that the greater the happiness we spread, the happier we ourselves become. It is the lesson of religion itself, which teaches us that the Ideal, which all men pursue, has sacrificed Himself for the benefit of mankind. And who would venture to deny these truths?

When once we have chosen the profession which affords us the greatest opportunity to work for the benefit of mankind, we shall not find any burden too great; for it involves sacrifice on behalf of all of mankind. In that profession we do not experience a paltry, narrow-minded, selfish pleasure—millions have a part

c   33

in our happiness, our deeds have a silent, but eternal life, and our very ashes will be moistened by the burning tears of noble hearted people!

The rather quaint sentiments that conclude this essay should not mislead us as to its profound honesty and its importance when it comes to interpreting Karl Marx's early development. This paper bears all the marks of a confession of faith, recorded at a stage which for many of his fellow-pupils involved the rite of confirmation and the business of entering the membership of the Christian church. Since we have come to know this paper in some detail, it may be worthwhile now to approach it as a whole and to analyse it from three different points of view: from the standpoint of Christian theology; from the angle of idealist neo-humanism; and in the perspective of Marx's own career.

Considered from a theological viewpoint, the essay is noteworthy for the religious setting of its opening and closing sentences. It begins with a reference to the guidance offered to man by the Godhead; and it closes with an allusion to the sacrificial death of Jesus Christ. A trinitarian interpretation appears plausible enough, therefore.

The term "Godhead" is used with strict consistency and nowhere is it replaced with the word "God". The term was familiar in the tradition of the Enlightenment and within the framework of classical tradition is recalled the Latin term *deitas*. Its abstract character is accentuated by the consistent use Marx makes of the feminine pronoun. But this does not imply that the term refers merely to an abstract idea. From the very outset it is connected with man, in contradistinction to the animal; with history as distinguished from nature; with man as having individuality in contrast with the animal species. There is not the slightest tendency to identify the Godhead with a divine Nature, nor to fuse the Godhead with a divine man. This Godhead is the wise and fatherly guide and educator who leads mankind as a whole, and every individual man, towards the final goal of perfection. The Godhead is less related to the beginning, as Creator, than to the end, the perfect education of man. Theology is determined by teleology. But man, as distinguished from the animal, is not led blindly and automatically. The Godhead, as a wise educator, had only set

34

the general goal, and it is up to man himself, in his freedom, to find the way. Nevertheless, man in his freedom is not left completely to his own devices. The fact that man has the vision of a lofty, final goal derives from the Godhead's guidance, its gentle but unmistakable voice speaking in man's deep-rooted conviction, in the inner voice of his heart. In dogmatic terms, from the First Person of the Trinity we have switched to the Third Person; and we are faced with the question of the *testimonium spiritus sancti*, the testimony of the Holy Spirit. As a matter of fact this is the proper subject of the essay. Translated into theological terminology, his essay wrestles with the problem of the relationship between the First and Third Persons of the Trinity. The Godhead has posited perfection as the final goal for man to achieve. Man sees a goal and, in his inmost heart, feels irresistibly fascinated by its greatness. Moreover, it is certain that the Godhead speaks through the voice of our private conviction.

This proposition could easily be translated in terms of the traditional Christian doctrine of God's self-revelation through the testimony of the Holy Spirit in the heart of the believer. Of course, that doctrine is dependent upon a circular argument which solves the question of inner certainty by means of a predetermined theological standpoint. It is precisely that hidden circular reasoning which, for Marx, precludes a traditional answer. His questions arise at the very point where dogmatics has already pronounced the discussion closed. How do we acquire a really invincible conviction; how do we attain complete certainty; how can we be sure that it is the voice of the Godhead and not the deceitful voice of our own imaginings? In terms of the theme of the essay, how can we be sure that the profession we have chosen is really the Godhead's own calling for us; how can we attain certainty that it will really lead us towards the goal of perfection which the Godhead has established, rather than toward our own phantasmagoria?

The second problem to be solved relates to the external aspect: how can we be sure that we really possess the physical and psychic proclivities for realizing our calling and for achieving the final goal? The solutions of these problems, as presented by traditional theology or by a rationalist philosophy, are unsatisfactory. Marx rejects both procedures, though not explicitly. His denial of a theological procedure follows from the postulate of man's complete freedom, granted him by the educative wisdom of the Godhead, to seek the divine goal by his autonomous efforts. He cannot therefore, assuage his doubts and questionings with the Augustinian exclamation: *"cor inquietum donec requiescat in te!"*, nor by a deductive, dogmatic argument. On the other hand, just as the theological procedure conceals a *petitio principii*, the same weakness is inherent in a rationalist solution. Therefore, the evidence of reason is no less emphatically discounted as a basis for man's inner certainty.

The solution of the dilemma, which Marx then proposes, reminds one of the procedure involved by a scientific experiment like the first flight to the moon. Once the general goal, namely a landing on the moon, has been decided upon, man has to find a means of achieving this goal. Neither the greatness of the goal nor the rationality of the scientific procedure in general are sufficient to bring us there. The endeavour depends upon two basic conditions. The first of these is the accumulation of past experience, which means in terms of Marx's reflections: the life-experience of an older generation, of our parents. The second condition is a conscientious and patient testing of the materials, or in the words of Marx's essay: a scrupulous self-investigation with an eye to the physical and mental conditions for the implementation of one's calling. All this having been completed, all the risks considered and all the instruments tested, the adventure may be undertaken with faith and assurance, the calling may be realized.

As—to speak in dogmatic terms—the essay starts with the First Person of the Trinity, and likewise the middle part is given over to the problem of the testimony of the Holy Spirit, so the essay closes with a christological passage. Though the name of Jesus is not explicitly mentioned, the reference is unmistakable. In this way, the trinitarian pattern provides the composition with a logical structure. The opening proposition which proclaimed the general goal of perfection, granted to man by the Godhead, was followed by an analysis of the subjective conditions required for the achievement of that goal. In conclusion, the opening proposition returns in the final statement that the perfection of mankind as a whole is identical with individual self-perfection. Man's nature is so constituted that he only achieves his own perfection by working on behalf of mankind.

This truth is evidenced by three different factors: history, personal experience and religion. The term "religion" is used in the classical sense of "the Christian faith" or *religio christiana*. After the testimonies of history and personal experience, the testimony of "religion itself" is cited as a conclusive argument. The fact that "the ideal which all men pursue has sacrificed himself for mankind" confirms the lessons of history and of personal experience: real human greatness consists in a life of service to the perfection of mankind. The conclusive christological argument proves the cornerstone of the composition as a whole. What matters is the choice of that *Stand* which affords the best opportunity for a sacrificial life in the service of mankind. This is not the *Stand* of a famous scholar, a great philosopher, a superb poet; it is the *Stand* of true, perfect humanity. It is the *Stand* of Jesus Christ crucified.

The moment of doubt and despair which Marx's analysis of the right choice and the true conviction has passed through appear in this light as the heart-searching of one who has heard the voice of the Master and submits himself to a painful examination of his readiness to follow. Whoever wants to build a tower must begin by counting the cost! The cost of sacrifice, of complete abandonment of one's own self-centred interests, pride, ambition. Every one who exalts himself will be humbled. Despair and self-contempt will be his reward.

If we sacrifice ourselves for mankind's sake, so much the greater will be our happiness. "Our happiness belongs to millions, our deeds have life eternal, our ashes are moistened by the burning tears of noble-minded people." Thus the essay closes with a vista of the communion of saints, of everlasting life and a vision of mankind united around the sacrifice of those who have fulfilled their calling to pursue the common good and universal perfection. The essay does not contain any explicit reference to the Church; nevertheless, there is, under the surface, a specific ecclesiological framework. Many are called, but few are chosen. The terrible burden of this truth rests upon Marx's reflections. What is lacking is only the recognition of a communion of the elect. It seems to be everybody's individual calling to strive for his own salvation. There is, in the ultimate perspective, a unity of mankind, but not the slightest hint of a communion of those who follow their calling.

This consideration brings us to the second viewpoint, that of idealist neo-humanism. As a matter of fact, the preceding theological interpretation would be an overstatement of the Christian motives, were we not to make due allowance for the idealist fashion and the neo-humanist style of expression here. I have already pointed to the classical background of the term *Würde*, virtue, *virtus*, as an essential quality of the true *Stand*. The aristocratic ideal of the noble man, of nobility and self-ennoblement, points in the same direction. This classical ideal is based upon the Greek, and particularly the Platonic, norm of the true life as a life devoted to abstract truth, to lofty ideas of perfection and happiness and the common good. It suits with this neo-humanist idealism that the Godhead should function as an idea, that Christ be referred to as "the ideal". As seen from this viewpoint, the loneliness of those who follow this ideal, who engage in these lofty truths, derives from an individualist anthropology.

These features, however, pale before the splendour of the dynamic spirit which runs through the essay as a whole. Standing on the threshold of a dramatic career, the adolescent surveys the visible horizon: and his eyes try to penetrate the invisible distance beyond, the unknown vista of his future. What is most impressive about this essay, which is by way of being a confession, is the dialectical style of analysis. Man, elevated above the animal, has a terrible freedom, the capacity to ruin himself. The voice of the Godhead may be the voice of our own delusions. The greatness of the goal may arouse the very ambitions by which we are blinded and brought to ruin. If the tower of our career is built on the quicksand of inadequate physical and mental faculties, then its end will be despair and self-annihilation.

Marx's dialectical style of thinking is the expression of an inner struggle between contradictory tendencies which threaten to tear his soul asunder: between self-seeking ambition and the call to self-sacrifice for the benefit of mankind; between a craving for perfection and fear of failure and self-destruction: between the voice of the Godhead and an agonizing consciousness of self-deception; between the loftiness of the ideal and the weakness of his capacities; between the spiritual and the corporeal principles or—in biblical language—between the spirit and the flesh.

Out of this inner disruption he seeks a sphere beyond these contrasts, an inner peace and harmony in which the contradictions will be reconciled. For great and beautiful deeds cannot arise, save out of inner peace.

I have said that this paper on the choice of a profession has the character of a confession. As a matter of fact, the essay as a whole has strongly religious overtones; and it could very well have served as an essay on religion. However, for his finals at a high school in Lutheran Germany a pupil was required to submit a paper specifically on a religious subject. Marx fulfilled this duty with an essay bearing the title: "The union of believers with Christ, according to St. John's Gospel 15:1–14, an exposition of its basic essence, its absolute necessity and its consequences". A careful reading of this religious essay would seem to confirm my theological interpretation of the German essay on the choice of a profession.

Since the religious essay was written in order to meet a formal requirement, a careful reproduction of the religious instruction he had received during the preceding years would have been sufficient. However, when one looks at it more closely, the religious essay discloses a pattern of thought and a train of argument remarkably analogous to the German essay. Such an analogy works in both directions. Marx had no reason, in the German essay, to follow a theological or religious trend of thinking. The theological background of that essay suggests, therefore, the deeper roots of his reflections. On the other hand, the religious essay might be expected to conceal under its formal surface some really independent thinking.

The trinitarian line of argument that we discovered in the German essay is also recognizable in the framework of the religious essay. The paper starts by demonstrating the necessity of union with Christ and poses the question: is that union really conditioned by man's nature; is it impossible to achieve by one's own efforts the goal for which God destined man when He called him forth out of Nothingness? As in several other instances, Marx here uses the term "God", although in other parts of the essay we find the term "Godhead". This mixed use may depend upon the alternative function of both terms in the religious instruction that he had received. The paper on the choice of a profession indicates Marx's personal preference for the abstract term "Godhead".

The necessity of union with Christ is demonstrated in accordance with a trinitarian scheme; the general guidance of God in history, the inner testimony of His voice in our hearts and the word of Christ. First, in studying history, the great teacher of mankind, we discover that even the highest stage of culture does not enable man to liberate himself from the shackles of idolatry, to acquire right notions about himself and about the Godhead, to purify his morals from untamed egoism and ambition. The primitive peoples display their fear of the anger of the gods, whom they try to assuage by expiatory sacrifices. Even the greatest sage of classical antiquity, the divine Plato, several times expresses his deep longing for the revelation of a higher Being which would implement the unsatisfied pursuit of truth and light.

Second, the spark of the Godhead is inherent in man's nature, in a longing for truth and goodness: but time and again the spark of eternity is stifled by the flame of lust and the seductive power of falsehood. Thus, man appears to be the only being within nature who does not fulfil his destiny, the only member in the whole of creation who is unworthy of the God who created him.

The third and most convincing proof of the necessity of union with Christ is the Word of Christ Himself, which we find in St. John's Gospel, chapter 15, in the parable of the union of vine and branches. Thus our heart, reason, history and the word of Christ convince us that without Him we cannot achieve our goal, that without Him we are doomed by God, that only Christ can save us.

This trinitarian demonstration of the necessity of union with Christ is followed by an exposition of the cause and essence of union with Christ. The cause is our need of salvation, our sinful nature, our erring reason, our depraved heart, our reprehensibility before God. Its essence consists in God's revelation in Christ as forgiving Father and gentle Educator, the very God who had beforehand presented Himself as offended Majesty. Our heart, in union with Christ filled with the highest love, at the same time turns to the brothers for whose sake Christ has sacrificed Himself and whom He has united with us. This leads up to the third part of the paper, the fruits of union with Christ. Our love of Christ results into our desire to follow His commandments and to sacrifice ourselves for our fellow men. This is the true virtue, the virtue emerging from love to Christ.

In conclusion, the paper goes back to the beginning and gives us an exposition of the radical divide separating Christian virtue from any other virtue, in a word, of its absolute excellence. Virtue in Stoic philosophy is but a gloomy phantom: among the Gentiles, virtue is the product of an unfeeling sense of duty. But virtue having love for Christ as its source is spotless, gentle, humane. The fruit of union with Christ is a joy which the Epicureans in their superficial philosophy sought in vain, just as did the more profound thinkers in the hidden grounds of knowledge. It is a joy known only to the innocent heart united with Christ, and through Christ with God.

Marx's paper on religion is, in fact, an exegetical sermon on John 15. So far as religious instruction to adolescent pupils is concerned, the paper witnesses to the success of traditional Lutheran catechesis: and indeed we might wonder why Marx did not proceed to confirmation, for his heart and mind seemed fully prepared for membership in the Lutheran church. What, then, are we to make of this paper? I have already hinted at the remarkable parallel between the argumentation followed in this and in the first paper, a parallel which rules out the possibility of reading this paper as no more than the fulfilment of an examination requirement. Marx seems in his reflections on a future profession to have made a most personal application of the insights which, in a more formal and impersonal style, we find in his paper on religion. The shift of accent is so much the more significant. The radical Christocentrism, so characteristic of the paper on religion and, we may suppose, of the Lutheran catechetical instruction Marx had undergone, has, so to speak, submerged in his reflections on the choice of a profession. Obviously, the theological part of these reflections has been strongly influenced by Marx's inclination to entertain an abstract idea of the Godhead. But conversely, the treatment of the subjective aspect, of the inner voice of the Godhead and of commitment to our calling, has in this personal meditation assumed a dramatic depth and dialectical vigour which in the paper on religion is lacking. To sum up, the Christocentric religion of traditional Lutheranism has, in Marx's adolescent period, been translated into a broad perspective of the goal of history, the happiness and perfection of mankind, for the sake of which every individual man is called upon to sacrifice himself, passing through an agonizing struggle with his pride, passions and radical doubts.

There has also been preserved a third paper written for the final examination. It is an essay in Latin called: "Is the Principate of Augustus rightly reckoned among the happier periods of the Roman Empire?" Marx's method in this essay is to compare the republican period prior to the Punic wars with the imperial reign of the Emperor Augustus. His conclusion is that both periods enjoyed a form of government befitting the specific needs of that time. Augustus had to reign during a period of moral enervation and corruption; in such a time public freedom is better guaranteed by a monarch than by a free republic. Augustus' reign was characterized by the mildness of his despotism, which helped the Roman citizens to believe that they still enjoyed the traditional freedoms. Augustus deserves our respect, since the only goal he had in mind was the salvation of the State.

This paper illustrates the effect on Marx of such instruction in the classics as he had enjoyed. It illuminates the all but complete isolation of classical education. The lessons in Greek and Roman history, literature, philosophy and politics were given in a purely classical atmosphere, unaffected by the teaching given in other subjects related to contemporary life and civilization and were kept in a watertight compartment, quite separate from the religious instruction. Thus it was quite a normal thing to write a splendid exegesis on a chapter of St. John's Gospel—required for the examination on the Christian religion—and at the same time to offer an evaluation of Augustus' emperorship, as if it had never occurred to the pupil that Jesus Christ had been born during Augustus' reign and had been crucified under Pontius Pilate. Again, it was nothing out of the ordinary to praise, in one paper, a life of self-denial dedicated to the happiness of mankind, after Christ's example, and yet in the Latin essay to extol the Roman emperor Augustus, a man deified by his subjects, and to represent the salvation of the State as the highest goal.

For an adolescent with Marx's depth of mind and lucidity of intelligence, this splendid isolation could not last for long. The walls of those neatly separated, watertight compartments, filled to the brim with knowledge accumulated at the gymnasium, were on the point of collapse. The choice of his profession could not be kept isolated from his insights into classical history; nor could the instruction he had received in religion remain divorced from his classical education. A confrontation was unavoidable; and it affected each of the three dimensions: the choice of his career, his relationship to the State, and his attitude to the Christian religion.

3

New gods in the centre of the earth

ARX's early development carried him, in a sense,
through the various stages of European, and particularly of German, civilization. The Gymnasium had
presented him with the tradition of classical antiquity,
coloured by the idealist outlook of German neo-humanism, it
had made him familiar with the world-view of the Enlightenment; and, last but not least, he had received there a Lutheran
type of catechetical instruction. The objective elements of a
more or less complete tradition were spread before him.

It would have been quite normal if in the two following
years, which he spent at the Universities of Bonn and Berlin,
Marx had simply proceeded along this path. However, in his
examination-paper on the choice of a profession he had already
evinced the inner dilemma of a youth who felt torn asunder, as
it were, between the heights of man's calling and the abysm of
human failure. This inner disruption is reflected in the deep
anxiety felt by his father, Heinrich Marx, with whom he
enjoyed an intimate relationship. In a letter of March 1837,
written when Marx was still a student in Berlin, the father
revealed his solicitude for his son's future career, his agonizing
doubt as to whether Karl's heart was not at odds with his head
and his talents. The father wondered whether there was room
in his son's heart for the milder, more earthly sentiments which,
in this vale of tears, are an essential source of consolation. Since
Karl's heart was evidently possessed by an extraordinary demon,
was that demon heavenly or Faustian, would his heart ever be

44

susceptible to truly human, domestic happiness, would he be able to extend that happiness to his immediate environment? The older man saw Karl's outstanding talents threatened by an unbridled ambition, a Luciferian reaching for the stars, an incompatibility with the common measure of things, the homely, the practical.

Of course, such an inner restlessness is a fairly normal feature of adolescence; but in Marx's development it also reflected the influence of the Romanticism which had flowered among the previous generation. In the context of German history, Romanticism was the peculiarly German reaction to the impact of the French Revolution. Whereas the socio-political development of France was marked by a radical break, Germany's semi-feudal order displayed a surprising resilience, resulting in an emotional protest against the impotent rationality of the Enlightenment. The flame which could not strike outward was driven in. As compared with the forest-conflagration of the French Revolution, German Romanticism was a mere domestic outbreak; but the movement showed a surprising depth and vehemence. The literary products of Marx's first academic years in Bonn and Berlin give evidence of an intense receptivity for the Romantic inspiration. The documents which have been preserved contain a collection of poems, a fragment of a "phantastic drama" titled *Ulanem*, the torso of a "humorous novel" entitled *Scorpion and Felix*, and a collection of folk-songs.

The verse collection, though worthless as poetry, is a remarkable biographical document. Some of the poems reveal Marx wrestling with the ineluctible powers of God and Fate, powers which cast their thunderbolts down upon the fragile target proffered by mortal men. But the mortal man, seeing his most cherished possessions in ruins, takes revenge: he builds a throne for himself, so that his work, although destroyed by God and Fate, is reconstructed by Eternity. It is the "Prayer of a desperate man" (the title of one poem) but at the same time it is the expression of an immense "Human Pride" (the heading of another poem). Man's supreme prayer is his own greatness. If man be doomed to perish through his own greatness, then his fall amounts to a cosmic catastrophe, and he dies the death of a god-like being, mourned by demons.

This volcanic fire and its catastrophic eruptions, revelations of man's god-like nature, are the explosive forces of the supreme, divine energy dwelling in the human soul, that is to say, the power of love. In a series of poems, Marx celebrates his burning love for Jenny von Westphalen, to whom, as a young student of 18 years old, he had been engaged. Romantic sentiment elevates earthly love to those divine heights where man can see himself and his beloved in the likeness of gods. When the stream of love flows through the human soul, man walks like a victorious god through the ruins of a world consumed by his devouring fire; every word spoken is sheer, burning activity, and his breast resembles the bosom of the Creator himself.

Yet this blessed feeling of godlikeness cannot last for long: almost at once this divine being falls headlong from his phantasmal throne and stands confronted with his mortal nothingness, beneath a soulless, starry sky. The "Ode to the Stars" is an exclamation of misery, yearning and despair. We mortal beings are doomed to suffer and to perish, while, lifting up our eyes, we discover that heaven and earth stand as before· Whereas within our heart a world is drowned, the outside world remains totally unaffected; no tree splinters, nor is any star descending.

At the same time, man's nothingness in face of the infinite Universe is only the negative side of his participation and union with the Infinite. Around us is a restless Eternity, above us, underneath us, beyond our understanding and endless, and, like single atoms, we are drowned in it. But—this poem is called "Awakening"—our setting is an endless rising, and that endless rising is a flaming, eternal kiss of the Godhead. The same mystical truth is acknowledged by the hero of the dramatic fragment *Ulanem*: to be drowned in Nothingness, completely to perish, to be nothing, that would indeed be life!

Death is the entrance to eternal life. Lifting up his eyes from this cold life, this miserable earth, man sees heaven open and feels the longing to die, to enter heaven and to see a more beautiful country. "Torn to pieces" is the title of the poem in which this longing for death finds expression. Essential to all these utterances is the inner pain of self-disruption, the consciousness of being swung like a pendulum between extremes. There is no fixed standpoint in the objective world, either on earth or in heaven. Heaven, one moment the inaccessible height of the starry sky, at the next turns into the blissful object of the longing for death. The crushing consciousness of man's nothingness in face of God and Fate can also turn into mystical absorption, the absorption of a dwindling atom into the infinite divine Universe. In this aesthetic subjectivism there is certainly no room for anything like positive religion. "Do you believe in God?" is the question in the drama *Ulanem*, to which the reply is given: "I don't believe in Him, at least not according to the common notion of belief: but I know Him as I know myself."

In the same drama the terrific idea of being unconditionally surrendered to an objective, changeless Being is sketched in impressive colours: "Bound, for ever, fearful, splintered, empty, fastened to the marbleblock of Being, bound, fastened for ever, for ever!" It sounds like a hint at the fate of Prometheus, who was fettered to a rock and suffered the eternal judgment passed by the gods on his heroic but criminal action in stealing the heavenly fire. Here, in fact, we touch the heart of Marx's inner wrestling during these years. His father wondered whether the demon which possessed him were heavenly or Faustian. Marx himself confesses his admiration for Faust, with whom he wishes to identify himself.

The torso of the novel *Scorpion and Felix* presents a Faustian uncertainty with regard to truth and reality. In a passage which reads like an ironic comment on the New Testament parable of the Last Judgment (Matthew 25), the contrast between right and left is reduced to absurdity. Of course, if God's countenance sported a nose, it would be evident what is right and what is left. But they are completely relative concepts. If God were to turn over, after He had dreamt the previous night, then the goats would be standing at His right hand and the sheep at His left. If we could define what is right and what is left, therefore, the whole problem of creation would be solved. But as a matter of fact we are all in the position of Faust: we don't know which side is right and which is left: our life is a circus, we run in a circle, we look about us in all directions, until we bite the dust at last and are killed by the gladiator, life itself. We desperately need a new Saviour, because—agonizing thought that keeps me awake, ruins my health, slays me!—we cannot distinguish the left from the right side, we cannot tell the location of either.

Obviously, Marx is already on his way to an horizon beyond the positions so far familiar to him. Beyond the classical idea of a well-ordered macrocosmic whole which is in full harmony with our microcosmic viewpoint. Beyond the positive or agnostic rationality of Enlightenment. Beyond the aesthetic religiosity of a Goethean and a Romanticist world view. Beyond the message of the Gospel, the proclamation of a Judge who is at the same time the Saviour and in face of whom we are—in Luther's words—*"simul justus, simul peccator"*, at once sinner and justified. The dilemma that emerged in his examination paper on the choice of a profession, the agonizing question of certainty which beset his mind, has grown in depth and intensity. If there is a Judge, if there exists an absolute distinction between right and left, between good and evil, between salvation and doom, and if this Judge is a conscious person rather than the insensible marble-block of objective Being, then he must be like us, capable of turning suddenly in the opposite direction so that what was right becomes left, so that good changes into evil, so that the doomed acquire salvation. No; this message too fails to give a saving answer; what we need is an answer beyond this answer: we need a new Saviour.

Reading this poetry with care, one is struck by one outstanding feature. It is the ever-recurrent use of the symbolism of an ocean, in most cases an ocean of water, but sometimes an ocean of fire and light. Closer investigation from a psychoanalytic viewpoint is likely to discover a strong inclination towards maternalistic symbols, arising out of a latent desire to return to the pre-natal and pre-conscious bliss of the womb. In terms of the phenomenology of religion, there is an evident tendency towards the symbols of a mother-religion.

Two poems which Marx dedicated to his father contain the mystery of the complete union and identity of the divine and the human person, connected by the bond of love. One poem, called "Creation", celebrates the mystery of the origination of the Universe, proceeding from its eternal source in the uncreated spirit of the Creator, like the waves of ocean emerging from their primeval origin, like waves of fire condensed into the firmament of golden stars. The divine Eros expresses itself within the limitations of the created world, just as the poet has to express his ineffable feelings by means of forms and words. But the divine Eros that creates the world is identical with the poetic Eros ascending to the divine source of All, the latter being its pure image. The waves of Love coming forth from the bosom of the eternal Father are the very waves of love that emanate from the bosom of the poet. Harmony binds together what is alike; souls can be captured only by the divine Soul; in the eternal Eros creature and Creator become one.

Two poems, called "Wild Songs", are the only products of his Muse which Marx himself caused to be printed (in 1841). These poems reflect yet another aspect of man's participation in the divine, eternal Love, namely, the connection of Eros with death. "The Minstrel" is a ballad which again is marked by the symbolism of water and waves. While the fiddler-minstrel is performing, the blood springs in waves; and from his violin waves of music stream forth. The poet tries to whip up the fiddler's playing until the music swells into a dance of the stars; for his art is a gift of God. But the minstrel replies that God neither knows nor respects his art. It emerges from the dark abyss of hell, bedevilling the mind and bewitching the heart; and his dance is the dance of death. The minstrel draws his sword and thrusts it into the poet's soul. "Nightlove", the title of the second poem, described as a "romance", continues the same theme. Love, the burning union between two souls, is an ecstasy that raises them to the glowing stars. But the heart, set aglow by the flame of love, turns out to have drunk a poisonous drink, the drink of night; the heart writhes with the pains of death; and the eye closes, never to be opened again.

In the collection of poems which in 1837 Marx dedicated to his father in honour of his sixtieth birthday, the romance, "Night-Love", is followed by two ballads. The water-symbolism is already present in the titles "Siren-Song" and "The Old Man in the Water". As we shall see, the siren-theme has obsessed Marx's mind. In the ballad of the minstrel it says that the waves of his music dash thunderously against the rock, the eye is dazzled, the bosom explodes and its sound descends into hell. The ballad of "The Old Man in the Water" also opens with a lamentation about the water which is undulating in a

D 49

circular, never-ending rhythm: the water does not sense how the waves are shattered: it has a cold, unfeeling heart. But the next strophe introduces a change: within the hot abyss inside the heaving water an old man is sitting; he dances when the moon and the stars have appeared, and he tries to swallow up the waters. But they are his executioner, consuming the old man's bones; and by daybreak the old man has died. It is worthwhile to compare this ballad with the poem on creation. Whereas in the latter poem the eternal undulation of the Universe is blessed by the all-inspiring Spirit of the Creator and Father, the ballad on the other hand stresses the gloomy aspect of its terrifying and soulless automatism, which destroys "the old man"—apparently a symbol of God the Father. His mystical element is the moonlight and the night sky, threatened by the invincible logic of the physical order, exposed to the sunlight of man's analysing intellect.

The agonizing pain caused by the soulless undulation of the Universe is not Marx's last word, however. Just as the water-symbols tend to lure his mind into the magic circle of mother-religion and aesthetic romanticism, so the same symbolism can become a challenge to action. The water becomes the river on which the boat of his career is sailing towards unknown vistas. The cold, soul-less, objective world can be mastered by man's intelligence, courage and imagination. In the "Song of a Bargeman on the Lake", the poet swears on oath, deep in his heart, by the waves blue and wet, that he will inflict on them the griefs with which they have afflicted him; and he undertakes to lash them uninterruptedly. The poet indeed keeps his word: he lashes the cold waves without intermission, he is seldom on dry land. The poem ends with a bold challenge to the waves: "You may play and scourge as much as you can, you may roll around my barge. You must bear it towards its goal: for I am your master!"

At last, through all the vicissitudes of romantic subjectivism, he appears to have achieved his goal. It had already been defined, in his examination paper on the choice of a profession, as the goal which the Godhead has determined for mankind and for every human being individually. At that time, however, Marx had still not measured the immense distance separating him from it, the tempting waters that had to be traversed, the tremendous sufferings which the soul had to overcome. Now he has come to know the force which will raise him beyond the contemplative peace of Romantic aestheticism. In a fragment of a poem, written in the autumn of 1836, Marx declares that he is never able, in a peaceful and comfortable state of mind, to deal with things that have fascinated his soul. He refuses to let himself fall into a mood of fearful, brooding resignation, since his mind remains filled with an intense longing and, above all, with a desire for activity! "The Song of a Bargeman on the Lake" describes how he is fascinated by the raging storm, how he is driven forth from his bed, from his safe, warm and peaceful abode, to sail in storm and lightning, to fight with wind and waves. While praying to God, the Lord, and while allowing his sail to swell, he keeps his eyes fixed on the polar star. This resolute mood betrays a romantic feeling of superiority to the narrow-minded mentality of the average, middle-class citizen. In a series of epigrams, Marx launches the arrows of his biting sarcasm against the philistine attitude which a vulgarized version of the Enlightenment had imprinted upon the ordinary German citizen; the philistine remains deaf and blind to the literature produced by great poets like Goethe and Schiller. Marx pokes fun at the pious stupidity of the average church member, who fails to see the point of Faust's wanderings, his doubts about God and world, his pact with the devil: this sort of piety believes the faith of Moses and the glory of Easter to be infallible safeguards against the temptations of hell and Satan. But Romanticism, in the years of Marx's adolescence, was already decaying: his critical eye had discovered its weakness as a socio-political phenomenon. One epigram of his is an ironic comment on the German mentality which, after the defeat of Napoleon and when the great expectations of a liberation and renewal of German society had been disappointed, became absorbed in literature and philosophy. Another epigram sketches with biting sarcasm the stupid complacency of the German bourgeoisie: like the spectators in a theatre, they watch the stormy scene of world events and, after the storm is over, begin to develop phantastic philosophies embracing the Universe. But they are only interested in the dead past. They would do better to let the Universe take its own way, better to try and understand the present time; for earth and heaven proceed upon their accustomed courses, and the waves continue to lap quietly along the rock.

At the end of this epigram we once again encounter the symbolism of the waves rushing past the rock. The Universe follows its eternal, circular course, undisturbed by any resistance or human encroachment. It is man's calling to be present at the point where the waves are breaking against the rock, that is, amid the decisive events of contemporary world history.

Among the epigrams ridiculing the political escapism of German literature and philosophy, there are four on Hegel, with whose philosophical system Marx had come into contact at the University of Berlin. These epigrams give evidence of the contradictory feelings that the encounter with Hegel's philosophy aroused in his mind. Being in a period of vehement inner ferment, while trying to cope with the lure of aestheticism and to grope his way beyond romanticism, his first reaction to Hegel's authority was one of confusion and perplexity. Epigrammatic irony was the form most adequate for expressing these ambivalent feelings.

With the exception of the last, the epigrams are presented as if Hegel himself were speaking in the first person. The first two reflect Marx's puzzlement at the abstruseness of Hegelian dialectics. "Since I have discovered the highest top and since my meditations have found the depth, I am wrapped in inaccessible darkness, like a God," says Hegel. "I have been exploring a long time, floating on the waving sea of thoughts, and there I found the word. Now I hold fast what I have found."

The epigram reads like a reference to the biblical story of creation, beginning with the Word of God which is spoken in the midst of the primeval waters. The second epigram is a comment upon this suggestion that Hegel's thinking is based on the word. Hegel teaching consists in words, mixed up in demonic confusion: their interpretation is left to private initiative, unhampered by any restrictive limitations. Just as the poet meditates upon the words and thoughts of his sweetheart, which well up, as it were, from the seething torrent gushing out of the protruding rock, so is everybody allowed to sip the refreshing nectar of wisdom. "I say All to you," concludes Hegel, "since I have said Nothing to you!"

The symbolism in these two epigrams is closely akin to the symbolism of the poem "Creation": even the words are very much alike. In the latter poem it is God the Father and Creator who, bringing forth the Universe from the infinite waves of the primeval waters, shrouds himself in poetic forms and words which are only to be interpreted by the divine love, the "Eros" in which man's soul meets his own divine image. "The blissful images of My Spirit," says God the Father, "have to be recaptured and reflected by the spirit", that is, by man's spirit which is God's Spirit indwelling man. The two epigrams take up this theme: this time it is Hegel himself who is speaking as God. The irony of these epigrams is extremely ambiguous. Marx encounters in Hegel's reconciliation of objective and subjective reality and in his dialectical identification of the divine and the human spirit the very temptations of pure mysticism which he is just now wrestling to overcome. Hegel's dialectical identification of All and Nothing, of pure Being and pure Nothingness, of affirmation and the negation of negation, threatens to drag him into the terrifying relativization of right and left, good and evil, true and false, in a word, into the magic circle of the truly Faustian spirit dwelling in every man. What attracts and frightens him in Hegel's thinking is the siren-like seduction of the rushing waters gushing out of the rock.

However, this is not the whole of Marx's comment on the first encounter with Hegel. The third epigram reverses the coin and shows a surprisingly new aspect. Once again it is Hegel who is speaking: "Kant and Fichte," he says, "were fond of flying off into the ether, seeking there a distant land; I only try thoroughly to understand what I found on the roadway."

This third epigram is, apparently, the very antithesis of the first and the second. Whereas in the latter Hegel is presented as the mysterious Godhead, shrouding his thoughts in words which may mean all or nothing, here, conversely, he is depicted as a pedestrian thinker. As contrasted with Kant and Fichte, Hegel is the down-to-earth philosopher. As a matter of fact, what Hegel had arraigned in the philosophical systems of Kant and Fichte was their incapacity to reconcile objective reality with the spirit, their blindness to the self-realization of the spirit through the material world. In other words, what is illuminated in this third epigram is Hegel's realism.

53

Did Marx himself not recognize the amazing contradiction between these epigrammatic comments on one and the same philosopher? On the one hand, Hegel is sketched as a mysterious God whose spirit is moving on the primeval waters and whose abstruse words leave us wretched mortals to the pre-rational chaos of contradictory interpretations. On the other hand, Hegel, like a rag-picker, gathers his truths from the dust beneath our feet. Rather than believe Marx to have overlooked these contradictions, we should regard them as symptomatic of Hegel's contradictory impact upon his over-sensitive mind. Perhaps the fourth epigram on Hegel is to be read as an ironic comment on these contradictory statements. Its apology for the preceding epigrams which "sing fatal melodies" refers to Marx's study of Hegel, which had not yet been completed with "a study of his Aesthetics". This sounds, in part like an ironic resistance on the part of Marx's original and independent mind to the pedantic cocksureness of the Hegelian system. But the reference to "fatal melodies" which the preceding epigrams are said to contain, seems to hint at the demonic power of Hegel's philosophy: his contradictory evaluations cannot be reconciled in some sort of aestheticist harmony. "Fatal melodies" is apparently synonymous with the "Siren-Song" emerging from the rushing waters of this abstruse thinking. In order to understand these metaphors, we have to turn to another document belonging to Marx's early academic years.

The letter which Karl Marx wrote from Berlin on November 10, 1837, is the only letter to his father now extant. This extraordinary *document humain* affords us a deep insight into his spiritual development at that time. Written as an attempt at self-investigation at a turning point in his life, the letter matches the intimacy of a conversion story with the depth of a confession of faith.

Already in its first phrases the letter shows a sense of history that reminds us of earlier writings. We have met with this feature in the examination paper on the choice of a profession, just as we shall meet it again in the dissertation: it has proved to be one of the most characteristic features of Marx's life and thinking. History was to him at once world history and individual biography; both aspects were to his way of thinking inseparable. Though the encounter with Hegel's thinking doubtless gave depth to this notion, the examination paper already expressed his conviction that the goal of world history and the goal of the individual are essentially identical. That paper was written before Marx knew anything of Hegel beyond his name. He derived his notion of history from the ideas, handed down by the traditions of the Enlightenment, of classical neo-humanism and of Lutheranism. But, above all, it found a response in the inner recesses of his mind.

Selbstverständigung, the absorption of literature, philosophy, and science as the way of self-understanding and self-analysis, had been a driving force in Marx's life from his youth on. This factor explains the devastating criticism that he was wont to hurl at other thinkers. It also explains the merciless self-criticism which led him to annihilate several of his own philosophical productions and made him work continuously on his manuscripts.

Moreover, this desire for *Selbstverständigung* was closely connected with his sense of historical decisions. In the letter to his father he calls it the "necessary consciousness of one's real position". In November 1837, a year after he had moved from Bonn to Berlin, such a decisive moment in his life had come. "World history also knows these moments," Marx wrote, in this way introducing world history as though it had a personal consciousness. Just as we human beings at a turning point in our life, want to survey with the eagle's-eye-view of thought the past and the present in order to realize our position, so world history itself loves such a retrospective view, and takes a moment of rest for self-inspection. Although it has the appearance of going back or standing still, in such moments world history settles down comfortably in an attempt at self-understanding and spiritual penetration of its own activity, that is, the activity of the Spirit.

The phraseology used is significant. At its turning-points world-history is engaged in reflection on its own activity as an activity of the objective Spirit. We are strongly reminded of that poetry of his which described the mystical union as a reflex of the divine spirit in the human Spirit. But this mystical concept has now turned into a historical concept. The self-expression of the Creator-Spirit within the creative human eros has shifted from the inner dimension of the soul to the public field of history: the timeless eternity of mystical bliss is transformed into the activity of the objective Spirit as realized in the concrete acts of human history. What in his meditation on the choice of a profession was still an external goal of history determined by the Godhead, has, through a stage of radical subjectivism, developed into the self-reflection of history in which objective Spirit and subjective spirit become identical.

Just as two years before, at the moment of finishing high school, Marx had tried to map out his future course, so now he is looking back at the trajectory. There is a close parallel between the patterns of thought followed in both meditations; after an initial proposition about the general goal of world-history, the argument focuses on personal biography. Rooted in the conviction that there exists an intimate relationship between individual and universal history, his view of the history of mankind seems inspired by intimate personal experiences. The main theme of the letter is the so-called "metamorphosis" he has just been passing through. The prospect of a new period he is now entering, arouses lyrical sentiments in him, as if this moment were the overture to a great new poem he has in mind. On the other hand, he sees his letter as a swan-song, a retrospective view. Peering into the future which is dawning with radiant, though still vague colours, seems incomparably more attractive than meditating upon the recent past. Nevertheless, a memorial should be erected in honour of past experiences in order to restore in our subjective feelings the place these experiences have lost on the field of action.

We have to dwell for a moment on this important phrase; and, once more, a comparison with the examination paper would seem to be relevant. In that paper, where he is mapping out a future career, his feelings of doubt, uncertainty and despair are assuaged by two considerations: the guidance received from his parents, and the divine goal of history. This time, thinking of the future puts him in a lyrical mood; for it is the field of his own designing, of his personal action. Nothing is said about a goal set by the Godhead; now, his own passionate conviction of having discovered the right course for his life appears to be wholly sufficient. The problem which makes him uncertain this time is confrontation with the past, since in such a retrospective encounter reflection is substituted for action.

At this moment of uncertainty he finds support in two considerations.

The first will already be familiar to the readers of his examination paper. The most sacred place for a memorial of the past is the heart of our parents: there exists our mildest judge, our dearest companion, the sun of love warming the inmost recesses of our aspirations!

The second consideration is new. We may trust forgiveness of our failures and errors if we understand their necessity, so that our heart need not be worried any longer at the repugnant vagaries of accident and mental aberration which have tricked us in the past.

What is striking in these considerations is the unmistakably religious overtones, the more so as the letter is devoid of any explicit reference to God or the Godhead. Marx's development up to this moment might be aptly described in terms of three different types of religiosity. The general mood of the examination paper might be characterized as reflecting the sentiments of "father-religion", derived from an optimistic Enlightenment-belief in a Godhead, whose kindly and instructive wisdom leads history towards perfection. The Romantic period of the early academic years is steeped in the emotions of "mother-religion". The last traces of Enlightenment-belief have been drowned in the flood-tide of mysticism; but its features of father-religion can still be detected in the unbroken personal relationship with his parents, particularly with his father.

There is yet a third type of religiosity to be traced in this letter: the belief in necessity. As distinct from the types of father-religion and mother-religion, this might be defined as the type of "neutral religion". An understanding of necessity saves us from the threat of persistent self-reproach in the face of past failures and accidents; it is the genuine source of forgiveness.

Once more, however, Marx returns to the field of action. Whenever he leaves this field, to indulge in retrospective meditation or in romantic introspection, religious tendencies come to the surface. The field of action is the place where he feels quite on home ground. He sees life as the expression of a spiritual activity which appears in a whole variety of manifestations, such as science, art, private life, and so forth. Individual life, like the movement of world-history, reveals the inner activity of the spirit. The essence of objective and subjective reality is action.

Marx begins by describing the first academic year in Berlin as a period marked by his discovery of a new world, the world of love, that is, initially, of a hopeless love, drunk with desire. On his journey to Berlin all the new and fascinating things around had been lost upon him: their beauty was nothing as compared with the beauty of his sweetheart, Jenny. Even the beauty of art could not match her beauty.

In the summer of 1836 Marx had become engaged to Jenny von Westphalen, four years his senior, daughter of an aristocratic family, a playmate since early childhood. Though he had promised, on account of his youth, to forgo any direct contact with her for the next few years, his passionate mind—which was never content with doing things by halves—suffered intensely from the enforced separation. He found a substitute in an immoderate devotion to science and art.

The fruit of his artistic activities were three collections of poems which he sent to his Jenny. Some of the poems which have been discussed in this lecture belong to these collections. From his present standpoint, Marx evaluates the so-called "lyrical poetry" as "purely idealistic". What he means by "purely idealistic" is described thus: "a *jenseits* (hereafter, beyond) as remote as my love became my heaven, my art. All reality vanishes, all things become boundless; attacks on the present time, expansive and formless sentiment, nothing natural, all things constructed from the moon; the full contrast between that which exists and that which ought to be, rhetorical reflections instead of poetic thoughts." Although these poems might enshrine a certain emotional ardour, a struggle for vitality, this is still to be condemned as the expansion of an unlimited desire.

The key to this radical rejection of his own poetry lies in the analogy between the remoteness of his love and the remoteness of his art, which he characterizes as his *jenseits*, his "heaven"; which is the same as "pure idealism". Since in the "*Introduction to a critique of Hegel's Philosophy of Law*" Marx's evaluation of religion uses a phraseology closely akin to the self-criticism of this letter, it should be worthwhile to look at these words more closely. Marx had just described his love for his sweetheart, Jenny, in its full ambiguity. Love was for him the discovery of a new world. It was a very real world; for, before his departure to Berlin, Jenny and he had become engaged and had spent the summer in regular contact in Trier, where both families were living. But he had to leave her; and marriage was still years ahead. He would have to wait until he had finished his studies and could provide for a family. This very real love for a girl of flesh and blood was at the same time terribly unreal, since it remained unfulfilled. It was a love drunk with desire. Its glory was the very source of his despair; its reality was at the same time infused with a terrible emptiness that nothing was able to fill. All that he experienced in the external world and all his artistic creations could not match the reality of his beloved, from whom he was separated. Therefore, all his lyrical poetry, which sang his love and was dedicated to his sweetheart, all this he had discovered to be a mere substitute, a miserable makeshift.

"A *Jenseits*, as remote as my love, became my heaven, my art!" What he blames in his art is its artificiality. His beloved was real, she existed, he had not created her, nor had he created his love by himself, but he had found his beloved and their mutual love like a gift. What lacked reality, therefore, was not his love, but the way his love had to linger on, a shadow of its true being. True love means union between the beloved, physical proximity. For the reality of this union no substitute exists. Of course, spiritual love may bridge physical distance, and poetry may express one's devotion to the absent sweetheart. But the bridge is an illusory bridge, constructed by an imagination which meets no resistance and therefore sees no boundaries.

The analogy between "my love", "my art" and "my heaven" has to be interpreted against this background. His lyrical poetry had indeed elevated his earthly love to heaven and identified divine and human eros as emerging from, and striving towards, one and the same mystical union, rooted in boundless and timeless eternity. This was, of course, not nonsensical; on the contrary, these artistic creations belonged to the new world that he had just been exploring, the world of love. His "heaven" was not a pure phantasmagoria, it possessed the same degree of reality as his love. But it was a *Jenseits*, in both the objective and the subjective sense. It was, from the objective viewpoint, as remote a reality as his beloved herself was far away. It was left to a subjective, impotent desire, to the devices of imagination, to bring near what in reality was remote. His "heaven" was the hopeless substitute for a very real desire felt for a very real, and yet remote, beloved.

Poetry, much as he might devote time and energy to it, could not during this first year in Berlin be more than a subsidiary occupation. More important were his legal studies and, notably, his wrestling with philosophy. The critique of Hegel's philosophy of right, which Marx was to write several years later, is obviously the fruit of a process of study and thinking that started with his first academic years. Marx reports how he continued the study of jurisprudence which he had begun in Bonn; he translated, merely for the exercise, two volumes of Roman jurisprudence from Latin into German. Besides that, he tried to develop a philosophy of law, one entirely on his own making, applicable to jurisprudence as a whole. He started with a series of metaphysical propositions. The result, which he calls a "miserable piece of work", ran to almost 300 pages. Its size gives evidence of the almost demonic explosion of Marx's enthusiasm and intelligence, already displayed by the young student; just as the fact that this early work has not been preserved points to the devastating seriousness of his self-criticism. What is more important, these first attempts reveal the close combination, displayed throughout his life, of an almost pedantic zeal for scrutinizing sources and facts with a profound need for philosophical reflection and creative thinking.

Looking back at these attempts to develop a philosophy of law, Marx denounces them as purely idealistic products, meaning that they conform to the pattern of Fichte's "Foundation of Natural Law according to the Principles of the Theory of Science" (*Grundlage des Naturrechts nach Prinzipien der Wissenschaftslehre*) and Kant's "Metaphysical Principles of the Theory of Law" (*Metaphysische Anfangsgründe der Rechtslehre*). By "pure idealism" he means the construction of a radical opposition between what is in reality and what ought to be (*Gegensatz des Wirklichen und des Sollenden*), the separation of form from matter. In accordance with this idealistic pattern he first designed a purely formal metaphysics of law, divorced from all actual jurisprudence and from any actual form of law; it was followed by a second volume, a philosophy of law that dealt with the pattern of development in concrete Roman jurisprudence, as if concrete law could be considered as totally separate from the purely formal, abstract propositions contained in the first volume.

He rejects this kind of purely formal metaphysics of law as an unscientific form of mathematical dogmatism, which allows the subject to circle round the object, to fence about the matter. This method fails to get at the truth, because it does not allow the object to display the fullness of its own organic essence. The mathematician designs his geometrical constructions and demonstrations; but his triangle remains a product of pure imagination in space. It does not develop a life of its own, but is dependent on artificial relationships to other imaginations. On the other hand, in the concrete manifestations of the living thought-world, that is, in law, state, nature, philosophy, the object is to be observed in its development, free from arbitrary distinctions. "The contradictory reason of the thing itself has to roll along until it finds its unity in itself." (*Die Vernunft des Dinges selbst muss als in sich Widerstreitendes fortrollen und in sich seine Einheit finden.*)

Of course, this philosophical conclusion anticipates the standpoint Marx had reached at the time of writing the letter to his father. Picking up the threads of his report, he continues the story of his trials and errors before the new truth had been revealed to him. Before he could even finish his design for a philosophy of law, and having tried in vain to force Roman jurisprudence into the framework of a tripartite concept, he discovered the fundamental error of his design, closely akin to Kant's philosophical system. Leaving the manuscript of almost 300 pages to its own devices, he made a fresh start and began to develop a completely new metaphysical system. But once again the result was so miserable that he called a premature halt to the whole enterprise.

Meanwhile, driven by restless anxiety for universal knowledge, he continued making excerpts of all sorts of literary and historical works, which he provided with his personal reflections. He translated works of Tacitus and Ovid, began to learn English and Italian and simultaneously devoured a wide

variety of literary, juridical and historical works. At the end of the semester he resumed writing his poetry, which ended up in pure formalism. The total frustration of his artistic creativity touched off the latent crisis. All of a sudden he saw, as if illuminated by a flash of lightning, the domain of real poetry revealed like some remote, ethereal palace; and all his creations crumbled to nothing. This crushing blow was followed by a physical breakdown, which obliged him, on medical advice, to seek recovery in the countryside.

"A curtain had fallen, my Holy of Holies had been rent asunder, and new gods had to be substituted"; so runs Marx's terse description of his first, terrible crisis. Just as he had at the beginning of his letter, once again Marx resorts to religious phraseology, this time of an unmistakably Christian character. We are reminded of the christocentric allusions at the end of his examination-paper on the choice of a profession, referring to Christ's sacrifice for the sake of universal happiness, a sacrifice which we are called upon to imitate in our personal life. Now, two years later, recalling the moment of his mental and physical breakdown, he seems to be remembering the gospel-story which records that, at the very moment of Christ's death on the cross, the veil of the temple was torn in two. The description reminds us also of what is reported in John 12:29, that a clap of thunder was heard at the moment when Jesus prophesied regarding his death and resurrection. Marx describes his personal crisis in such terms as to identify it with the end of the Old Covenant. The curtain which veiled the Holy of Holies, was torn asunder, the old God had died. The old God, that is the "idealism" which he has left behind in order "to seek the ideal in the real itself. As formerly the gods had been dwelling beyond the earth, so they had now become its very centre".

In philosophical terms, what Marx describes is the substitution of Hegel's philosophy for the rejected idealism of Kant and Fichte. He explicitly mentions the names of these three thinkers, so that one might be inclined simply to identify the old gods dwelling above the earth with Kantian and Fichtean idealism and the new gods, living at its centre, with Hegel's reconciliation of the ideal with the real. Had Hegel's philosophy become the end-point of Marx's wanderings, then this turning-point in his life could, indeed, have been aptly described as the substitution of one philosophy for another. But such a simplification is ruled out by the ambiguous and paradoxical character of Marx's relationship to Hegel.

Up to this moment Marx had not mentioned Hegel's philosophy. Now the time had come to pronounce the magic name. Marx tells his father how already earlier, during his first year in Berlin, he had been reading fragments of Hegel's philosophy; but its "grotesque melody of the rock" did not please him. "Once more," he goes on, "I wanted to dive into the sea, this time, however, with the fixed purpose of bringing the pure pearls to the surface and to hold them in the sunlight; I resolved to stop fencing with ideas and to find the spiritual nature as necessary, concrete and palpable as the corporeal nature."

With this purpose in mind, he wrote a dialogue of approximately twenty-four pages, entitled *Cleanthes, a treatise on the starting-point and the necessary development of philosophy*. In this philosophical essay he succeeded, up to a point, in uniting the completely separate domains of art and science. He began patiently to design a philosophical-dialectical development of the Godhead, in its successive manifestations of pure concept, of religion, of nature, of history. He had prepared for this essay by studying physics, Schelling's philosophy and history. Designed as a kind of new logic, it had required an immense degree of cerebral exertion on his part. The conclusion is surprising: "My last sentence was the beginning of the Hegelian system. This very treatise this, my dearest child, nurtured in moonlight, bears me, like a false Siren, into the bosom of the enemy. Infuriated, I was for a few days incapable of thinking. Like a madman, I ran round the garden on the muddy waters of the Spree, in which souls are washed and tea is diluted; I even attended a hunting-party with my host, ran to Berlin and was in a mood to embrace every loafer." Shortly afterwards he continued with "merely concrete studies" and became absorbed in the immense task of reading, epitomizing or translating all sorts of classical, philosophical and scientific works.

The result was complete exhaustion of mind and body. "Consumed with grief over Jenny's illness and over the futile creations of my mind which had perished, devoured with anger because I was compelled to idolize a hateful conception, I fell ill. Having recovered, I burnt all poems and designs of novels and so forth,

63

in the illusion that I could leave off. So far I have not yet, after all, furnished proof to the contrary."

During his illness he had studied Hegel from beginning to end, as well as most of Hegel's disciples. In Stralau, the village to which his doctors had sent him to convalesce, he had several meetings with friends, who introduced him into a "Doctors' Club", a club of Young Hegelian academics at Berlin University. "In the conflict of opinions," Marx continues, "I chained myself up faster and faster to the present world-philosophy which I had thought to evade, but certainly not without silencing all music that was left in my heart; I was all irony at so much negation. Added to this was the fact that Jenny remained silent."

With a casual remark about some unsuccessful new writings he had produced, Marx ends the account of his experiences during the past year in Berlin. The rest of the letter deals with his post-university prospects. He acknowledges his sacred duty to complete his studies as soon as possible in order to enter the legal profession or begin an academic career as a lecturer or assistant professor. It is that duty, as well as strong doubts as to his father's consent which forces him to stay in Berlin, though he is consumed with desire to visit Trier and to see his family and his sweetheart.

The whole letter reveals the state of mind of a young man, torn between contradictory ideas and passions, desperately trying to steer a course through the breakers and into smoother waters. Philosophical reflections, artistic enthusiasm and the ardour of a consuming love are inextricably tangled together in him. It is this peculiar mixture which makes the letter a true revelation of Marx's inner development.

The document contains what is in every respect a genuine conversion-story. Just as the allusion to Christ's death and the rending of the Temple veil indicates the dimensions of his personal crisis, likewise there are several features that remind us of the story of Paul's conversion as reported by the apostle himself in the Book of Acts. The fact that Marx was mentally incapacitated, was quite unable to think for several days, reminds one of Paul's three-day blindness. The stroke of lightning which suddenly revealed to him the nothingness of all his creations, recalls the heavenly light which shone about Paul on his way to Damascus. There is even one feature of Marx's story that recalls the baptism which Paul received in Damascus after his conversion (Acts 9:19). Marx reports how he was walking like a madman along the bank of the river Spree in whose foul waters "souls are washed". The phrase is a quotation from Heinrich Heine's cycle of poems *Peace*, being the first part of a larger cycle which bears the title "North Sea". And to complete the analogy: just as after his baptism and recovery Paul was for several days with the disciples (Acts 9:20), so Marx, while recuperating in the village of Stralau, became a member of the "Doctors' Club", the club of Young Hegelian philosophers which became his first genuine, spiritual community.

As a matter of fact, the water-symbolism which had proved to be an essential element in his romantic poetry, also plays a prominent rôle in Marx's conversion-story, notably in connection with his paradoxical encounter with Hegel. After a casual reading of some fragments, he was displeased with the "grotesque melody of the rock" of Hegel's philosophy. Diving into the sea in a final effort to find the pearls of truth, he discovers in those depths the very philosophy which he had tried to rebut as a fatal temptation: the Hegelian system. His dearest child, nurtured in moonlight, was, like a false Siren, bearing him into the bosom of the enemy.

The expressions "grotesque melody of the rock" and "false Siren" remind us of the "protruding rock" and the "fatal melodies"—expressions which we encountered in two of the epigrams on Hegel. Obviously, these metaphors are related to the well-known saga of Lorelei, the demonic mermaid sitting upon the protruding rock in a dangerous bend of the Rhine. While she is singing her siren song, she seduces the heart of the bargeman and pulls his boat down into the fatal whirlpool.

In other words, the encounter with Hegel is permeated by all the blissful and terrifying features which make the water-symbolism such a striking expression of the *mysterium fascinosum et tremendum*, the fascinating and tremendous mystery of religion. We are particularly reminded of Marx's romantic "Ballad of the Old man in the Water", which I discussed in the preceding lecture. The endless undulation of the waters, above which shines the sun, is the murderer of the old man who is living in the water's abyss and dancing in the moonlight.

Comparing this ballad with the poem entitled "Creation", I ventured to interpret the "old man" as representing the Father-Creator, the uncreated Creator-Spirit whose images are reflected by man's spirit. The treatise which Marx wrote in a last effort to find in the oceanic abyss the pearls of truth, was a philosophical dialogue about the dialectical development of the Godhead in its manifestations of pure concept, of religion, of nature, of history. This dialectical self-manifestation of the Godhead was the truth he found in the "oceanic depths". An extremely ambiguous truth! It was the very truth which he feared as one would fear the pernicious fascination of the Siren's song.

In the encounter with Hegel, Marx is faced with the paradoxical riddle of his own mind, with the inner contradictions of his own thoughts and passions, of his mystical raptures and abysmal doubts. What he fears in Hegel is that same boundless mysticism which had permeated his own lyrical poetry and had expressed some of his deepest desires. On the other hand, he is fascinated by the concept of a Godhead which is no longer dwelling in a remote, illusory heaven, but is manifesting itself in all the dimensions of earthly reality of which it is the centre. His suspicion is aroused by the rationality of this philosophy, which brings the pearls of truth out from the abyss into the sunlight of reason and thus repels the mysteries of divine love and human eros. Much as he is fascinated by this comprehensive system of a powerful thinker, he dreads its tyrannical embrace, which threatens his own freedom of thought. But no choice remains; the die is already cast. Like the bargeman on the lake, described in one of his romantic poems, he will valiantly confront the Siren on her rock, he will castigate the waves and show himself their master.

4

Human self-consciousness as the highest divinity

MARX's personal crisis, his conversion and his subsequent
reception into the so-called "Doctors' Club" of Young
Hegelian academics present several features which
are only too familiar to the phenomenology and psychology of
religion. While from that viewpoint a comparison with Paul's
conversion is quite justifiable, the differences are no less significant. Although in the letter to his father Marx confesses how,
in the encounter with Hegel's philosophy, the light of truth was
suddenly revealed to him, the way he describes his relationship
remains, right up to the last sentence, extremely ambiguous.
What he encounters in the "Doctors' Club" is the very opposite
of a religious community of people devoted to a unifying faith;
rather is it an atmosphere of highly intellectual discussion between contradictory views. But this very climate of spiritual
reflection and competition is for him the indelible mark of
truth. Instead of raising his doubts, it corroborates his conviction that here the pearls of truth are being discovered and
brought to light. A conviction, however, unenlivened by any
expression of jubilation or gratitude such as often characterize
the religious pilgrim who, having accomplished his perilous
journey through lonely deserts of doubt and despair, at last
beholds the promised land, the city of salvation. Marx's
account of this reads like the story of a neurotic bachelor, who,
trapped by the fatal devices of a woman stronger and older than
himself, has finally succumbed to the inescapable snare of
marriage. His wedding-day is the day of his defeat, doomlike

and arousing the victim's mind to a fury of powerless indignation.

Such a state of mind would appear neither to mirror a state of happy love nor to provide the foundation for a stable marriage. As a matter of fact, a negative indication is to be found in the absence from Marx's writings of any unambiguously positive evaluation of Hegel's philosophy. Those rather scanty parts of his writings which contain a direct discussion of Hegel are intensely critical. His relationship to Hegel has from the very outset been of a dialectical nature. A number of factors serve to shed light on this.

One obvious reason is of a psychological nature. Marx's restless mind was continually engaged in the struggle to grasp unique truth and reality. He could not concede that the fullness of life which he perceived as the expression of a spiritual activity could be imprisoned within a fixed system. It is normal enough to find the younger generation inwardly resisting the maturity and established position of the older one. In Marx's case it drove his passionate mind, at one and the same time, to the extremes of unqualified respect for and aversion from the master-philosopher's authority.

One might wonder whether this ambivalent adherence was not, in fact, much more in conformity with Hegel's thinking than the blind adoration of his epigones. Even in his later works Hegel's philosophical system bears the marks of a long ripening process. Its evolution, traceable throughout the course of his writings, gives evidence of a continual wrestling with the thoughts he was burning to formulate in an intelligible language. What is yet more essential, the dialectical nature of Hegel's thinking is rooted in the process of reflection-in-actu, a living process which dies the very moment it allows itself to become imprisoned in fixed forms. The essentially historical character of this philosophy militates against its coagulating into a system. Since it claims not only to think about history but to be the self-fulfilment of the history of philosophy and the self-expression of history in the language of philosophy, it follows that the pulse and heartbeat of this philosophy is that very dialectical process of history which it claims to incorporate. Of course, the older Hegel had already tried to halt the dialectic of ongoing history and to enshrine his philosophical system, safeguarded against critical negation. His epigones could only be expected to build a mausoleum for the master's spirit. On the other hand, the character of Hegel's philosophy as comprehensive reflection upon the whole range of socio-political and cultural phenomena made it necessary for his school to remain in close touch with the social and political situation in Germany. In the peculiar structure of German society, one's philosophical position was bound up with the position one had, or desired to have, within the political order. The increasing political conservatism manifest in Hegel's development could be explained partly as an outcome of the socio-political situation. Whereas in France the principles of the Enlightenment had been incarnated in the Revolution of 1789, in Germany their only foothold was in the intellectual aspirations of a thinking élite. Germany's political encounter was not with the victorious French bourgeoisie but with Napoleon's enlightened despotism. The ambiguity of Hegel's political philosophy reflected the ambiguity of developments in France after the Revolution and the double ambiguity of their repercussions in a backward Germany.

The dissolution of the Hegelian school in several distinct currents was therefore both inevitable and justified. There was sufficient ambiguity in the master's philosophy to account for the subsequent, mutually contradictory interpretations presented by the Hegelian Right, Left and Centre. This process of disintegration was inevitable, since it merely reflected the increasing tensions which external and internal pressures alike inflicted upon German society. The French July Revolution of 1830, however slight its influence upon Germany may have been at the time, nevertheless had the effect of enhancing the critical forces already at work. It became the historical calling of the Hegelian Left to embody this criticism in philosophical reflection. The fact that this occurred within the setting of the Hegelian system increased its significance. Hegel's dialectics were, so to speak, congenial with the inner disruption from which the German intelligentsia was suffering as a consequence of the growing contradictions between progressive thinking and backward society. The philosophy of the French Enlightenment did not provide anything to match the depth of Hegel's thinking and the relevance of his methodology to these manifest contradictions.

The tools adequate to cope with his system had been forged by the master himself.

As a matter of fact, Hegel's philosophy had absorbed the thinking of the Enlightenment about social and political questions to such an extent that the criticism developed by his left-wing pupils became the most effective means of opposition to the political status quo. Hegel's philosophical sanctification of the Christian religion was closely linked with his philosophical justification of the German Christian monarchy. Since the Hegelian Left attempted to transform the master's philosophy into a philosophy of pure human self-consciousness, the political consequences of their attack upon the established position of the Christian religion were bound to become evident. It was not until ten years or so after Hegel's death that a clear stand had been made and the collision with the State began.

It was during this critical period around the year 1840 that Marx was busy writing his doctoral dissertation. This work is essential to any understanding of the philosophical foundations of Marx's thinking, its methodology and its structure. Some of the reasons that have induced me to pay special attention to this work have already been expounded in my opening lecture. I have already mentioned that Marx completed his dissertation in March 1841 and that in the following month he was awarded his doctorate by the University of Jena. The dissertation is entitled *The difference between the Democritean and Epicurean philosophies of nature,* supplemented with an Appendix, entitled *Critique of the Plutarchean polemic against Epicurus' theology.* Though at the end of 1841 Marx was still considering the desirability of publication, and with that in mind had even conceived a new preface, the dissertation has never been printed. Unfortunately, only a part of the manuscript has been preserved. Of the first part which deals with the difference between both Greek philosophies in general, the two concluding paragraphs, summarizing the results of his analysis, have been lost. Of the Appendix only the first paragraph of the first part has been preserved.

This loss is partly made good by the preservation of Marx's preparatory studies which he began during the winter semester of 1838–39. Seven exercise-books filled with excerpts, translations and a wealth of comments and remarks have been preserved. Their size far exceeds that of the dissertation; and their significance for the development of Marx's thinking during those years is, in fact, greater in some respects than that of the dissertation itself. The importance of the preparatory studies is also indicated by the title given them by Rjazanow (in the historical-critical edition of Marx's and Engels' collected writings), namely: *Preparatory studies on the history of the Epicurean, Stoic and Sceptic philosophies.* This title, which indeed describes the content of these exercises, suggests a wider and partly different theme, as compared with the theme of the dissertation proper. On the covers of five exercise-books Marx has written: "Epicurean philosophy". Democritus is hardly mentioned. The comparison between Democritean and Epicurean philosophy, which is the theme of the actual dissertation, is likely to have been a minor aspect of Marx's preparatory reflections.

As a matter of fact, in the Foreword to his dissertation Marx has explicitly stated his wider and more extensive plan to write a larger study on the cycle of Epicurean, Stoic and Sceptical philosophy in relation to Greek speculation as a whole. He regards his dissertation as only a preliminary to the proposed larger essay which, he promises, will correct the failings of the existing treatise. In the opening paragraph of the first part of the dissertation, which sets out its theme in general terms, this promise is repeated and explained in more detail.

The idea of this larger essay, which in point of fact Marx was never able to write, probably emerged from the discussions in the Young Hegelian Doctors' Club, which fostered a general interest in the post-Aristotelian period of Greek philosophy. This interest is particularly obvious in the writings of the two friends, Carl Köppen and Bruno Bauer, who together with Marx formed the so-called "philosophical Montagne" (a name invented by Ruge). In the foreword to his dissertation, Marx refers to *Köppen's* essay *Friedrich der Grosse und seine Widersacher* ("Frederick the Great and his Adversaries") as containing a more profound suggestion regarding the connection of post-Aristotelian philosophy with Greek life. The essay, dedicated by Köppen "to my friend Karl Heinrich Marx of Trier", was published in 1840 on the centenary of the accession of Frederick the Great of Prussia. It showed how this famous king-philosopher of the Enlightenment had assimilated the ideas of later Greek philosophy into his life. Köppen described Epicureanism,

Stoicism and Scepticism as "the nerve, muscle and intestinal system of the antique organism. Their direct and natural unity determined the beauty and morality of classical antiquity which collapsed when the latter died out." Drawing a parallel and trying to demonstrate the connection between classical philosophy and eighteenth-century Enlightenment, Köppen launched a vehement attack on the alliance of Romanticism and political reaction in his own days, which he compared with the decay of classical civilization and society.

While Köppen's polemical pamphlet had a clearly political purpose, Bruno Bauer's study of the three philosophical systems of late antiquity arose primarily out of his interest in the origins of Christianity. The audacity of Bauer's criticism of the Gospels went well beyond the attack which had been launched in 1835 by David Strauss's *Leben Jesu* ("Life of Jesus"). Bauer contended that the Gospels were devoid of any historical truth, that everything in them was the literary product of the Gospel writers' own fantasy; consequently, Christianity as a world-religion was merely the product of the classical Graeco-Roman world.

This proposition had far-reaching implications for the relationship of Young Hegelian philosophy to the dominant tradition of Christianity. The term "philosophy of self-consciousness", which the Young Hegelian school had adopted, was derived from the title which had formerly been given to the cycle of Sceptic, Epicurean and Stoic schools. It was the great merit of these philosophical systems, which could not match the speculative depth and universality of knowledge of Plato and Aristotle, to have salvaged the inner happiness of individual man from the ruins of Greek civilization. The immortal principle of individual self-consciousness had, as Bauer contended, been absorbed by the Christian religion, which had thus received the strength to outlive a dying antiquity. But Christianity had absorbed it in an alienated form, in that the individual spirit became deified into a divine, almighty Sovereign and Judge, the heavenly counterpart to the world ruler in Rome. Nevertheless, under the slavery of the Christian religion, humanity had been prepared for the attainment of the final goal of liberty. Now the time had come for the philosophy of self-consciousness, that is to say, for the Hegelian Left, to liberate mankind from the alienated products of the Christian religion, much as formerly the spirit of primitive Christianity had been able to defeat a decaying Graeco-Roman civilization.

The parallel also applied to the political and social field. The national limitations of Hellenism and the social limitations of slavery-limitations which neither Plato nor Aristotle had dreamed of overstepping—had once before been broken down by the "philosophy of self-consciousness". It had greatly fructified primitive Christianity, which was the world-religion of the suffering and the oppressed and which did not go over to Plato and Aristotle until it had become the religion of an oppressive and exploiting power. Now it was likewise the task of the modern philosophy of self-consciousness to liberate man from the oppression of a tyrannical Church and religion. Thus it was in reality picking up again the threads of the eighteenth-century Enlightenment. Bruno Bauer was filled with an almost apocalyptic consciousness. "The impending catastrophe will be great," he wrote in a letter to Marx, "greater and more vehement than the catastrophe of the past, when Christianity made its appearance."

Viewed in this context, it is obvious that Marx's dissertation is much more than a scholarly historical study of a detail of classical philosophy. In the mirror of a stage of the Greek past he finds the burning questions of his own existence focused and reflected. Before plunging into the political arena of his own day, he turns to pre-Christian history. On this seemingly secure field of study the vehemence of his emotions and the force of his critical intellect are to be trained for the coming battle.

Since the preparatory studies provide such a wealth of insights in addition to the text of the dissertation, it would be inept of me to deal with that text in isolation. I shall therefore continue to treat these two kinds of writings as being the successive stages of an indivisible process of thinking on this philosophical subject. In the Foreword to the dissertation, Marx has summed up the significance of his theme against the background of far-reaching perspectives. A discussion of this text may serve as an excellent introduction to Marx's thinking at this stage of his development.

The purpose of the dissertation, which is to demonstrate that the Epicurean philosophy of nature is basically different from the Democritean philosophy, enshrines an explicitly polemical point. It is Epicurus' originality in relation to his predecessor Democritus that has to be demonstrated. Since, as we shall see, Marx's interest in Epicurus is rooted in his personal struggle for the adequate philosophy and for the invincible truth, his defence of Epicurus' philosophical importance springs from an intimate inspiration. In a sense, Epicurus acts as Marx's double. Every time the name of Epicurus is mentioned, we are to think of Marx reflecting his own problems in the mirror of Greek philosophy. When he begins his preface by presenting a claim to have solved a heretofore unsolved problem in the history of Greek philosophy, he leads his readers straight to the heart of the matter. This conviction of having made a revolutionary discovery in turning upside down the whole history of philosophy and in revealing its hidden truth is the backbone of Marx's reflections; and from it they derive their peculiar vigour. The unsolved problem on which the dissertation focuses is not the kind of specialized subject calculated to serve the average student of the history of philosophy as preparation for his academic career. It is Marx's belief that he has found the key to the inner sanctum of Greek philosophy and, probably, of all philosophy whatever.

He begins by stressing the fact that no even remotely applicable preliminary studies exist for the subject of his treatise. Epicurus' philosophy of nature has always remained open to the gravest misunderstanding. An unbroken tradition of misapprehension runs from the Graeco-Roman philosophers of the centuries immediately before and after Christ, throughout the Middle Ages up to modern times. Even the philosophers of the Enlightenment were not able to liberate their judgment from this spell.

The basis of this bad tradition was laid by Cicero and Plutarch. The kind of thing they said has been repeated and repeated up to the present day. In the first part of the dissertation one paragraph is given over to a summary of the main judgments formulated during past centuries. According to Cicero and his contemporaries, Epicurus had copied his philosophy from Democritus; where Epicurus had deviated from his master and had tried to improve his philosophy, he had succeeded only in spoiling it. Plutarch, living in the first and the beginning of the second century A.D., went even farther, endeavouring to show that Epicurus had appropriated from Greek philosophy only what was false, and lacked any understanding of the true.

This unfavourable opinion voiced by older writers turns up again in the Church fathers. Modern writers, in line with tradition, represent Epicurus as a mere plagiarist of Democritus, where the philosophy of nature is concerned. Leibniz denies him even the capacity to excerpt competently from Democritus, while Leibniz's contemporary, Pierre Bayle, merely copies the opinions about Epicurus derived from Cicero and St. Augustine.

Three authorities in particular are mentioned in the Preface to the dissertation as representing this false tradition. Plutarch's influence is held to be so detrimental that a critique of Plutarch's polemic against Epicurus' theology has been added as an Appendix. This polemic is not an isolated product, but is representative of a species; it strikingly presents the relation of the theologizing intellect to philosophy. Typical of Plutarch's standpoint is his endeavour to bring philosophy before the bar of religion.

A more ambivalent position is adopted by the seventeenth-century philosopher, Pierre Gassendi. His merit consists in the attempt to free Epicurus from the interdict which the Church fathers and the whole Middle Ages (which Marx calls "the period of consummate unreason") had placed upon him. Gassendi seeks to accommodate his Catholic conscience to his pagan knowledge and Epicurus to the Church, which was certainly so much wasted effort. It is like trying to throw the habit of a Christian nun over the splendid body of a pagan Greek beauty. It would be more correct to say that Gassendi learns philosophy from Epicurus than that he in any way enlightens us about Epicurus' philosophy.

In the second exercise-book of the preparatory studies, Marx even accuses Gassendi of having misunderstood Epicurus completely. Gassendi tried the impossible, namely, to be an Epicurean and, at the same time, to conserve the doctrines of the Church regarding divine inspiration, eternal life, and so on. He is a worthy teacher of Epicurean philosophy; but as soon as his religious presuppositions are threatened, Gassendi tries to meddle with the rigid consistency of Epicurus' opinions.

Marx's judgment about Gassendi is important, because this philosopher of Enlightenment had pioneered the renewal of Epicurean philosophy in the modern era. The first two exercise-books of Marx's preparatory studies contain excerpts from the work of the Greek author, Diogenes Laertius, about the life and opinions of famous philosophers, including a wealth of quotations from, and opinions about, his older contemporary, Epicurus. In the middle of the seventeenth century, Gassendi wrote a commentary on Diogenes Laertius' work, from which Marx derives valuable knowledge for his dissertation. He also makes use of the discussion of Gassendi's philosophy contained in Feuerbach's *Geschichte der neueren Philosophie* ("History of Modern Philosophy"). Thus there runs a line from Epicurus via Gassendi and Feuerbach to Marx.

What Marx definitely rejects in Gassendi's thinking is the latter's attempt to compromise between pagan philosophy and Christian faith. Historically speaking, this harsh judgment is scarcely justified. What from the vantage-point of a nineteenth-century critique might appear as deliberate accommodation, in the first half of the seventeenth century was on the contrary a struggle to draw a clear distinction between philosophy and theology. Gassendi, a catholic canon and a member of the secular clergy, was in regular contact with scholars like Francis Bacon and Thomas Hobbes. His work contains a typical combination of elements of sceptic philosophy and rationalist thinking with religious convictions. The pioneering study he wrote on the life and doctrine of Epicurus was inspired by his zeal for modern science and the philosophy of nature. It prompted the renewal of atomism and aimed a sharp attack on Aristotelian philosophy and the medieval tradition of Scholastic theology.

Like Bacon, Gassendi made a sharp distinction between the knowledge belonging to the sphere of "natural light" and the super-sensual truths which are only to be known by means of revelation, under the authority of the doctrines of the Church. His sceptical sensualism, which was to become a dominant feature in the spiritual atmosphere of the French Enlightenment, enabled him to keep separate his faith and his scientific insights. This brought him in vehement opposition to his contemporary, Descartes; he combated Descartes' attempt to extend the method of rational thinking to the knowledge of the Godhead and of the essence of the human soul. Like Hobbes, Gassendi defended the sensualist position, contending that man as an object of scientific knowledge has a merely sensual nature, determined by corporeal impressions and affections. The atheistic consequences of this stand-point, evident in Hobbes' writings, met with opposition not only from orthodox Christian theology but from Neoplatonic philosophers, who defended the divine essence of man and world. Thus the renewal of Epicurean philosophy, as promoted by Gassendi, became an important element in the breakthrough of the scientific method and its confrontation with theology and religion.

The third thinker, mentioned by Marx in the Preface as being responsible for having distorted the significance of Epicurus, is Hegel. To be sure, Hegel had correctly defined the general aspects of the cycle of Epicurean, Stoic and Sceptic philosophies. But this tremendous thinker was hindered by his view of what he called the speculative idea *par excellence* from recognizing in these systems the great importance that they have for the history of Greek philosophy and for the Greek mind in general. He did not recognize them as the key to the true history of Greek philosophy.

Plutarch, Gassendi, Hegel: by contrasting his approach to Epicurus with the opinions of these three thinkers, Marx is in discussion with three stages of the history of philosophy and theology. In Plutarch, a representative of religious Platonism during the early part of the Christian era, he attacks the religious metaphysics which have set an almost indelible mark upon the tradition of Christian theology up to modern times. Gassendi is the Christian theologian who, seeing the true light of natural science and philosophy, has allowed it to get hopelessly blurred with theological ideas. Finally, while Hegel succeeded in incorporating and defeating the Christian theological tradition by the power of his philosophy, his speculative tendency confused his insight and prevented him from recognizing the point where the liberating function of Greek philosophy is to be discovered.

Polemicizing thus against the whole European tradition up to the present time, Marx sets himself to clear a way for the true Epicurus. It is interesting to see how Epicurus had already begun to exercise his mind in his adolescent years. The closing sentence of the religious treatise written for his final examination contains a sharp attack upon this pagan philosopher. Union with Christ yields a happiness which the Epicurean with his superficial philosophy seeks in vain. On the other hand, this spiritual happiness is also beyond the grasp of the deeper thinker who vainly pursues it in the hidden depths of knowledge. It is known only to the childlike simplicity of the heart united with God in Christ.

Between the radical denunciation of Epicurus which concludes this paper and the no less radical defence which is the core of the dissertation lies a period of five years, years during which Marx passed through several stages of personal evolution and through a decisive crisis and conversion. Apparently, Epicurus represents the climax of that evolution and becomes the turning-point of Marx's thinking. From two kinds of indictment Epicurus has to be exonerated: the accusation of superficiality and the accusation of paganism. The first can be refuted by an analysis of the religious and philosophical idealism from which it emerges: such an analysis has to demonstrate that the truth of Epicurus' philosophy consists in those very elements which are rejected for their superficiality. The second accusation, aimed at Epicurus' paganism, seems to be rooted in the primitive tradition of Christian theology. Its misjudgment of Epicurus' apostasy from Greek religion could have suspect motives, in that Christian theology has not been able to resist the spell of antique religious tradition.

The importance of the inner revolution which Marx passed through consists in the discovery of a basic connection between the two kinds of accusation. Both of them, the Platonic and the Christian-theological rejection of Epicurus' philosophy, have a common source in their religio-metaphysical premises. In the first chapter of the dissertation, a straight line is drawn from the Platonic Greek thinker Plutarch to the Christian Church fathers who have simply conserved his viewpoint. As a significant example, Marx cites a passage from Clement of Alexandria, a Church father who with regard to Epicurus deserves prominent mention, because he re-interprets St. Paul's general warning against philosophy as a specific warning against Epicurean philosophy. The passage refers to St. Paul's letter to the Colossians, chapter 2, verse 8: "See to it that no one makes a prey of you by philosophy and empty deceit, according to human tradition, according to the elemental spirits of the universe, and not according to Christ." Clement bases his interpretation that Epicurean philosophy in particular is denounced by St. Paul upon the account in Acts 7:18 of the debate between some Epicurean (and Stoic) philosophers and St. Paul during his stay in Athens.

Epicurean philosophy is regarded by Clement as the prototype of all philosophies which idolize the "elements" instead of submitting them to the creative primeval cause, i.e. all philosophies which do not recognize the Creator. The term "elements" (Greek: *stoicheia*) is a reference to the passage from Colossians.

Marx (in the fifth exercise-book of the preparatory studies) provides Clement's interpretation with the sarcastic comment: "It is a good thing that those philosophers who did not indulge in fancies about God are rejected!" And he adds the remark that modern interpretation of the letter to the Colossians recognizes that St. Paul had in mind all philosophy. This comment is only understandable with reference to the Greek text, quoted by Marx. In the phrase "which do not recognize the Creator", the Greek term for "recognize" makes use of the verb *phantazomai*, from which the English word "fantasy" is derived. Recognition of the Creator is thus ridiculed by Marx as producing fantasies, fantastic ideas about God.

Viewed in this light, Marx's remark that in reality all philosophies are rejected by St. Paul is the more significant. For in this way Marx refutes the tendency to make a contradistinction between philosophies which recognize a Creator and those which deny His existence. According to this distinction, the first category is acceptable to Christian theology, whereas any positive relationship with the second category is rejected. The passage quoted from Clement of Alexandria is typical of the presuppositions which from the second century A.D. onwards have throughout the course of Church history dominated a good deal of Christian theological approach to philosophy.

The Greek term for "Creator", namely, *Demiurgos*, has simply been adopted from the terminology of Greek philosophers like Plato and Aristotle. Marx, however, enlightened by the criticism of secular philosophers since the seventeenth century, has broken with the age-long theological tradition. On the one hand, the idea of a divine Creator, an idea which has simply been transplanted in unbroken continuity from pagan Greek religion and philosophy to the Christian era, is unmasked as a product of man's fantasy, man's capacity for spinning ideas and images out of his own mind. On the other hand, Marx remains peculiarly loyal to the insight expressed in the closing sentence of his final examination-treatise on *Union with Christ*, namely, that the Christian faith is not only opposed to Epicurean and other so-called materialist or atheist philosophies, but no less radically to spiritualist and idealist philosophies, which seek a union with God in the inner recesses of the human mind. The dividing-line does not run between atheistic and theistic philosophies, but between philosophy and theology.

Such, as a matter of fact, is Marx's interpretation of St. Paul's denunciation of philosophy. The situation is, however, a little more complicated. Marx's use of the terms "philosophy" and "theology" is anything but distinct. The Appendix to the dissertation, entitled *Critique of the Plutarchean polemic against Epicurus' theology*, uses the term theology with reference to the Epicurean ideas about man's relationship to God, about individual immortality, and so on. Strictly speaking, these so-called theological ideas are part of Epicurean philosophy. As a matter of fact, this Plutarchean polemic is described in the Preface as being a typical example of the approach of the theologizing intellect *(theologisierendes Verstandes)* to philosophy. In other words, Plutarch is the prototype of the theologian in opposition to philosophy, of which Epicurus is the representative *par excellence*. Since this is Marx's opinion, his explicit and deliberate use of the term "theology" with reference to Epicurus has striking implications. Obviously, he not only opposes philosophy to theology, but wants to oppose true theology, contained in philosophy, with false theology. His dissertation, considered from this viewpoint, in part bears a theological character.

What he has in mind is the idea of a philosophy or, as part of that, of a theology free from religious admixtures. Philosophy should not, as with Plutarch, be brought before the bar of religion. A passage from David Hume is quoted, claiming for philosophy a sovereign authority which ought to be acknowledged on all sides; it is a kind of insult to philosophy, if one forces it to defend itself on every occasion because of its conclusions and to justify itself against every art and science that takes offence at it. "One thinks of a king accused of high treason against his own subjects."

Philosophy has taken the royal seat which during the Middle Ages had been claimed by theology. The next sentence reveals, indeed, Marx's essentially theological pretensions. Philosophy, he writes, as long as one drop of blood still beats in its heart, being absolutely free and master of the universe, will never grow tired of throwing in the teeth of its adversaries the cry of Epicurus: "The blasphemous is not he who scorns the gods of the masses, but he who imputes to the gods the ideas of the masses."

On the last page of the dissertation, Epicurus is called the greatest Greek representative of Enlightenment and, in his honour, the eulogy of Lucretius is quoted: "When man's life lay for all to see foully grovelling upon the ground, crushed beneath the weight of Religion, which displayed her head in the regions of heaven, threatening mortals from on high with horrible aspect, a man of Greece was the first that dared to uplift mortals against her, the first to make stand against her; for neither babbles of the gods could quell him, nor thunderbolts, nor heaven with menacing roar. . . . Wherefore Religion is now in her turn cast down and trampled underfoot, whilst we by that victory are exalted high as heaven."

Lucretius praises Epicurus as the true Prometheus. So does Marx when, almost imperceptibly, the Preface passes on to the Greek mythological hero. The Promethean profession: "In simple words, I hate the pack of gods" (quoted from Aeschylus' tragedy), is the peculiar profession of philosophy, its own aphorism against all divine and earthly gods who do not acknowledge human self-consciousness as the highest divinity. It allows no rivals.

But to the knights of the rueful countenance, who rejoice over the apparently weakened social position of philosophy, it responds again, as Prometheus replied to Hermes, the servant of the gods:

> Be sure of this, I would not change my state
> of evil fortune for your servitude.
> Better to be the servant of this rock
> than to be faithful boy to Father Zeus.

Prometheus—thus the proud profession which concludes the Preface—is the most eminent "saint and martyr in the philosophic kalendar".

Thus the Preface issues in a confession of faith. The real hero of the dissertation seems to be Prometheus in the guise of Epicurus. The hitherto unsolved problem in the history of Greek philosophy which Marx set himself to solve, appears to have more than intellectual dimensions. It is the problem of Prometheus. As a matter of fact, this Greek mythological hero had served as prototype and ideal for several anti-religious currents of the modern Enlightenment, as well as for the circle of Young Hegelian philosophers. Marx's mind was evidently deeply fascinated and intrigued by the enigmatic figure of Prometheus. His biographer, Franz Mehring, noticed that his confession to this "saint and martyr of the philosophic kalendar" anticipates the struggle and sufferings of Marx's own career. Marx appears to have been captivated in particular by Aeschylus' tragedy *Prometheus Bound*. His sensitivity to the tragic features of Prometheus' revolution against the gods adds to his approach a dimension lacking in the general notion of Prometheus as the heroic champion of Enlightenment and saviour from idolatry and stupidity.

The phrase "saint and martyr" should be understood as an interpretation of the verses from Aeschylus' tragedy that are quoted in the Greek text. The answer of Prometheus to Hermes contains a subtle ambiguity, embedded in the double use of the Greek terms for "service" and "to serve", namely *latreia* and *latreuein*. These terms are preserved in the English word "idolatry", but they are in general related to worship, veneration, service of the gods. The gist of Prometheus' argument consists in their polemical use. In preference to Hermes' subservience as faithful to Father Zeus, he would rather "serve this rock" to which he is bound by way of punishment. Prometheus' profession is the service of man over against Hermes' service of the gods. The latter enjoys an apparent freedom, whereas the liberator of man is subjected to eternal sufferings and bondage. But in these sufferings and bondage he is free, because it is his own conscious and deliberate choice. His martyrdom for the sake of man makes him the real saint.

We may remember how the fragment of the tragedy *Oulanem*, one of the literary products of Marx's early academic years, contains a Promethean verse which speaks of being "fixed, for ever, fearful, shivered, empty, fixed to the marmorblock of Being, fixed, bound forever, forever!" This verse sounds like a reference to the verse quoted from Aeschylus' tragedy which concludes the Preface of the dissertation. In the preface to a somewhat later work, the *Introduction to a critique of Hegel's philosophy of law*, we find yet another reference to the tragic aspects of Prometheus' act. The gods of Greece are said to have already been "tragically wounded to death in Aeschylus's *Prometheus Bound*". In other words, the real victim in the tragedy is not the human saint and martyr Prometheus, but rather the gods whose dominance has been fatally undermined by man's disbelief.

However, the martyr is a saint and a saviour. His sufferings do not outweigh the glory of the freedom he has acquired. In the last paragraph of the Dissertation, another verse from Aeschylus's *Prometheus Bound* is quoted, describing Atlas standing in the distant West and supporting on his shoulders the pillars of heaven and earth. The quotation functions within the context of a comparison between Aristotle's views and those of Epicurus. If Aristotle reproaches the ancients for believing that the heavens require the support of Atlas, Epicurus on the other hand criticizes those who believe that man needs heaven; and Atlas himself, upon whose back the heavens are supported, he sees as in the grip of human stupidity and superstition. Stupidity and superstition are also Titans.

Prometheus' act is the true task of philosophy. In the sixth exercise-book of the preparatory studies, Marx discusses the turning-points in the history of philosophy. He compares the practical realization of Hegelian philosophy with the act of Prometheus. Just as Prometheus, having stolen fire from heaven, begins to build houses and to establish himself on earth, so philosophy, having embraced the whole world, rebels against the world of phenomena.

If Prometheus was the real philosopher, then philosophy cannot be different from activity, encroaching upon human and worldly reality. In the *Economic-philosophic Manuscripts* of 1844, Marx discusses the appalling circumstances the proletariat is doomed to live in. Their houses have become abodes of death. The dwelling full of light which Prometheus, in Aeschylus, indicates as one of the great gifts by which he has changed savages into men ceases to exist for the worker. The implications are evident: what we need is a new Prometheus.

Having thus recognized the saviour-rôle assigned to Prometheus in Marx's early writings, we would do well to return, in conclusion, to the closing sentences of the Preface to the dissertation. Prometheus' challenging answer to Hermes, the servant of the gods, is applied to the actual political situation at the time of writing, March 1841. During that and the preceding year the Young Hegelian academics' prospects of making a career at one of the German universities had all but vanished. Through the death of the Minister of Public Worship, Altenstein, in May 1840, their circle had lost the semi-official support so far accorded it by the government. One of the measures taken by Altenstein's successor, Eichhorn, in order to put paid to the Hegelian radicals, was the appointment to the University of Berlin of the philosopher Schelling, who in his old age had developed a mystical philosophy with politically conservative implications. Another result of the changed governmental policy was to encourage the theological faculty in Bonn to reject the appointment of Marx's friend Bruno Bauer as professor. These measures were not only a death blow to Marx's prospects of an academic career in Bonn, but also made him decide to break off his studies in Berlin and take his doctor's degree at one of the smaller universities. As a matter of fact, in April 1841 the University of Jena awarded him the degree of Doctor of Philosophy *in absentia*, on the strength of the dissertation which he proposed shortly to publish. Marx had written the Preface in the preceding month, that is, in March of the same year. Its aggressive style and content represent his immediate reaction to the political situation.

By the "knights of the rueful countenance, who rejoice over the apparently weakened social position of philosophy" are meant all those in the Universities who collaborated with the government, and so helped to stifle the academic freedom of the Young Hegelian philosophers. The official government policy aimed at maintaining the familiar union of throne and altar, in a word, the settled ties between a semi-feudal political order and a conservative Christian church. The political subservience of the theological faculties is compared by Marx to Hermes' servile obedience to Father Zeus. The gods of the state and of the established religion had their trustworthy messengers throughout the country.

Against the background of this current political reality, the verses quoted from Aeschylus' tragedy acquired a surplus value over and above their original meaning in the pre-Christian era. Christianity, firmly established in the course of the age-long history of the *Corpus Christianum*, had been transformed into a Cult over which a Ministry of Public Worship presided, into an institution required to serve as the religious sanction of the State. In other words, it had returned to that very position which religion had formerly possessed in the Greek *polis* during the classical period. The quotation from Aeschylus should therefore be read as an indirect assault on the analogous position of the Christian religion in nineteenth-century Germany. The word *latreia* is the *terminus technicus* for "Cult". Over against the dominating Christian "Cult", what Marx champions is the Promethean freedom of the martyr and the saint. There is another tacit implication of Marx's polemic that cuts deeper still into the flesh of the established Christian religion. The Church had its long list of saints and martyrs whom it had turned into harmless objects of the Cult, administered by faithful servants of the State. Its truth had migrated, so to speak, to philosophy, which in the current struggle for freedom was developing its own kalendar of saints, with the name of Prometheus heading the list.

If such an interpretation fits the prevailing state of affairs, hardly concealed in Marx's polemic, then it seems tempting to make a comparison with the situation of the primitive Church, although such a parallel is likely to go beyond Marx's conscious intentions. In the Acts of the Apostles, Chapter 14, a vivid account has been preserved of the visit paid by Barnabas and Paul to the town of Lystra in Asia Minor. Under the impact made by Paul's ministry in curing a paralysed inhabitant, the multitude was convinced that "the gods have come down to us in the likeness of men!" Barnabas they called Zeus, and Paul, because he was the chief speaker, they called Hermes.

In other words, the pagan multitude tends to turn the Christian message into a pagan cult. But that is the very thing which is radically rejected by the apostles, because it would corrupt their message the moment it began striking root in such virgin soil. When the apostles Barnabas and Paul heard of it, they tore their garments and rushed out among the multitude, crying: "Men, why are you doing this? We are also men, of like nature with you, and bring you good news, that you should turn from these vain things to a living God who made the heaven and the earth and the sea and all that is in them."

The story ends with the report that, with these words they scarcely restrained the people from offering sacrifice to them. The reaction of the apostles signified an unprecedented and radical encroachment upon all that a pagan multitude had ever envisaged as the essence of religion.

Nineteen centuries later, Marx returns to a pre-Christian polemic against the Greek gods, Zeus and his messenger Hermes, in order to express his radical opposition to a Christian religion that had been transformed into a pseudo-pagan Cult.

5

The natural science of self-consciousness

As a matter of fact, the main themes of Marx's letter to his father of November 1837 are the very issues basic to his dissertation. This points to the intimate connection between, on the one hand, the personal problems which emotionally disrupted his inner life and, on the other hand, his philosophical thinking. His first scholarly work, although apparently a dry, historical comparison between two ancient Greek philosophers, could be read as a philosophical elaboration of his conversion story. This close relationship seems to confirm the identity of his personal conversion experiences with his reflections about a historical turning-point, marking the contemporary situation of his society and civilization.

This insight may serve to guide us through the labyrinth of the seven exercise-books that contain Marx's preparatory studies for the dissertation. The dissertation proper is a relatively short document which, though marked to some extent by clarity of exposition and simplicity of structure, deals with a difficult subject in a special terminology. It cannot be adequately understood except in close connection with the studies preparatory to it; for they contain a wealth of insights and arguments calculated to enrich and illuminate the line of thought developed in the dissertation. Although in some respects the dissertation itself may reveal a slight development in Marx's thinking, as over against the preparatory studies, it is quite feasible to deal with the study process as an indivisible whole. In the following discussion we shall not make any

87

distinction between the stages of the study process, so that the term "dissertation" is normally intended to include the preparatory studies.

The opening sentence of Marx's letter of November 1837, addressed to his father, refers to the turning-point which his life has undergone. Looking back on the past years of his personal life, he draws a parallel with the retrospection which world history itself sometimes seems to love. It was the discovery of Hegel's philosophy—a philosophy to which he felt irresistibly drawn as by the fatal power of a magical attraction —which allowed him consciously to participate in the turning-point of his own period of history.

Marx's struggle with the overwhelming power of Hegel's philosophical system has left its mark on the dissertation and is indeed its driving force. But the speed of his mental evolution had within three years propelled him to a further stage. The main question which now challenged his penetrating mind was the post-Hegelian situation of philosophy, the vacuum which the death of that philosophical giant had left behind. The pivot around which the dissertation revolves is the parallel between Marx's situation as a philosopher after Hegel and the situation of Epicurus as a philosopher in the wake of Aristotle. Just as Aristotle had gathered the ripe fruits of a rich tradition of classical Greek philosophy, so Hegel had reaped the harvest of western philosophical thinking throughout successive periods. At the same time, Hegel could not simply be treated as an Aristotle *redivivus*. There is a qualitative difference between modern western and classical Greek philosophy which accounts for the chasm dividing Aristotle from Hegel. This dialectical relationship between close analogy and essential difference also determines Marx's approach to Epicurus. The Greek philosopher is a strange kind of mirror, enabling him to discover and define his own historical identity.

What does it mean to live after the heyday of a "total philosophy", i.e., after the reign of a philosopher like Aristotle or Hegel? A total philosophy represents a junction or conjunction in the history of philosophy. Such junctions have the effect of concentering several abstract principles which during the preceding period had been developed separately, along parallel lines. Abstractions are tied together into one concrete knot.

Such a focus is, however, not only an end but a beginning. The convergent lines subsequently diverge outwards again and radiate. A philosophy which has passed such a focal point begins to turn its gaze towards the outer world. It has passed the stage of comprehension and begins to plot, as it were, to intrigue with the world.

It is a psychological law that the theoretical spirit, having become free within itself, is transformed into practical energy and will. Appearing from Amenthes' shadowy realm, it challenges the earthly reality existing apart from it. Philosophy throws itself into the bosom of the worldly Siren. That is the "Shrove Tuesday" *(Fastnachtzeit)* of philosophy, the time for philosophy to put on a mask. In the post-Aristotelian period philosophy takes on a canine appearance as the Cynics, dons the sacerdotal cloak as the Alexandrinian, or fresh spring apparel as the Epicurean.

Such a turning-point in the history of philosophy is a metamorphosis comparable to the creation of the world. What it means is only to be conveyed in mythical terms. We have been told that the Greek mythical hero Deucalion, a son of Prometheus, after the flood produced by the supreme god Zeus, founded a new mankind by throwing backwards a number of stones which changed into human beings. In the same way, when in her heart the desire has emerged to create a world, philosophy throws her eyes backwards. Her shining eyes are the bones of her mother.

Marx tries to express in the language of Greek mythology the enigmatic situation in which he finds himself, grappling with the riddle of his own philosophical identity. Hegel had, in his *Phenomenology of Mind,* described the course of self-conscious mind, arriving at the key-point of totality; his very philosophy as a whole was conceived as a representation of that key-point. Marx describes the ambiguous character of Hegel's philosophy as analogous with the paradoxical way Deucalion created a new mankind, as it were by a retrospective act. It was Hegel's intention to embrace the world, but it was a thought-world, not yet the real world. Since his reflection had a retrospective character, the prospective meaning of his philosophy merely existed in his reflection. The totality of his mind was an end in itself, but it did not create a real future.

Marx appears to be continually wrestling with this terrific ambiguity of Hegel's thought. In the letter to his father of a few years before, he had described his encounter with Hegel's philosophy as the moment of descent of the gods who had been living beyond the earth and were going now to be living in the very centre of the earth. Meditating on the problem of a post-Hegelian situation, he begins now to be aware that the descent of the gods is not yet the creation of a new world. He is, as it were, living between the time of descent of the gods and the moment of a new creation. The world is now waiting for a new Prometheus whose fire, stolen from heaven, will become the source of light and energy for mankind. In an analogous twilight-period, after the sun of Greek philosophy had set and before the dawning of a new day, the post-Aristotelian schools of philosophy had played their historical rôle.

A total philosophy is a complete world in itself. Having reached like a fruit the stage of maturity, it has grown into a closed system leading an independent inner life. Subsequently the moment arrives when the skin can no longer bear the pressure from within; the process which had been prepared secretly now turns into open manifestation. The inner self-sufficiency is broken; that which was an inner light becomes a consuming flame, turned outward. The theoretical system turns into practice, reflection changes into will. Of course, the practice pursued by philosophy continues to be of a theoretical nature. It is the critique which measures specific existence according to the general idea. This immediate realization of philosophy, however, is essentially burdened with contradictions, contradictions which inevitably become manifest and impress their stamp on the world of phenomena.

When a total philosophy turns itself as will against the world of phenomena, it can no longer maintain its totality. It comes to grips with external reality and, in that confrontation, it displays its one-sided, merely abstract comprehensiveness. Its relationship to the outside world is a reflective relationship, full of paradoxes. Its ambition of self-realization creates tensions with the reality it desires to master. Consequently, in the degree to which the world becomes philosophical, philosophy becomes worldly; its realization is simultaneously its loss; that which it attacks on the outside is its own inner deficiency. While fighting, it falls a victim to the very failures it wants to combat; only by becoming sick is it able to cure the diseases of its opponent. Its counterpart in the duel is its second self—but in an inverted image.

As a consequence of this paradoxical partnership of combat between an externalized philosophy and the outside world, the totality of the world is rent asunder. The impact of a great philosophy tears the world to pieces by its own contradictions; its aftermath is a storm. The force of this storm is commensurate with the heroic greatness of the preceding philosophy. Common harps can be plucked easily enough by common hands; but the harp of the god Aeolus only begins to sound when the force of the storm beats upon it.

Unless a man learns to understand this historical necessity, he is not likely to admit the right of anyone to live on, to survive the reign of a total philosophy. Without this historical necessity philosophers like Zeno, Epicurus and even Sextus Empiricus could hardly have made their appearance after Aristotle; no more could the for the most part miserable products of present-day philosophers have appeared after Hegel.

The problem which a post-Hegelian and a post-Aristotelian period bring with them resembles the dilemma of a people confronted with an impending catastrophe. The half-hearted commanders see reduction or dispersion of the army as possible solutions; whereas Themistocles, when Athens was threatened with destruction, persuaded the Athenians to abandon their city and to found a new Athens on a different element, on the sea.

Such catastrophes are, as a matter of fact, succeeded by an iron age, which will be deplorable if it is anything like the centuries of epigones that follow on periods of great achievement in the arts. The iron age will be a welcome one, however, if it is marked by titanic struggles. The times following upon the reign of a total philosophy and its successive, subjective forms of development have indeed a titanic appearance, since the unity of a total philosophy conceals a gigantic schism. The post-Aristotelian systems of Stoic, Sceptic and Epicurean philosophy, for example, are succeeded by the Roman period.

The iron age is an unhappy one, in so far as, its gods having died, the new goddess retains, for the time being, the dark shape of Fate, that is to say, the appearance of pure light or of pure darkness. She has not so far assumed the colours of the day. The soul of such an epoch, like a spiritual Monad saturated and self-sufficient in its universal ideality, cannot recognize any reality but its own concept. This impotence is precisely what makes the epoch an unhappy one. On the other hand, the happiness concealed within this unhappiness is the subjective form of philosophy, its relationship to reality in the form of subjective consciousness. In this respect Epicurean and Stoic philosophy, for example, were the happiness of their time; when the general sun has set, the night moth seeks the lamp light of privacy.

This is one side of the question. However, the historian of philosophy is more interested in the other side. He is inclined to turn the medal over and read the drama in reverse, starting from the end. The turning-point in the evolution of a total philosophy, its "transubstantiation" into flesh and blood, will vary with its initial destination. In the final stage of its development the *curriculum vitae* of a total philosophy is focused in one subjective point, just as the whole career of a hero is manifested in his death.

That is why a study of Epicurean philosophy is, at one and the same time, a treatise on the whole history of Greek philosophy. Rather than begin with a description of those elements in the preceding philosophical systems which have shaped the thinking of Epicurus, Marx's dissertation prefers the reverse order: it allows his favourite philosopher to speak for himself, so as to demonstrate his precise position in relationship to his predecessors.

Following this critical method, Marx's analysis reaches a result at radical variance with that familiar approach to the history of Greek philosophy which considers the objective history of philosophy in Greece as ending with Aristotle. What should not occur in a good tragedy seems to happen here: a weak ending. Epicureans, Stoics and Sceptics are generally regarded as an almost improper postscript to Aristotelianism, being out of all proportion to its powerful premises, Epicurean philosophy is regarded as a syncretistic combination of Democritean physics and Cyrenaic morality; Stoicism as a compendium of Heraclitic nature-speculation, the ethical world-view of the Cynics and perhaps also Aristotelian logic; and Scepticism as the necessary evil which opposes these dogmatisms. One unconsciously links these philosophies to Alexandrinian philosophy in making of them a narrow and tendentious eclecticism. Finally, Alexandrinian philosophy is itself regarded as a form of complete fanaticism, of collapse, of a confusion in which, at most, a universality of intention is still just recognizable.

Now it is a truism, to be sure, that origin, fluorescence and decay constitute the cycle in which everything human is caught up; so that it is not surprising if Greek philosophy, after reaching its zenith in Aristotle, should then have withered away. But whereas the death of a hero is like a glorious sunset, the demise of Greek philosophy, according to commonly held opinion, more closely resembles the final rupture of an over-inflated frog!

Then again, origin, fluorescence and decay are very general, very vague, ideas, in which everything may be included, of course, but through which nothing is to be comprehended. Death itself is prefigured in the living thing; its form is therefore to be grasped equally in its specific individual character, just as is the form of life.

Finally, if we take a glance at history, are Epicureanism, Stoicism and Scepticism isolated phenomena? Are they not rather prototypes of the Roman mind, the form in which Greece can be said to have "emigrated" to Rome? Are they not such intense and eternal entities, so full of character, that even the modern world has to allow to them their full spiritual citizenship?

With these preliminary questions Marx opposes himself, from the very outset, to the familiar view of the history of Greek philosophy. Against the background of his reflections on the crucial significance of turning-points in the history of philosophy (reflections which we have derived from his preparatory studies) his position is clear. His methodology is different from the familiar historical approach in three respects. Instead of explaining the later stage as the outcome of those that came before it, he begins with the outcome and attempts, from this final point of view, to explain the character of the earlier development. Secondly, he is not content with a general explanation of historical evolution by means of a hypothetical analogy with the organic cycle of life and death, since that analogy fails to point the specific character of a historical succession. Marx's protest against this organicist model is indeed not only directed against its tendency to fallacious generalization; it is also a corollary of his reversed approach to history. His argument that death itself is prefigured in the living thing, therefore, implies the reverse argument that the process of life is to be understood from its culmination, i.e. death.

However, this reverse argument is deployed in such a strange fashion that it renders the organicist model absurd. The thesis concerning the death of the hero as the mirror in which his preceding career is reflected and revealed receives a surprising application, in that the death of the hero is compared with the final rupture of an over-inflated frog. The comparison reminds one of Köppen's approach to the three post-Aristotelian systems of philosophy as representations of the nerves, muscles and intestinal system of the organism of Antiquity, which were falling to pieces when the latter expired. The historical stage of these philosophical schools parallels the *post mortem* disintegration of what had once been an organic unity. Having, in this way, weakened the organicist model, Marx reverses the argument once more; what, from the viewpoint of preceding history, resembled a *post-mortem* stage of dissolution, is now considered the prenatal stage of subsequent history. These post-Aristotelian systems represent the transition from the Greek to the Roman epoch. Evincing as they do the character of eternal youth, they are prototypes not only of the Roman but even of the modern mind. In other words, in the mirror of this transition-period between Greek and Roman civilization, Marx sees his own situation, as a "living between the times", reflected.

Having thus alluded to their great significance for the understanding of present history, he returns to the historical framework and mentions a number of reasons why the relationship of these systems to previous Greek philosophy should prompt further enquiry. Why is it that Greek philosophy issues in two distinct groups of eclectic systems, one of which constitutes the cycle of Epicurean, Stoic and Sceptic philosophies, the other of which goes by the name of Alexandrinian philosophy? Furthermore, is it not remarkable that after the Platonic and Aristotelian philosophies, which extend to universality, new systems appear which do not refer back to these great intellectual figures, but, looking beyond them into the past, seek contact with the simplest schools—in regard to physics, with the philosophers of nature, in regard to ethics, with the Socratic school? Furthermore, what is the basis for the fact that the systems that follow Aristotle find their foundations, as it were, laid in the past; so that Democritus is related to the Cyrenaics and Heraclitus to the Cynics? Is it an accident that with the Epicureans, Stoics and Sceptics all the elements of self-consciousness are represented as complete, except that each element is represented as a particular existence? Is it an accident that these systems, taken together, form the complete structure of self-consciousness? Finally, consider the character with which Greek philosophy begins, mythically speaking, in the seven sages, consider its centre-point embodied in Socrates—is it an accident that the very character of the sage is presented in those post-Aristotelian systems as the reality of science?

If the preceding systems are more significant and more interesting because of their content, the post-Aristotelian ones, and particularly the cycle of Epicurean, Stoic and Sceptic schools, are more important because of the subjective form, the character of Greek philosophy. It is precisely the subjective form, the mental vehicle of philosophical systems, which had almost entirely been ignored, owing to a one-sided consideration of their metaphysical pronouncements.

These arguments so greatly fascinated Marx's mind that it was his firm intention to write, at a later date, a study of the Epicurean, Stoic and Sceptical philosophies in their totality and in their total relationship to earlier and later Greek philosophy. His dissertation was intended as an illustration of this relationship with a single example, developing only one aspect of it, namely, its relation to earlier speculation. As such an example he selected the relationship of the Epicurean to the Democritean philosophy of nature.

Marx realized very well that this was not the simplest point of contact. Because, on the one hand, it was a well-established prejudice to identify the Democritean and the Epicurean physics, so that people saw in Epicurus' modifications only arbitrary ideas. On the other hand, he was forced to go into detail concerning phenomenal atomism. But precisely because this prejudice was as old as the history of philosophy, because the differences are so concealed that they can be detected as it were only under the microscope, the result promised to be all the more important if, despite the relation between the Democritean and the Epicurean physics, an essential difference extending to the smallest detail could be demonstrated. What can be demonstrated on a small scale can be demonstrated even more easily where the relationships are understood in larger dimensions, while, conversely, completely general discussions leave doubt as to whether the result will hold good when applied to details.

The prejudice which he had to rebut had become deeply entrenched in the course of history; from Cicero to Leibniz and Bayle, Epicurus had been regarded as a mere plagiarist of Democritus, when it came to the philosophy of nature. This traditional approach could indeed point to a general identity of Democritean and Epicurean physics. The principle elements —atoms and the void—are undeniably the same. Only in specific statements does there seem to be an arbitrary, therefore unessential, difference.

But here is an insoluble riddle! Two philosophers teach exactly the same science, in exactly the same way but—how inconsistent!—they stand diametrically opposed upon every point of truth, of certainty, and as to the application of this science, where the relationship of thought and reality in general is concerned.

Democritus' opinion concerning the truth and certainty of human knowledge seems difficult to ascertain. His aphorism may be cited: "In truth we know nothing, because the truth lies at the unfathomable bottom of the well." His sceptical, uncertain and internally contradictory view is developed still further in the way in which the relationship of the atom and the sensible world is determined. On the one hand, the sensible appearance of things is not ascribed to the atoms. On the other hand, the sensible appearance is the only true object. To say that the phenomenal is the true is contradictory, however. Consequently, Democritus makes sensible reality subjective illusion; but the antinomy, banned from the world of objects, exists now in his own self-consciousness, where the concept of the atom and the sensory perception meet in opposition. Thus Democritus does not escape the antinomy.

On the other hand, let us listen to Epicurus. "The sage," he says, "takes a dogmatic, not a sceptical position." "All the senses are heralds of the true." "Nothing can refute sensory perception." While Democritus reduces the sensible world to subjective illusion, Epicurus reduces it to objective appearance. Cicero's conclusion is right: "The sun seems large to Democritus because he is a scientist trained in geometry; to Epicurus it seems to be about two feet in diameter because he claims it *is* as large as it *seems*."

Second, this difference in the theoretical judgments of Democritus and Epicurus about the certainty of science and the truth of their objects manifests itself in the disparate scientific practice of these men. Democritus, for whom the principle element does not enter appearance and remains without reality and existence is on the other hand faced with the world of sensible perception as a real and concrete world. Democritus is consequently driven to empirical observation. Dissatisfied with philosophy, he throws himself into the arms of positive knowledge. So we see him travelling through half the world in order to exchange experiences, pieces of knowledge and observations. On the one hand, it is the lust for knowledge, that drives him afar. The knowledge which he considers true is contentless; the knowledge that gives it content is without truth. Democritus is supposed to have blinded himself so that the sensible light in the eye would not darken sharpness of intellect.

In Epicurus an opposite figure appears to us. He is satisfied and blissful in philosophy. For "to serve philosophy is freedom itself." While Democritus, dissatisfied with philosophy, throws himself into the arms of empirical knowledge, Epicurus scorns the positive sciences because in his opinion they contribute nothing to true perfection. But while Democritus seeks to learn from sages and scientific observers throughout the world, Epicurus prides himself for not having had a teacher, for being self-taught, and he hardly leaves his garden in Athens. While finally Democritus, despairing of knowledge, blinds himself, Epicurus, feeling the hour of his death coming, takes a warm bath and calls for pure wine and recommends to his friends that they remain faithful to philosophy. We see as a difference in practical energy that which expresses itself, in the first instance, as a difference in the theoretical consciousness.

We consider, finally, the form of reflection, which expresses the relation of thought to being in their reciprocity. In the general relationship which the philosopher establishes between the world and thought, he merely makes objective the relation between his particular consciousness and the real world.

Now Democritus uses necessity as a form of reflection of reality. By contrast Epicurus writes: "Necessity, which some make the absolute master, does not exist. There are some fortuitous things, others depend on our free will. The ways to freedom remain open everywhere."

The most important consequence of this difference appears in the manner of explaining individual phenomena. Democritus declares that he would rather discover a new etiology than acquire the dignity of the Persian crown. On the other hand, Epicurus proceeds with a boundless nonchalance in explaining individual physical phenomena. He is not at all interested in investigating the real causes of objects. He is merely interested in soothing the explaining subject. His manner of explanation, he admits, has in view only the ataraxy of self-consciousness, not the knowledge of nature in and of itself.

Thus, the sceptic and empiricist who holds nature to be subjective illusion, considers it from the point of view of necessity and endeavours to explain and to understand the real existence of things. On the other hand, the philosopher and dogmatist who considers the appearance real, sees only chance everywhere, and his manner of explanation tends rather to destroy all the objective reality of nature. There seems to be a certain perversity in these contrasts.

One can hardly expect that these men, contradicting each other in everything, will become disciples of one and the same teaching. And yet they seem to be firmly chained to one another.

This is the preliminary conclusion drawn by Marx from a careful analysis of the difference between the Democritean and Epicurean philosophies of nature. The difficulties with regard to their, traditionally postulated, identity have guided his research to a deeper level of apperception. The method followed by his penetrating gaze is typical of the trend of thought which can be traced as the continuous pattern of his subsequent writings. He begins by laying bare, underneath the surface of generally accepted appearance, hidden differences which stand in contrast with phenomenal evidence. Subsequently, these differences are exposed as symptoms of basic contradictions, which, in conclusion, are analysed with an eye to their reciprocal relationship and dialectical unity.

The next chapter, which was intended to deal with this relationship in general, has not been preserved; nor has the final chapter, which purported to summarize the results of the first part of the dissertation. Whereas the first part had dealt with the difference between the Democritean and Epicurean physics in general, the second part goes into greater detail.

The first point of difference, when analysed, concerns the question of the declination of atoms from a straight line. Epicurus assumes a threefold motion of the atoms in the void. One motion is that of a fall in a straight line, the second envisages the atom as deviating from a straight line, and the third is established through the repulsion of the multiplicity of atoms. The postulate of the first and last motions Democritus shares with Epicurus; the point of difference between them lies in the declination of the atom from the straight line. At this juncture, therefore, Marx turns to consider that declination. Just as the point is absorbed in the line, so every falling body is absorbed in the straight line which it describes. The consequence of this for atoms would be, since they are in constant motion, that the atom does not exist, but rather disappears into the straight line. For the solidity of the atom does not exist as long as it is understood as falling in a straight line. How then can Epicurus give reality to the purely formal determination of the atom, the concept of pure individuality, which excludes any mode of being determined by another thing?

The relative existence which is opposed to the atom, the mode of being which it should negate, is the straight line. The direct negation of this motion is another motion, thus, as conceived in spatial terms, the declination from the straight line.

Atoms are purely autonomous bodies, or, rather, are bodies conceived in an absolute autonomy, like the heavenly bodies. Therefore, like the latter, they also move, not in straight but in oblique lines. The motion of falling is the motion of non-autonomy.

If therefore Epicurus represents the materiality of the atom in its motion in a straight line, he has realized its formal determination in the declination from the straight line. And these opposed determinations are represented as directly opposed motions.

Lucretius, the only one of the ancients to understand the Epicurean physics, therefore maintains correctly that the declination breaks through the *fati foedera*, i.e. the decrees of fate, and, as he applies this directly to consciousness, it can be said of the atom that declination is that within it which can fight back and resist.

Epicurus feels with special force the contradiction implicit in his theory. He therefore endeavours to give to declination a representation as little sensory in character as possible. It is neither in a certain place nor at a fixed time; it comes into being in the smallest possible space.

Pierre Bayle, supported by the authority of Augustine, according to whom Democritus ascribed to the atoms a spiritual principle, reproaches Epicurus for having thought in terms of declination instead of this spiritual principle. Marx rebuts this opinion with the contrary viewpoint that to speak of the soul of the atom would be mere verbiage; while in declination the *real* soul of the atom, the concept of abstract individuality, is represented.

The declination of the atom from the straight line is in fact not a particular determination appearing accidentally in Epicurean physics. The law which it expresses runs through the whole of Epicurean philosophy.

As a matter of fact, the abstract individuality can affirm its pure being-for-itself only by making an abstraction of the being that comes into opposition to it. Thus as the atom frees itself from its relative existence, the straight line, by making an abstraction of it, by evading it, so the whole Epicurean philosophy evades the restrictive mode of being whenever the concept of abstract individuality, the autonomy and negation of all relation to other things, has to be represented in its existence.

Thus the goal of action is abstraction, the avoidance of pain and confusion, ataraxy. The good consists, therefore, in avoiding the bad; and happiness is avoidance of pain. Finally, where abstract individuality appears at the highest point of its freedom and autonomy, in its totality, then logically the mode of being that is evaded is all existence. Thus the gods evade the world and do not concern themselves with it and dwell outside it.

These gods, says Marx, are not a fiction of Epicurus. They have existed. They are the plastic gods of Greek art. Theoretical calm is a chief element in the character of Greek divinities. As Aristotle says: "What is best requires no action, for it itself is its own end."

Having demonstrated the key function of the concept of declination within the framework of Epicurean philosophy as a whole, Marx turns to discussing the consequence arising directly out of the declination of the atom. Its negation of all relation to something else can only be made real, positively established, if the being to which it refers is none other than itself, thus equally an atom, and, since it itself is directly determined, many atoms. Thus the repulsion of the many atoms is a necessary realization of the *lex atomi*, as Lucretius calls the declination, i.e. of the law of the atom. Lucretius says correctly that if the atoms were not accustomed to decline, neither repulsion nor encounter would have arisen, and the world would never have been created.

Thus it is that man ceases to be a product of nature only if the other thing, to which he is related, is not a different existence but rather itself an individual human being, although it is not yet the spirit. But in order for man to become his only true object, he must have crushed within himself his relative mode of being, the force of passion and of mere nature. Repulsion is the first form of self-consciousness; it corresponds therefore to the self-consciousness which comprehends itself as an imme-diately existing entity, an abstractly individual thing.

Hence in repulsion that concept of the atom is realized according to which it is abstract form, but the contrary is also realized, according to which it is abstract matter; for that to which it refers is indeed atoms, but other atoms. Now if I relate to myself as to something directly other, then my relating is a material one. This is the highest degree of externality that can be conceived. In the repulsion of the atoms, therefore, their materiality which was established as the downward fall in a straight line and their formal determination which was estab-lished in declination, they are synthetically united.

Democritus transforms into an act of blind necessity, a forcible movement, that which for Epicurus is a realization of the concept of the atom. The Epicurean declination of the atom thus changed the whole inner construction of the realm of the atoms, by making valid the determination of form and by realizing the contradiction which lies in the concept of the atom. Consequently, Epicurus was the first, even if only in sensible form, to have grasped the essence of repulsion, while Democritus only understood its material existence.

Therefore we also find more concrete forms of repulsion applied by Epicurus; in the political sphere it is the contract, in the social sphere friendship, which is praised as the highest.

With this very casual allusion to the consequences of the principle of repulsion in other realms than the atomic one, Marx concludes his chapter on the declination of the atom. Since in the course of these lectures the implications of this allusion will be discussed, I will content myself, at this point, by calling particular attention to its importance. This is the only passage in Marx's dissertation where we glimpse a wider intention to draw consequences from Epicurean physics, as applied to the social and political realm. The preparatory studies contain reflections about the close affinity between the religious and the political foundations of Greek life in general; but even those reflections have no direct bearing on Epicurus' atomistic philosophy.

Conversely, although the implications of Marx's approach to Epicurean physics in relation to the social and political realm can be traced in Marx's later writings, we look in vain for any explicit reference, in these later writings, to Epicurean philosophy. One of the reasons for this surprising silence could perhaps lie in the political consequences the Epicureans themselves drew from their principle of isolated individuality, in that they adopted an attitude of passivity towards the authorities. We shall not at this moment, however, pursue this question further.

The apparently casual nature of the reference to Epicurus' political and social ideas should not make us overlook its importance. Marx stresses the fact that the Epicurean principle of declination has changed the whole inner construction of the realm of the atom. Just as the real soul of the atom is represented in this principle, so the repulsion of the multiplicity of atoms, being the realization of this principle, is the first form of self-consciousness. Repulsion, says Marx, is in the social and political realm the reciprocal relationship between one individual human being and his second self, another individual being. Thus he has implicitly formulated the principle of a civil society, which is based on the concept of abstract individuality.

We have to think of these implicit consequences also in relation to Marx's account of the qualities of the atom, which forms the subject of the second chapter of the second part of the dissertation. Marx sees his understanding of the peculiar character of Epicurus' atomic theory confirmed in the consideration of the qualities of the atom. The very concept of the atom in fact rules out the attribution of qualities, because, as Epicurus says, every quality is changeable but the atoms do not change. Even so, it is a necessary consequence of his approach to attribute qualities to atoms. For the plurality of atoms in repulsion, separated by sensible space, must necessarily be directly different one from another and be different from the pure essence of the atom, i.e. must possess qualities.

Through those qualities the atom acquires an existence which contradicts its concept; it is presented in a mode of alienated being differentiated from its essence. It is this contradiction which constitutes the main interest of Epicurus. Therefore, as soon as he postulates a quality and thus has drawn the consequence of the material nature of the atom, he counter-postulates at the same time determinations which again destroy this quality in its own sphere and, on the other hand, validate the concept of the atom. He determines, therefore, all qualities —size, form and weight—in such a way that they contradict themselves. Democritus, on the other hand, nowhere considers the qualities in relation to the atom itself, nor does he objectify the internal contradiction between concept and existence.

The consideration of the qualities of the atom provides us therefore with the same result as the consideration of declination, namely, that Epicurus objectifies the contradiction in the concept of the atom between essence and existence and thus creates the science of atomism, while in Democritus no realization of the principle element itself takes place, but only the material side is maintained and only hypotheses are offered in support of empirical investigation.

In Epicurus' view, the world of appearance can only proceed from the perfected atom, i.e. from the qualified atom, which has been alienated from its concept. Epicurus expresses this by saying that only the qualified atom becomes *stoicheion* or that only the *atomon stoicheion* is endowed with qualities. This distinction between the atom as *arche* and *stoicheion*, as principle element and basis, belongs to Epicurus. For Democritus, on the other hand, the atom has only the meaning of *stoicheion*, of material substratum. The importance of this difference will become clear from what now follows.

The contradiction between existence and essence, between matter and form, which lies in the concept of the atom is attributed to the individual atom by endowing it with qualities. Through its quality the atom is alienated from its concept, but at the same time perfected in its construction. Out of repulsion and the consequent conglomerations of the qualified atoms there now emerges the world of appearance.

In this passage from the world of essence into the world of appearance the contradiction in the concept of the atom reaches its most vivid realization. For according to its concept, the atom is the absolute, essential form of nature. This absolute form is now degraded to absolute matter, to the formless substratum of the world of appearance.

Atoms are, to be sure, the substance of nature out of which everything arises, into which everything dissolves; but the constant annihilation of the world of appearance yields no final result. New appearances are formed; the atom itself remains always at the bottom, like a sediment. Thus in so far as the atom is envisaged in terms of its pure concept, its existence is empty space, annihilated nature; in so far as it comes into reality it is degraded to a material basis which, as the bearer of a world of multitudinous relations, never exists except in its external forms that are indifferent to that material basis. This is a necessary consequence because the atom, conceived as an abstract and complete particular, cannot affirm itself as an idealizing and dominating power over that multiplicity.

Abstract particularity is freedom *from* being, not freedom *in* being. It cannot shine in the light of being. There it is an

element, and so loses its character and becomes material. Therefore, the atom does not manifest itself in the light of appearance,
or it sinks down to a material basis when it does enter it. The
atom as such exists only in the void. Thus the death of nature
has become its immortal subsistence, and Lucretius correctly
asserts: "It is as if we had never been born, when immortal
death has taken away our mortal life." It could be said that in
Epicurean philosophy it is death itself which is immortal.

Epicurus grasps this contradiction at this its highest point
and objectifies it. He distinguishes the atom where it becomes a
basis of appearance as *stoicheion* from the atom as it exists in the
void as *arché*. This is what constitutes his philosophical difference
from Democritus, who only objectifies the one element, the
atom as *stoicheion*, material substratum.

Since in the atom matter, as pure relationship to itself, is
removed from all mutability and relativity, it immediately
follows that time is to be excluded from the concept of the
atom, from the world of essence. For matter is only external
and autonomous in so far as one makes an abstraction of the
temporal element within it. Here Democritus and Epicurus
agree. But they differ as to the manner in which time, removed
from the world of atoms, is determined, whither it is transferred.

For Democritus time is not important; nor is it necessary to
the system. He explains it in order to dispose of it. Time, excluded from the world of essence, is transferred to the self-
consciousness of the philosophizing subject, but does not make
contact with the world itself.

Epicurus treats it differently. Excluded from the world of
essence, time for him becomes the absolute form of appearance. Time is to the world of appearance what the concept of
the atom is to the world of essence, namely the abstraction,
annihilation and reduction of all determined being into being-
for-itself.

From this consideration Marx draws the following conclusions. First, Epicurus makes the contradiction between matter
and form the character of phenomenal nature, which thus becomes the counterpart of essential nature, the atom. This
happens in that time is opposed to space, the active form of
appearance is opposed to the passive.

Second, only in Epicurus is appearance apprehended as appearance, that is, as an alienation of the essence which asserts itself as alienation in its reality. On the other hand, in Democritus time is the fire of essence which eternally consumes appearance and stamps it with the character of dependence and non-being.

Finally, time is, according to Epicurus, change as change, reflection of appearance in itself. Consequently, phenomenal nature is correctly posited as objective; sensory perception is correctly made the real criterion of concrete nature, although the atom, its basis, is only grasped through reason. The mutability of the sensible world as mutability, its change as change, this reflection of appearance in itself which forms the concept of time, has its particular existence in conscious sensibility. The sensibility of man is therefore embodied time, the existing reflection of the world of sense in itself.

By means of this connection between time and sensibility the *eidōla*, images, which are also found in Democritus, acquire a more consistent status. The *eidōla* are the forms of natural bodies which peel off from them, as it were, as skins and cause them to enter into appearance. These forms of things constantly flow from them and press against the senses and in this way allow objects to appear. Therefore, in hearing nature hears itself, in smelling smells itself, in seeing sees itself. Human sensibility is thus the medium in which, as in a focal glass, natural processes reflect themselves and ignite to become the light of appearance.

In Democritus this is an inconsistency, since appearance is only subjective; in Epicurus it is a necessary conclusion, since sensibility is the reflection of the phenomenal world in itself, its embodied time. The relation of sensibility and time exhibits itself in such a way that the temporality of things and their appearance to the senses are posited as intrinsically one. It is precisely because bodies appear to the senses that they pass away. Indeed, the *eidōla*, by perpetually separating themselves from the bodies and flowing into the senses, by having their sensibility outside themselves as another nature, not in themselves, i.e. by not returning out of the diremption—for these reasons they dissolve and perish.

Thus as the atom is nothing but the natural form of the abstract, individual self-consciousness, so sensible nature is only the objectivity of the empirical, individual self-consciousness; and this is what constitutes sensibility. The senses are therefore the only criteria in concrete nature, as abstract reason is the only criterion in the world of atoms.

This important conclusion with which Marx completes his exposition of Epicurus' concept of time, serves at the same time as the indispensable starting-point for the final chapter of the dissertation, which will apply these notions to the realm of religion. In that realm Marx's exposition will reach its climax. In a sense, his preceding argument about the specific character of Epicurus' philosophy of nature provided the preliminary stages leading to this apex. It will be my task in my next lecture to discuss this concluding chapter.

6

From Platonism to Christianity

MARX's insight into the crucial importance of Epicurus' theory of the declination of atoms is quintessentially revealed in the final chapter of the dissertation, which deals with Epicurus' ideas about meteors. It is in this celestial dimension that the full range and depth of Epicurus' critique of religion become evident.

The difference between Democritus and Epicurus in the field of atomistic philosophy is reproduced in the macro-dimension. Whatever may be said in favour of Democritus' astronomical views in the context of his own time, they are of no philosophical interest. They do not go beyond empirical reflection; nor are they in any definite way related to the doctrine of atoms.

Epicurus' theory of the meteors—a term which includes both the heavenly bodies and the processes connected with them— stands in contrast to Democritus' opinion. After all we have learnt in the earlier chapters of the dissertation about the differences between these two philosophers, this may neither surprise us nor appear to deserve any special attention.

But the difference proves to be still more crucial at this point, where what is at issue is Greek philosophy *in toto*. It is only in this closing chapter, therefore, that the full impact of their disagreement in the field of atomistic philosophy becomes obvious. Epicurus' total disagreement with Democritus is essentially rooted in his dissent from the opinion of Greek philosophy in general. This contrast is revealed in that dimension where the ultimate religious background of the whole of Greek philosophy is to be found, namely, in the celestial dimension.

The adoration of the heavenly bodies is a cult which all Greek philosophers celebrate. The system of the heavenly bodies is the first kind of naïve and naturally determined existence of true reason. Greek self-consciousness occupies the same position in the realm of the mind. It is the intellectual solar system. Thus Greek philosophers worshipped their own mind in the heavenly bodies.

Marx illustrates his bold thesis with reference to a number of Greek philosophers. Anaxagoras, who was the first to give a physical explanation to the heavens and thus drew them down to earth, when asked why he had been born answered in this way: *eis theorian heliou kai selènès kai ouranou*, which means: "for the observation and contemplation of sun, moon and heaven." Xenophanes, however, looked at the heavens and said: "The one is God." The religious association accorded to the heavenly bodies in the Pythagoreans, Plato and Aristotle, is well known.

Aristotle refers to the fact that all men have an idea of gods and assign the highest place to the divine Being, the barbarians as well as the Hellenes. The ancients assigned the heavens and the highest place to the gods because they alone are immortal. As many as believe in the existence of the gods obviously connect the immortal with the immortal, because the contrary is impossible. Thus Aristotle concludes that, if a divine Being exists—as indeed it does—then our common statement about the substance of the heavenly bodies must also be correct. There is one heaven, indestructible, uncreated, totally removed from every mortal ill. Thus the divinely given concept of the divine encompassing all of nature bears testimony to the phenomenon of the one heaven, just as, conversely, that phenomenon bears testimony to the concept.

Of course, Aristotle makes a distinction between the mythological form in which the ancestral traditions were cast and their philosophical essence. But basically Aristotle's views are in line with the whole tradition of Greek philosophy. Epicurus, on the other hand, opposed the view of the whole Greek people. Whereas, for instance, Aristotle merely rejects the belief that the heavens require the support of Atlas, Epicurus takes a radically new step. He attacks the belief that man needs the heavens; and Atlas himself, upon whose back the heavens are supported, he sees as incarnating human stupidity and superstition. Stupidity and superstition are also Titans.

The theory of the meteors is a matter of conscience for Epicurus. What he denies is the pre-eminence which the theory of the meteors is supposed to enjoy over the other sciences. He puts this theory on a level with the rest of natural science. He does not believe that from knowledge of the meteors, whether they be considered in general or in detail, any other goal can be reached than ataraxis, that is mental tranquillity, and solid assurance, as is the case with the other sciences. Our life does not need ideologies and empty hypotheses, but requires that we live without confusion.

But this having been said, the radical contrast between the theory of the meteors and the rest of natural sciences, is stated by Epicurus with considerable emphasis. Aristotle, in agreement with the other Greek philosophers, makes the heavenly bodies eternal and immortal because they always behave in the same way, while he ascribes to them their own, higher element, not subjected to the force of gravity. Epicurus claims that it is exactly the other way round. His theory of the meteors is specifically different from all other physical theory, in that everything happens in the meteors in multifarious and unregulated fashion, everything in them is to be explained by a variety of reasons. Indeed he rejects, angrily and with some vehemence, the opposite opinion which holds to one method of explanation to the exclusion of all others, which assumes something unified and therefore eternal and divine in the meteors, which falls into vain explanation and is led astray by the servile tricks of the astrologers. Those who think thus overstep the bounds of natural science and throw themselves into the arms of myth.

In Epicurus' view, any explanation which respects the limits of natural science is satisfactory. Only let myth be avoided. It will be avoided if, attending strictly to the phenomena, one draws conclusions from them concerning what is invisible. One must hold fast to the appearance of things, to what is perceived by the senses. The analogy is applicable, therefore. One can thus explain away fear and free one's self from it, giving reasons concerning the meteors and the other things which dismay the rest of mankind. There is only one absolute norm: that nothing can be ascribed to an indestructible and eternal nature that destroys ataraxy, that gives rise to alarm.

Thus Epicurus concludes: Because the eternity of the heavenly bodies would disturb the ataraxy of self-consciousness, the absolute tranquillity of mind, it is a necessary, stringent conclusion that the heavenly bodies are not eternal.

It is this strange conclusion which puzzles Marx. He is not satisfied with any explanation given thus far by authors writing on Epicurean philosophy. They present this theory of the meteors as something incongruous with the rest of his physics, with his atomistic theory. The battle against the Stoics, superstition and astrology are the three factors cited by these authors as sufficient explanation for it.

In Marx's analysis, however, Epicurus' opposition to the Stoics explains nothing. Their superstition and indeed their whole view had already been refuted by Democritus' thesis that the celestial bodies were accidental complexes of atoms and their processes the accidental motion of these atoms. The supposed eternal nature of these bodies was annihilated by this —a conclusion which Democritus was satisfied to draw from that premise. Indeed, their very existence had been nullified.

Consequently, atomistics needed no new method. Epicurus does nonetheless differentiate the method applied in his theory of meteors from the method employed in the rest of his physics. Where does he get this idea from?

Marx finds the solution of this problem in the relationship between Epicurus' specific atomistic theory and his special theory of the meteors. For Epicurus, the heavenly bodies are atoms become real. The atom is matter in the form of autonomy, of individuality, as it were, the representation of weight. But the heavenly bodies are the highest reality of weight. In them, all antinomies between form and matter, between concept and existence, which formed the development of the atom are solved; in them, all determinations which were demanded are realized. The celestial bodies are eternal and unchanging; they have their centre of gravity in themselves, not outside themselves. Their only action is motion; and separated by empty space, they deviate from the straight line, form a system of repulsion and attraction in which they maintain all their autonomy and finally engender time out of themselves as the form of their appearance. Thus in the heavenly bodies matter has become endowed with individuality.

Epicurus must have seen in this the highest existence of his principal element, the peak and finale of his system. But at this very culmination a puzzling antinomy arises. Epicurus declared that he had postulated the atoms so that immortal foundations would lie at the basis of nature. He alleged himself concerned about the substantial individuality of matter. But where he finds the reality of his nature—because he knows only the mechanical—in autonomous, indestructible matter, in the heavenly bodies, whose eternal existence and immutability are proven by the belief of the people, the judgment of philosophy and the evidence of the senses—there it is his single aim to draw them back down into earthly transitoriness. It is at this juncture that he turns jealously against the worshippers of autonomous nature, which contains the point of individuality in itself. This is his greatest contradiction.

Therefore Epicurus feels that his earlier categories go to pieces here, that the method of his theory becomes a different one. And this is the deepest wisdom of his system, the most thorough consistency, that he feels this and expresses it consciously.

The whole Epicurean philosophy of nature is steeped in the contradiction between essence and existence, between form and matter. But in the heavenly bodies this contradiction is resolved, the conflicting elements are reconciled. In the celestial system matter has received form within itself, has taken into itself individuality and has thus achieved autonomy. But at this point matter stops being an affirmation of the abstract self-consciousness. In the world of atoms as in the world of appearance, form battled with matter; one determination destroyed the other, and precisely in this contradiction the abstract, individual self-consciousness sensed its nature to have been objectified. The abstract form which battled with abstract matter under the form of matter was individual self-consciousness itself. But now, where matter has reconciled itself with form and is objectified, the individual self-consciousness emerges from its husk, announces itself as the true principal element and contends against nature, which has become autonomous.

From another point of view it can be expressed in this way:

matter, by receiving individuality within itself, that is by receiving form, has ceased to be an abstract individual. This is the case with celestial bodies, in which matter has become concrete individuality. But at this point the analogy between the atoms and the celestial bodies turns into its opposite. We have learned that the declination of the atom from the straight line is for Epicurus the decisive principle whereby the atom breaks through the law of blind necessity and maintains its absolute autonomy. Indeed, the concept of declination from the straight line was derived by Epicurus from the motion of the celestial bodies and was applied to the movement of the atoms. His sole purpose was to guarantee the pure freedom of the atoms. But he does not recognize this freedom in the actual motions of the celestial bodies. On the contrary, though their movement declines from the straight line, it does not mirror their autonomy but, since their movement is eternally recurrent and unchanging, is the expression of blind necessity, of mere passivity under the immutable law of nature. The abstract individuality of the atom, the moment it becomes concrete in the celestial bodies, turns into generality.

Thus in the meteors the abstract, individual self-consciousness is confronted with its objective refutation—the general attains existence and nature. Therefore, it recognizes in them its mortal enemy. Thus it attributes to them, as Epicurus does, all the fear and confusion of human beings, because the fear and dissolution of the abstract individual is the general. So here the true principal element of Epicurus, the abstract, individual self-consciousness, is concealed no longer. It steps out from its hiding-place and, freed from material disguise, it seeks to destroy the reality of autonomous nature in terms of abstract possibility—what is possible can also be different; the opposite of the possible is also possible. From this comes the polemic against those who explain the heavenly bodies *haplos*, that is, simply, absolutely, only in one way, instead of *pollachos*, that is, in many ways. For the One is necessary and autonomous in itself; and this is precisely what Epicurus, in defence of the abstract, individual self-consciousness, denies and attacks in the concrete manifestations of heaven.

Thus as long as nature, as atom and appearance, expresses the individual self-consciousness and its contradiction, the subjectivity of the latter appears only in the form of matter itself; where, on the other hand, this subjectivity becomes autonomous, the individual self-consciousness is reflected in itself, and opposes nature in its own shape as autonomous form.

It could have been predicted from the beginning that when Epicurus' principal element is realized, it will stop having any reality for him. If the individual self-consciousness had been placed in reality under the determination of nature or nature under its determination, then its determination, that is, its existence, would have ceased, because only the general in free differentiation from itself can at the same time know its affirmation.

In the theory of the meteors, therefore, Marx discovers the heart of the Epicurean philosophy of nature. Its absolute principle is the *ataraxy*, the mental tranquillity of the individual self-consciousness; and therefore nothing is eternal which annihilates this principle. The heavenly bodies disturb the ataraxy of the individual self-consciousness, its identity with itself, because they are existing generality, because nature has become autonomous in them. The absolute character and freedom of self-consciousness is the principal element of Epicurean philosophy, even if self-consciousness is only conceived in the form of individuality.

This analysis brings Marx to a twofold conclusion of first importance. If the abstract, individual self-consciousness is posited as an absolute principal element, then the effect is double-edged—it cuts both ways!

On the one hand, this principle undermines all true science, in so far as individuality is not paramount in the nature of things themselves. Since Marx does not elaborate this aspect, his statement concerning this negative side of Epicurus' philosophy of nature might easily be overlooked. Indeed, when in the closing sentences of the dissertation Marx proclaims Epicurus the greatest Greek representative of enlightenment, what he has in mind is the other side of Epicurus' philosophy, its radical opposition to Greek religion. But Marx's clear and explicit recognition of the basic impotence of this philosophy as regards the creation of true science, means, in fact, that we are to stress the adjective "Greek". Epicurus' opposition to Greek philosophy as a whole and his pioneering rôle in anticipating the modern European Enlightenment remain imprisoned in the magic circle of Greek civilization; they have no direct and intrinsic relationship to the birth of modern science.

In this respect Democritus and Epicurus stand on the same ground. One must see their differences as contrasts within one and the same circle. In Epicurus the atomistic theory with all its contradictions is carried through as the natural science of self-consciousness. The absolute principle of self-consciousness in the form of abstract individuality is raised to its highest conclusion, that is, its dissolution and conscious opposition to the universal. For Democritus, on the other hand, the atom is only the general, objective expression of the empirical investigation of nature in general. The atom remains for him a pure and abstract category, a hypothesis, which is the outcome of experience, not its energizing principal element. The atom remains unrealized, just as the real investigation of nature is no further affected by it.

The fact that neither Democritus' nor Epicurus' atomistic philosophy—albeit for opposite reasons—has affected the real investigation of nature, is one side of the question. It was not this aspect, however, which formed the main theme of Marx's dissertation. What fascinated him was the other edge to Epicurus' sword, his opposition to all forms of transcendence. If the abstract, individual consciousness is posited as an absolute principal element, then everything collapses which behaves transcendentally over and against human consciousness, that is, which belongs to the imaginative intellect. Full stress has to be laid on the adjective "individual", in radical contrast with "general". For if self-consciousness, which knows itself only under the form of abstract generality, is made to become an absolute principal element, then the door is opened wide to superstitious mysticism. The historical proof of this Marx finds in Stoic philosophy. The abstract, general self-consciousness has an urge to affirm itself in things in which it is only affirmed by denying them. As the radical enemy of mystical and superstitious self-consciousness, Epicurus, in Marx's eyes, is the great forerunner of the modern Enlightenment. He has cast down religion, as Lucretius' eulogistic poem says of him, whilst we are exalted high as heaven by the victory.

In the inner contradiction which impelled Epicurus to deny

in the heavenly realm the consequences of his own atomistic principle, Marx has tried to lay bare the inner contradiction of the whole of Greek philosophy. It would be a grave misunderstanding, therefore, to regard Marx's dissertation as simply a polemical treatise against religion. On the contrary, his analysis is an attempt to reveal the inner dialectics of the human self-consciousness which needs and produces religious objects and at the same time denies and rejects them.

Marx therefore unleashes his bitter criticism against that total lack of understanding which describes Epicurus' philosophy as "gastrology", that is, a belly-doctrine. Plutarch, who took this false idea from the Stoic philosophers, is the typical representative of religious apologetics, and so becomes a special target for Marx's attacks. For Epicurus, the highest happiness is freedom from pain, is total indifference. His supreme good, where the world is concerned, is to be freed from the world. The heart of all evil is that the individual is imprisoned in his own empirical nature and excludes his eternal nature, that is, conceives his own eternal nature as an empirical god outside of himself. What is deified by Epicurus is the free individuality, liberated from its familiar shackles. The centre of his adoration is the non-existence of God as God, God's existence as the supreme happiness of the individual, God as ataraxy, as perfect peace of mind. The *makariotès*, the pure bliss, the perfect satisfaction of nothingness, the being totally void of any determination, *that* is God. Epicurus' God is a *deus otiosus*, a completely inactive God who dwells not inside but outside the world.

Therefore, Plutarch's allegation that Epicurus destroys all belief in immortality, and so deprives the masses of their sweetest and greatest hope, is false. Far from destroying this notion, Epicurus explains it and elevates it to the level of real understanding. His doctrine of immortality consists in the doctrine of the eternity of atoms. That is the hope and consolation for every individual. The personal import of this doctrine is stressed by Marx with reference to a poem of the seventeenth-century mystic, Jacob Böhme: "Whoever conceives eternity as time and time as eternity, is freed from all discord."

People have indeed poked fun at the gods of Epicurus, who live a life of bliss in the intermundia, the empty spaces between the worlds. These gods have no body but a quasi-body, no blood but quasi-blood; and subsisting in blissful peace, they hear no supplication. They are unconcerned about men and the world, are venerated for their beauty, their majesty and their superior nature, not for any gain. But they are entirely consonant with Epicurus' doctrine. Much as the atom frees itself from its relative existence, the straight line, by evading it, so the goal of action is the avoidance of pain and confusion, ataraxy, and so likewise the gods avoid the world and do not concern themselves with it. In this respect, too, Epicurus' philosophy is the culmination of the Greek tradition. For these gods are not a fiction created by Epicurus; they do exist. They are the plastic gods of Greek art. Plutarch is blamed by Marx for having forgotten every Greek concept when he opines that this theory of the gods destroys fear and superstition, without providing joy and gratitude for favour of the gods, but rather it gives man the relationship to them that we have to Hyrkanian fishes, from which we expect neither harm nor advantage. Plutarch has apparently forgotten that theoretical calm is a chief element in the character of Greek divinities. As Aristotle says: "What is best requires no action, for it itself is its own end."

This total inactivity and indifference which for the Greek mind have always been the supreme image of pure theory, of perfect contemplation, in the closing period of Greek philosophy found their adequate expression in the philosophy of Epicurus. His greatness is that he has applied his principal element of ataraxy both in his theoretical considerations—his atomistic theory and his theory of the meteors and of the gods—and in his practical philosophy, his ethics of mental tranquillity as the supreme good.

There is also a second thread connecting Epicurus with the whole tradition of Greek thinking. The ideal of the sage is a key issue in all the post-Aristotelian systems; but in Epicurus' atomistic philosophy this theme has received its most consistent treatment. Marx fastens upon it as a telling illustration of the way classical Greek philosophy issued in the complete objectivization of Epicurus' thinking.

As the *nous*, the cosmic material spirit, of Anaxagoras begins to move in the reflection of the Sophists (in whose philosophy the *nous* becomes, in fact, the non-being of the world), and this motion receives an objective form in the *daimonion* of Socrates, so in its turn the practical motion of Socrates' reflection becomes a general and ideal motion in Plato's philosophy, so that the *nous* widens into a realm of ideas. In Aristotle, this process is once more comprehended in its particularity, which has now become a real and conceptual one.

Thus there is one and the same spirit linking up the tradition of Greek thought from the beginning to the end, from Anaxagoras to Epicurus. The figure which we see finally emerging from the workshop of the Greek philosophical consciousness, from the darkness of abstraction and wrapped in its dark folds, is the same figure in which Greek philosophy has trodden the stage of the world, the same which saw gods even in the fire upon the hearth, the same which drank the poison cup, the same which, as the god of Aristotle, enjoys the supreme bliss, the bliss of theory, pure contemplation.

That figure has been given a classical embodiment in the ideal of the sage. The sage, *sophos,* is to be understood under two aspects, one theoretical and one practical, which have one and the same root. The notion of the sage is the practical expression of an idea theoretically manifested in philosophical thinking about the material world. Greek philosophy begins with seven sages, one of whom is the Ionian philosopher of nature, Thales; and it ends with an attempt to portray the stage in a clear-cut concept. This history of the Greek sage is, as a whole, dominated by one *sophos,* namely, Socrates. Of course, this is not to be taken as an exoteric fact, any more than Greece was politically ruined when Alexander the Great lost his wisdom in Babylon.

The Greek philosopher is a *demiurgos,* he creates a world of his own, a different world from that which flourishes in the natural sunlight of substantial reality. This ideal substance is embodied in the very philosophers who testify to it. These sages are no more popular, therefore, than the statues of the Olympic gods. Their way of life is a self-sufficient calm, their attitude towards the people is the same objective stance they assume towards substantial reality. This dualism becomes acute when, in the Sophists, the ideal world created by the philosopher, the sage, appears in its direct form, that is, in the subjective spirit which opposes substantial reality. The nucleus of this development appears in the person of Socrates, who is called by the delphic oracle, *sophotatos,* sagest of all.

The paramount importance of Socrates consists in his having represented the relationship between Greek philosophy and the Greek spirit, between consciousness of the ideal world and substantial reality. In Socrates the intrinsic limitations of Greek philosophy become obvious; and this is true in three respects.

First, the fact that the ideal aspect of substantial reality has acquired autonomy in the form of the subjective spirit means a leap, a decisive break with substantial reality. This leap, this apostasy, is represented in the *daimonion,* the enigmatic and irrepressible conscience which Socrates finds in the inner recesses of his own mind. Socrates is a no less substantial individual than the earlier philosophers, but in a subjective way, not in the form of a complete substance, not an image of the gods, but a human image; not mysterious, but clear and light; not a seer, but a "cheerful companion".

Secondly, this subject which stands in opposition to substantial reality, has become a judge; it sets a purpose for the world, which is at the same time its own purpose. The sage presents the purpose, the supreme good, in his own life as well as in his teachings. He is the subjective spirit which has begun to pass into practice.

Finally, while enacting the judgment of subjective understanding over against the world, the individuality of the sage is inwardly divided and becomes the object of its own judgment. On the one hand, his individuality is itself rooted in substantial reality, it has its right of existence only in the right of its state, its religion, in a word, in all substantial conditions which are manifest in its nature. On the other hand, the sage contains in himself the purpose which is the judge of all these substantial conditions. Thus his own substantial nature is judged inside himself. He is bound, therefore, to perish, for the very reason that his point of origin is the substantial spirit, and not the free spirit which endures all contradictions and overcomes them, because it owes nothing to any natural condition.

In the life and praxis of Socrates, the subjective spirit presents itself in its exponent, as an education whereby he leads each individual out of his substantial bonds into an autonomous existence. Setting aside this practical activity, his philosophy as a merely abstract definition of the supreme good becomes pointless. His philosophy is the act of emigrating out of the substantial images, differences, and so on, and of immigrating into the autonomy; but it has no other content than the very act of dissolving the reflection of which it is the vehicle. The philosophy of Socrates is therefore essentially his own wisdom; his own goodness in relation to the world is the sole fulfilment of his philosophy of the supreme good. In other words, the subjectivity of Socrates is something quite different from the presuppositions of Kant's categorical imperative. In Kant's philosophy, the attitude of the empirical subject towards the categorical imperative is of no importance.

From Socrates, Marx finally proceeds to Plato, in whose thinking the movement of Greek philosophy becomes ideal. As Socrates is the image and teacher of the world, so are Plato's ideas, his philosophical abstractions, the archetypes of the world.

In Plato, this abstract definition of the supreme good expands into an extensive, world-embracing philosophy. Whereas Socrates merely discovered the name of the ideal world which had moved from substantial reality into the subject, and while he was still himself this conscious movement, it is in Plato's consciousness that substantial reality becomes really and truly idealized. But the effect of this process is to render this ideal world itself no less pluriform than the really substantial world to which it stands in opposition. For the philosopher, the differentiation and pluriformity of the real world have moved to the ideal sphere beyond. The ideal world which, in Socrates' consciousness, had moved into the subject, had now abandoned this world.

Thus the philosopher as sage has become the truth beyond the substantial world over against him. This relationship is aptly exhibited in Plato's thesis that for the state to arrive at its destination, either the philosophers must become kings or the kings philosophers.

Plato contemplates his relationship to reality in such a manner that an independent realm of ideas hovers beyond reality, in which it is darkly mirrored; this beyond is the philosopher's own subjectivity. It is Plato's intention to transplant into the ideal realm not only things but the very sphere of being in its totality. This ideal realm is a closed, specifically distinguished realm within the philosopher's consciousness itself; it therefore lacks movement. This contradiction within the philosopher's consciousness is bound to be objectified and projected into the ideal realm itself. Ideas are paradigms not only of sensible objects but of the ideas themselves, so that the ideas are at once paradigms and images.

Marx's thoughts on the development of Greek philosophy up to Socrates and Plato, recorded in one of his preparatory studies, find a fascinating complement and conclusion in another part of the same studies—that part containing his comments on a book of Ferdinand Christian Baur, entitled "The Christian Element in Platonism, or: Socrates and Christ" (*Das Christliche des Platonismus oder Sokrates und Christus*). Baur, a theologian and church historian who had won fame as a leading scholar of the Tübingen school of historio-critical biblical research, had published his book in 1837.

Marx begins by reacting critically to Baur's thesis that Socratic philosophy and Christianity are related to each other as are self-knowledge and knowledge of sin. In Marx's view, the conclusion to be drawn from Baur's own exposition is the very opposite of an alleged analogy between Socrates and Christ. If self-knowledge and knowledge of sin are related to each other as are the general and the specific, then the so-called analogy between the Socratic irony—that is, the obstetrical method of that philosopher—on one hand, and grace on the other, is in fact a glaring contradiction. The Socratic irony, as conceived by Baur who follows in the footsteps of Hegel, is the dialectical trap whereby the common human understanding is liberated from its arterio-sclerosis and is precipitated into its own immanent truth. This irony is the subjective relationship of philosophy to the common understanding. The fact that this philosophy has assumed in Socrates the form of an ironic man, of a sage, follows from the basic character of Greek philosophy and its relationship to reality. But so far as the objective content of Greek philosophy is concerned, any philosopher, be it Heraclitus, Thales or Johann Gottlieb Fichte— whoever maintains the truth of immanence over against the empirical person—is an ironic man.

Conversely, in the case of grace and the knowledge of sin,

not only the subject who receives grace and is brought to knowledge of sin, but even the subject who bestows grace and the subject who rises from the knowledge of sin are empirical persons.

The only point of analogy between Socrates and Christ might be that Socrates is philosophy personified, as Christ is religion personified. But what matters is not the question of a general relationship between philosophy and religion, but the relationship between philosophy institutionalized and religion institutionalized. The general relationship between a philosopher, Socrates, and a teacher of religion, Christ, is no more relevant than the relationship between Plato's state as a general ethical expression of the Socratic idea and the general expression of the idea. Likewise, it is no more relevant than the relationship between Christ as a historical individual and the Church. Moreover, the important fact is neglected that Plato's Republic is a product of Plato's own mind, whereas the Church is, on the other hand, totally distinct from Christ.

If Hegel was right in saying that in his Republic Plato maintained Greek substantiality over against the invading principle of subjectivity, then Plato is the radical opposite of Christ. For Christ maintained this element of subjectivity over against the existing state, which he characterized as merely worldly and profane. That the Platonic Republic remained an ideal, whereas the Christian Church became a reality, was not in itself the true difference. The true difference lies in the fact that the Platonic idea followed reality, while the Christian idea preceded it.

Therefore it would be much more reasonable to find Platonic elements in Christianity than Christian elements in Plato, the more so since the early church fathers, historically speaking, originated in part from Platonic philosophy. From the philosophical point of view it is important that in the Platonic Republic the highest order is that of the sages. A similar relationship exists between the Platonic ideas and the Christian Logos, between the Platonic recollection and the Christian restoration of man to his original image, between the Platonic descent of souls and the Christian fall of man, the myth of the pre-existence of the soul.

Marx then goes on to comment on Baur's thesis that more

than any other philosophy in ancient times Platonism has the character of a religion. Baur points to Plato's definition of the task of philosophy as salvation, liberation, separation of the soul from the body, as a dying and a mortification.

Baur's thesis, which in itself is not wrong, is really pointing to the fact that no philosopher has brought more religious enthusiasm to his task than has Plato, whose philosophical commitment indeed had for him the meaning and character of a religious cult. But how should this religious dedication on his part be evaluated? Marx compares Plato's attitude with that of other great philosophers whose relationship to philosophy had a more general form, less imbued with empirical sentiment. Yet their enthusiasm was no less intense: Aristotle's enthusiasm, when he extols *theoria,* theoretical knowledge, contemplation, as the supreme good and happiness, or when he admires the Reason of Nature; Spinoza's, when he describes the experience of contemplation *sub specie aeternitatis,* the love of God or the freedom of the human mind; Hegel's, when he develops the eternal realization of the Idea, the magnificent organism of the Universe. The enthusiasm of these three philosophers is well founded, thorough, gratifying to the general educated mind. In contrast with Plato's religious devotion, which has functioned only as a kind of hot-water-bottle for individual minds, the enthusiasm of Aristotle, Spinoza and Hegel has become the animating Spirit of historical developments on a world scale. Whereas Plato's enthusiasm was totally consumed in the flames of ecstasy, the enthusiasm of these other great philosophers became the pure, ideal flame of science.

On the one hand, it is true that the Christian religion, as the apex of religious development, must have a closer relationship to the subjective form of Platonic philosophy than it has to the subjective form of other ancient philosophical systems. But conversely, it is equally true that no philosophy has revealed more distinctly the contradiction between religion and philosophy than Plato's has done. For whereas with Plato philosophy appears in the guise of religion, it is, conversely, in Christianity that religion appears in the guise of philosophy.

Why is it that Plato felt the desire to undergird his philosophical insights with a positively mythical foundation? In the development of those questions of ethics, religion and even natural philosophy, concerning which his negative explanation of the Absolute turns out to be unsatisfactory, Plato is forced to resort to a positive account of the Absolute. The appropriate form of such a positive explanation is myth and allegory. When the Absolute and the limited, positive reality are set in opposition to each other, and when the latter has to be supported at all costs, then positive reality turns into a transparent medium whereby the absolute light is refracted into a fantastic spectrum of colours, so that the positive and limited is made to refer to something else, to serve as a miraculous chrysalis for the hidden soul. The whole world has then turned into a world of myths. Every shape is an enigma.

Marx adds to this description a reference to a return of these mythological and allegorical tendencies in recent times, apparently engendered by not dissimilar reasons. This personal note is significant for the intimate relationship of Marx's own development to his confrontation with Plato's religious philosophy. He is still in intense discussion with the romanticist ideas which only a few years before had caught his mind and heart.

Marx continues his discussion of Plato's mythology by expounding its relationship to Christianity. The positive explanation of the Absolute and its mythical-allegorical garb is the source, the heart-beat, of the philosophy of transcendence, i.e. of a transcendence that is essentially related to and intersects the sphere of immanence. At this point Marx sees congeniality between Platonic philosophy and any positive religion, notably the Christian religion, which is the perfect philosophy of transcendence. From this point of view it is possible to show a profound connection of historical Christianity with the history of ancient philosophy. If one individual *par excellence* has been in Plato's view the mirror, indeed, the myth of wisdom, if he calls that man, Socrates, the philosopher of death and love, then this view is anchored in his positive account of the Absolute. This did not imply that Plato had to dispense with the historical Socrates; for a positive account of the Absolute is connected with the subjective character of Greek philosophy, as expressed in the figure of the sage. Death and love are the myths of a negative dialectic; for the dialectic is the inner, simple light, the penetrating eye of love, the inner soul which is not subdued by the body of material fragmentation, the inmost recesses of the mind. Thus its myth is love. At the same time, the dialectic is the sweeping torrent which breaks through the multiple and its limits, which destroys all distinct shapes, absorbing all things in the one ocean of eternity. Its myth is death.

Indeed, the dialectic is death; but it is at the same time the vehicle of creative life, blossoming in the garden of the spirit; it is the foaming potion, sparkling with seeds out of which buds the fiery flower of the one spirit. Plotinus calls the dialectic, the path to *haplosis*, simplification of the soul, direct union with God. In this term Aristotle's *theoria* is united with Plato's dialectic. Their absorption in the empirical, individual consciousness appears in Plotinus as the state of ecstasy.

The dialectic of death and love, leading up to the mystical union with God, to the point where Aristotle's contemplation is united with Plato's dialectic, to the highest religious experience, to the state of ecstasy! It is as if Marx's preparatory studies allow us to snatch a glimpse behind the curtain which, in the dissertation proper, prevents our gaze from penetrating beyond the margin of the visible heaven. While in that official treatise the view of the whole Greek people, as opposed by Epicurus, was described as Greek philosophy worshipping its own mind in the heavenly bodies, these preparatory reflections which were not destined for publication guide us beyond that visible boundary into the supreme sphere of the spirit, the sphere of the invisible heaven.

Marx leaves off at this point; and he leaves it to his readers to guess at his intentions. His defence of Epicurus, against the charge of irreligiosity, with reference to the concept of the immortality of the atom as the mirror of individual self-consciousness; his quoting a verse of the mystic, Jakob Böhme; his abstruse reflections on the contrast and parallel between Platonism and Christianity, leading up to the prospect of mystical ecstasy; these allusions and hints are ambiguous enough to remind us of the strange ambiguity of mind which we discovered in Marx's earlier stage of development. This ambiguity seems to have continued; so that we may well begin to wonder whether it is an essential aspect of Marx's life and thought.

7

From the visible heaven to the unsealed Word

IN the three preceding lectures I have tried carefully to follow
the main argument of Marx's dissertation and of the preparatory studies. It has not always been a simple matter to
understand his intentions, sometimes because of the extreme
conciseness of his style and sometimes owing to the abstruseness
of his style of thought. There is, however, a more profound
reason for the difficulty one has with Marx's first scholarly
writing. He is wrestling with a fascinating and puzzling
dilemma.

This dilemma is most explicitly formulated in two passages
closely related in content.

The first passage contains an attempt to understand the ambivalent attitude of the seventeenth-century scholar, Peter
Gassendi, who on the one hand admired Epicurus and presented his philosophy as an example of modern Enlightenment, but on the other hand rejected those Epicurean doctrines
which he could not square with his Christian faith. Marx does
more than cavil at this half-heartedness and vent his irritation
at the incapacity of a modern scholar radically to free himself
from obsolete Christian doctrines. He recognizes Gassendi's
indecision as a characteristic symptom of the dilemma lying at
the very foundations of modern philosophy.

The heart of the matter is to be found in the peculiar relationship between ancient and modern philosophy: the decay of
the former has emerged from the very principles out of which
the latter has been brought to birth. Modern philosophy starts

126

with Descartes' principle of universal doubt, whereas, conversely, the Sceptics sound the death-knell of Greek philosophy. Whilst it is the rational concept of nature that serves to deliver modern philosophy into the world, conversely, it is Epicurus who gives the *coup de grâce* to ancient philosophy, more thoroughly and decisively, even, than the Sceptics themselves. Antiquity was rooted in nature, in substantial reality. Its degradation, its profanation, entails a radical break with substantial, native life; the modern world is rooted in spirit, which has the required freedom to dispense with what is distinct from it, that is, nature, and to separate it from itself. But the opposite is also true; what for antiquity entailed the profanation of nature is for modern times a liberation from the shackles of servitude to the tyranny of faith; and the primeval intuition that in nature the divine, the idea, is immanent—the very intuition which inspired the birth of ancient Ionian philosophy—is still in advance of the modern rational apperception of nature.

The second passage, which is to be understood in close connection with the first one, is a comment on Epicurus' theory of the meteors. It draws a parallel with the modern world. For the ancient philosophers were the meteors, the *visible heaven*, the symbol and demonstration of their substantial constraint, so that even a philosopher like Aristotle envisages the stars as gods or, at least, associates them directly with the supreme energy. Analogously, the *written heaven*, the *sealed Word* of the God who has revealed himself in the course of world history, is the battle-cry of Christian philosophy. The presupposition of the ancients is the action of nature, for the moderns it is the action of the spirit. The battle of the ancients could not be concluded until the visible heaven, the substantial bond of life, the gravitation of political and religious existence, had been pulverized; for the spirit to become united with itself, nature has to be cleft in two. The Greek broke nature to pieces with the artistic hammer of Hephaestus, beating it into statues; the Roman dipped his sword in nature's heart, and the peoples died. But modern philosophy unseals the Word, causes it to vanish, consumed in the holy fire of the spirit; and not like some individual apostate who has fallen away from the gravitational field of nature, but as a warrior of the spirit contending with the spirit, modern philosophy works universally, melting down the forms which prevent the universal from making its appearance.

These passages, read together in a common perspective, afford a synopsis of Marx's three-dimensional thinking. More clearly than any other part of the dissertation or the preparatory studies, these pages reveal that Marx's historical discussion with the tradition of classical philosophy is at the same time a continuous struggle to clarify his own situation *vis-à-vis* his own time and his own world. It is especially clear that throughout his confrontation with the Greek past he is invariably puzzled by the problem of his relationship to the Christian tradition which had succeeded to the Greek and had left such a dominant mark on the civilization in which he himself had been born and was destined to live.

Indeed, what Marx calls Christian philosophy occupies a key position in his notion of world history. This strategic position is essentially ambiguous, being at once positive and negative. It represents the middle factor in a tripartite scheme that is dominated by the contrasting duality of nature and spirit. As far as antiquity is concerned, its character seems simple and unambiguous: antiquity was rooted in nature, in the substantial. But what does it mean when the modern world is said to be rooted in spirit? On the one hand, it is crystal clear that Marx's idea of modern philosophy is diametrically opposed to his conception of Christian philosophy. The modern world begins with the struggle for liberation from the tyranny of the Christian faith. Modern philosophy, embodied in Descartes' method of axiomatic doubt and in the rise of a rational approach to nature, is inspired by an urge to freedom from Christian tutelage, whether medieval or ancient. But this would seem to be only one side of the coin. The contradistinction between the ancients and the moderns, on the other hand, is identical with the contrast between ancient philosophy and Christian philosophy. The foundation of the ancients was the visible heaven, the symbol of their being imprisoned within the limits of nature. Conversely, the *"written heaven"*, the sealed Word, is the creed of Christian philosophy, which stands on the side of the spirit over against nature. Obviously, within the framework of the contrast between nature and spirit, Christian philosophy stands for spirit.

But there seems hardly to be room for a frank and explicit recognition of the rights of Christian philosophy. At the very moment the dual scheme of nature over against spirit is about to work in favour of the Christian spirit, it is already intersected by the tripartite scheme. The *"written heaven"* may, in itself, be very much a novelty as compared with the visible heaven which represented the ultimate horizon of antiquity; yet it is still a closed horizon. Visible nature has been replaced by audible Word; but this Word remains imprisoned in a written text which can be possessed, manipulated, a text which has, in fact, become an instrument of tyranny and suppression of spiritual freedom. The Word, as distinguished from nature, may bear testimony to the spirit; it still remains sealed. The true work of the spirit still lies ahead, therefore; but the intensity of its activity now appears to have assumed a new and higher quality. Whereas within the world of antiquity the struggle was directed against the ascendancy of natural bondage, now the front is directed against the powers of spiritual bondage. It is the sealed Word, the *"written heaven"*, which this time has become the antagonist. The arena in which the battle is to be fought is no longer the realm of nature but the realm of the spirit itself. The sealed Word has to be unsealed, the "written heaven" has to be "pulverized" the palpable, reified text of a canonized Bible, a frozen creed, a congealed tradition, has to be reduced to ashes, to be melted down and transformed in the devouring fire of the spirit.

This Utopian vision breaks through, it is true, in one or two passages where Marx's deepest inspiration shows through the husk of his philosophical analysis. It remains, however, a marginal aspect, which has not determined the main lines of his approach. To be sure, if it had become the dominant feature, Marx's dissertation might have looked like the polemical broadside of an Anabaptist prophet rather than an historical treatise. The tripartite scheme, in fact, turns out to be composed of two dual schemes which intersect one another. The battle between spirit and nature which, had Christian philosophy really lived up to its calling, would have become the indelible mark of the Christian era, has, owing to the failings of Christianity, assumed a contradictory character. The dominance of heaven has continued, albeit in a new guise. The visible heaven of antiquity has survived in the "written heaven" of the Christian era. The seals of bondage to the powers of nature have not really been broken, but have become seals of bondage to the domination of the written Word, in which the spirit remains sealed. Thus in a new form and in the realm of the spirit, the battle that started with the birth of ancient Ionian philosophy continues still.

This historical ambiguity has made its effects felt in two areas. On the one hand, the contradictions of the Christian era have certain features analogous to those which ran through the tradition of antiquity. In this respect, it is quite possible to project the problem underlying the Christian era into the period of antiquity itself. Marx's interest in the questions that dominated Greek philosophy is, in essence, a transposed version of his confrontation with Christian philosophy, because the battle of antiquity has continued through the Christian era. The end of classical philosophy is the prototype of the end of Christian philosophy. Within the tripartite scheme of history, divided into antiquity, Christendom and the modern world, the transition of the first into the second period is closely parallel to the transition of the second period into the third.

From this point of view, the reason for Marx's apparently negative approach to the beginnings of the Christian era becomes obvious. That era has failed of its purpose; the fulfilment of its task still lies ahead, it has still to be enacted by modern philosophy. The end of the Christian era is imminent—and is imminent by reason of its inner contradictions. This situation can be examined—and splendidly illustrated—by a scrutiny of the closing period of antiquity and of the philosophical systems which marked the end of classical philosophy. When we study its essential features, we see, as in a mirror, an image of ourselves.

But the contradictions which were concealed in the Christian period and are beginning to be discovered now by the spirit of modern thinking, should also be evaluated from the opposite point of view. If the bonds of nature have continued to hold sway in the tyranny of Christian logolatry, the worship of the written Word, then, conversely, the urge to freedom of the spirit was anticipated in the struggle that marked classical philosophy. The end of classical philosophy was more than a final chord of the ancient symphony. In retrospect, viewed from the bridge which leads from the Christian era towards the modern age, the death of antiquity bore the seeds of modernity. The rise of modern philosophy from its roots in Cartesian doubt and modern physics was prepared and foreshadowed in the fundamental questions raised by the school of Scepticism and, more radically, in the radical demythologization effected by Epicurean philosophy. The struggle of antiquity for the liberation of the spirit from nature's tutelage can, in retrospect, be observed in the mirror of the modern era. We are now in a better position to interpret the potentialities concealed in classical philosophy than was possible in the ancient period itself. The death of the hero can only be contemplated, and its meaning is only to be understood, by his successor on the stage of history.

Apart from these two viewpoints—one retrospective and the other prospective—which allow us to view the successive periods of history in a common perspective, it seems that lying in the background of Marx's interpretation there is yet another notion, which concerns the final destiny of nature. The battle of classical philosophy was prompted by the urge to freedom over against the pressure of nature. For spirit to become unified it is necessary to cleave nature asunder. It is this freedom which characterizes the modern world: the capacity of spirit to loose itself from nature and claim its own independent rights. Yet is it really the ultimate destiny of spirit to become totally autonomous, completely to separate itself from nature, in other words, to become natureless? Obviously, this is not Marx's deepest intention; for he seems to allude to an ultimate synthesis wherein nature and spirit will be reconciled. There is a noteworthy parallel between the way the dominance of a closed nature is terminated at the end of the classical period and the way the tyranny of the sealed Word is to be destroyed by the victory of modern philosophy, which will substitute the freedom of the spirit for the bondage of the Christian era. Of the end of the first period it is said that for spirit to be unified, nature has to be cleft into two. The end of the second era is marked by a conflict of the spirit with the spirit, that is, a fight of the free spirit against faith in a sealed Word. The spirit appears divided in itself, or, to put it more adequately, the seals of the spirit must be broken by the free spirit.

To what purpose? What is the ultimate destiny of this process? Marx realizes that the movement of modern philosophy, beginning with Descartes and with the birth of modern science, is only a first start. Modern philosophy, proclaiming rational man's independence of the powers of nature, was able to take up the thread of classical philosophy which had ended in Epicurus' complete profanation and degradation of nature. At the cradle of Greek philosophy, however, and implicit in the half-conscious meditations of the Ionian pioneers, stands the intuition that the divine spirit, the Idea, is incorporated in nature. Could it not be the ultimate destiny of history to realize this synthesis? For spirit to become one, nature had to be cleft asunder. Yet, spirit, far from attaining its own unity, has come to be divided in itself, and has become involved in a conflict of spirit with spirit. Apparently, the inner division of nature which marked the first period has repeated itself in the second period as an internal schism of the spirit. Is there a hidden meaning in this development, in that, for nature to become unified again in its turn the spirit has to become divided? Of course, nature cannot be unified without the inclusion of all that has accrued from history; nature will not return to that primeval self-sufficiency which left no room for the spirit to lay claim to its own. The unity of nature will be realized on a higher level. Once nature has become spiritualized, the spirit in its turn will become naturalized, that is, will celebrate its reunion with a spiritualized nature.

From this comprehensive viewpoint, let us now take a fresh look at the main insights presented in the dissertation and the preparatory studies. A striking illustration of what has been said about the current relevance of Marx's historical analysis is to be found in a passage which, at the same time, may serve as an apt starting point for our survey. The passage is part of the annotations to the Appendix: "Critique of Plutarch's polemic against Epicurus' theology", only a fragment of which has been preserved. As is clear from these annotations, the first chapter of the Appendix had been entitled: "Man's relationship to God", and divided into three paragraphs: 1. Fear and the transcendent being; 2. The cult and the individual; 3. Providence and the degraded God. Of the second chapter, called "Individual immortality" only a fragment of the first paragraph has been preserved: it is headed: "On religious feudalism. The hell of the populace".

The annotations to the first paragraph of the first chapter of the Appendix contain, besides quotations from Plutarch, one from the book *System of Nature,* written by the French eighteenth-century spokesman of mechanistic materialism, d'Holbach. The passage in question inveighs against the traditional fear of a transcendent Being which for thousands of years has held mankind under its sway. The notion of the Godhead always arouses in us depressing ideas. Every time we hear the name of the Godhead pronounced, there arise in our minds fears and gloomy thoughts. If our moral standard is founded upon the far from moral character of a capricious God, then man can never be sure of his duty to God, to himself or to other men. Thus nothing is more dangerous than the suggestion that there exists a supranatural Being before whom reason becomes speechless, a Being to whom everything on earth has to be forsaken in order to acquire salvation. The annotations to the third paragraph open with a quotation from Plutarch's reply to Epicurus' denial of a divine providence. Plutarch tries to demonstrate that Epicurus' argument concerning human fear of God is false. God is the Creator of all that is good, he is the father of all that is beautiful, he is capable neither of doing evil nor of suffering evil. Since wrath and grace, hate and love, are worlds apart, it is impossible for the Divinity to possess both qualities at once. God's essence is being gracious, so that wrath and evil-doing must be alien to him.

The annotations then turn back to modern philosophy. The philosopher Friedrich Wilhelm von Schelling is accused of having relinquished his youthful conviction in exchange for his present mystical philosophy. Marx recalls Schelling's pronouncement, formulated in 1795, refuting the rational ground of God's existence. If God is the object of human knowledge, He cannot at the same time be its precondition. Schelling had written the prophetic words, that now it was time to proclaim to mankind the freedom of human minds and to put an end to complaining about the loss of man's shackles.

These quotations from the early Schelling serve as introduction to some comments of Marx on the celebrated issue of the proofs of God's existence. Marx begins with a radical criticism of Hegel's treatment of the theological proofs of God's existence. For instance the cosmological proof had been interpreted by Hegel so as to mean: "Because of the non-being of the accidental, God or the Absolute is." However, this is just the reverse of the theological proof, which reads as follows: "Because the accidental has true being, God is." In the theological proof, God is the guarantee of the accidental world. Self-evidently, this also implies the reverse truth: that the accidental world is the guarantee of God's existence. Hegel's interpretation is, in fact, very much a maltreatment of these theological proofs. He has turned them upside down, that is to say, in order to justify them, he has rejected them. This manipulation leads Marx to exclaim: what a strange sort of client who must be killed by their advocate in order to be saved from condemnation!

It is noteworthy that at this early stage already Marx stands in such radical opposition to Hegel's philosophy of religion. A serious discussion of Marx's development in relation to Hegel must wait for my next lecture. For the moment I need only point out that Hegel's treatment of the cosmological proof of God's existence is based on an explicit refutation of Epicurus' concept of the accidental. In the second volume of his Lectures on the philosophy of religion, Hegel deals with the presupposition of the cosmological proof. This presupposition is: accidental being, namely, a being that lacks self-determination and so needs a cause outside itself by which it is determined. He rejects the Epicurean concept of accidental being as that sort of being to which it makes no matter whether it be thus or thus.

Obviously, Hegel's procedure draws the sting out of the religious consciousness as envisaged in Marx's dissertation. First, Hegel gives a definition of the accidental which already entails the conclusion drawn by the cosmological proof of God's existence; and then he interprets this theological proof in such a way that the properly religious problem which hinges on confrontation with the accidental evaporates into the only true and real being of absolute necessity.

There would have been no point to Marx's study of Epicurus, if Marx had followed Hegel in explaining the religious problem away. What fascinated him about Epicurus was the iron consistency with which the latter confronted the religious challenge. It is not surprising, therefore, that Marx approaches the question of God's existence in terms of a coercive alternative. He sees only two possibilities: the proofs of God's existence are either no more than empty tautologies, or they are merely proofs of the existence of the essential human self-consciousness.

He begins to explore the first possibility, that the proofs of God's existence are just empty tautologies. Take, for instance, the ontological proof, which from the thought of God's existence concludes His existence. This proof may have just this meaning: "that which I imagine as reality is to me a real imagining, it acts upon me" (N.B.: the German word *Wirklichkeit*, reality, is cognate with the verb *wirken*, to act). In this sense, all gods, the pagan gods as well as the Christian god, have had a real existence. Did not the ancient Moloch, the pagan Canaanite god to whom children were sacrificed, actually reign? Was the delphic Apollo not a real power in the life of the Greeks?

With this in mind, Marx develops his argument by examining Kant's critique of the ontological proof of God's existence. In his *Critique of Pure Reason* Kant illustrates his critique with the example of a sum of money. "The value of a hundred real crowns is not one penny greater than the value of a hundred imaginary crowns. Indeed, the concept of the possible sum is the adequate notion of its reality. However, regarded from my standpoint as a proprietor the case is quite different. If my property contains a hundred real crowns, it is larger than with only a hundred imaginary crowns. The reality of the object is not included in my concept as an analytical conclusion, but is something added, synthetically, to my concept. Yet the sum of possible crowns has not increased when the crowns become real."

In Marx's opinion this critique of Kant is pointless. Marx approaches the example from the subjective point of view. If somebody imagines himself possessed of a hundred crowns, if this imagining is more than a subjective emotion, if he really believes in it, then the hundred imagined crowns have for him the same value as a hundred real crowns would have. For instance, he will incur debts on the strength of his imagined property, it will act upon him and exert real influence, in the same way as mankind as a whole has incurred debts on the strength of its (belief in) gods. Far from having refuted the ontological proof, Kant's example might rather have served to confirm it. Real crowns have the same kind of existence as have imagined gods. Does a real crown exist anywhere else than in the imagination, even if this imagination has a universal, or rather a collective, character? If you were to import paper currency into a country where its function is unknown, you would be laughed at, because of your subjective imagination. If you were to introduce your gods into a country where the other gods are the ones recognized, people would soon show you to be suffering from delusions; and rightly so. Anyone who brought the god of a German tribe to the ancient Greeks, would have discovered proof of the non-existence of that god. For the Greeks he would have been non-existent. These examples concern the inanity of particular gods in particular countries; but an analogous conclusion may be drawn with regard to God's existence in general: in the country of Reason, God no longer exists. This is the logical conclusion of the first interpretation of the proofs of God's existence, that their meaning is merely tautological. The alternative interpretation explains these proofs to be merely proofs of the existence of the essential human consciousness, its logical explications. Take, for example, the ontological proof. What kind of being is immediately present, the very moment it is being thought of? It is the self-consciousness.

In this sense—thus Marx's triumphant conclusion—all proofs of God's existence are proofs of his non-existence, refutations of all imaginings about a god. The real proofs should read conversely: "Because nature is badly organized, God is." "Because an unreasonable world is, God is." "Because thought is not, God is." Do these pronouncements mean anything, however, other than: "Whoever conceives the world as unreasonable, in a word, whoever is unreasonable himself, for him God exists. In short, unreason is God's existence"? This conclusion is underlined by the addition of two other quotations from the early Schelling. The first says that the absolute autonomy and freedom of reason contradict any postulation of an objective God. The second passage condemns as a crime against humanity any attempt to conceal principles that are universally communicable.

Human consciousness is the highest divinity. It allows of no rival. This solemn Promethean proclamation, which was already formulated in the preface, is thus convincingly demonstrated and confirmed at the end of the dissertation. The historical analysis of Epicurean philosophy as the supreme philosophy of human self-consciousness gets a finishing touch in its application to contemporary philosophy. A study which at first sight might look like a dry treatise on a remote past, finally reveals its hidden purpose: it is in fact the arena for a tenacious struggle with the whole of religious tradition and a resolute reckoning with the claims of Christian theology.

When we try, from the vantage-point of this final demonstration, to recapitulate the milestones along the road we have travelled, the first thing to note is the key function of the religious imagination. The importance of Marx's approach consists in his insight that the root of the question lies in the phenomenon of the imagination as such. Therefore, when he lumps all gods indiscriminately together, pagan as well as Christian, this is not out of a malicious desire to ridicule Christianity, but as a result of his analysis of the imagination. The power of imagination is so strong that it makes an impact equal to that of reality. The reverse is also true: real crowns have the same existence as imaginary gods. Thanks to his faculty of imagination, man is able to create his own environment, a system to live in, in short, a world. Whether the system is a monetary system or a religious system is neither here nor there. What matters is that both money and gods really exist for those in whose imagination they are real, and that outside that circle they are non-existent.

It would have been a simple solution to leave the issue there, so reducing it to a matter of psychological observation. As there are various currencies, so there are various religions. But Marx does not allow himself to be misled by a fallacious answer of that sort. What puzzles him is whether the magic circle of imagination can be broken. If imagination is indeed equal to reality, if the objects of imagination really exist, if the world created by imagination is man's real world, then the crucial point is whether any escape from this imagined reality or this real imagination is possible.

Of course, the example of a sum of money has nothing to do with Marx's interest in economics—which as a matter of fact was not aroused until several years after this. Moreover, the example in question was not that Marx had chosen but was derived from Kant's treatment of the ontological proof of God's existence. Yet the difference between Kant's use of the example and Marx's approach is significant for that very reason. In Kant's thinking the factor common to a sum of money and God's existence consists in the alternative, applicable to each of these objects, between real existence and possible, that is, imagined existence. Marx, on the contrary, is intrigued by the enigmatic capacity, common to both objects, to identify possible and real existence, imagination and reality. What is posed by Kant as an essential distinction between an analytic conclusion, belonging to the sphere of thought, and a synthetic conclusion, making the leap to reality, is discovered by Marx to be a mere tautology, a semantic distinction. For as long as imagined reality can make the same impact as real existence, any distinction between them is fallacious.

I repeat that the example he uses of a sum of money has no relevance to Marx's economic interest of a later period. But again, for this very reason his interpretation is a striking indication of the deeper motives that impelled him. It is not the religious issue as such which preoccupies him during these early years, any more than it is the question of economics as such which will absorb his attention during the mature period of his life. The point at stake is an underlying problem, one which lies at the root of the religious as well as the economic question. The fundamental problem arises from man's obvious but enigmatic ability to create, by force of imagination, a world of his own, his real world. And the crucial question, the life-and-death issue, is where to find the Archimedean point on which to stand and from which this world is to be moved. So long as this world is a limited world, the problem is not yet a life-and-death issue. Just as, the moment we leave our country, our currency is replaced by a different currency, so our religious system obtains only within the region where our gods are believed in. The German gods and the Greek gods had a limited domain. However, when for the variety of systems we substitute one universal system, the case is altered. Then there are no longer any number of different worlds; what remains is one world, the world of all mankind. There is no longer a geographical frontier offering the possibility of escape.

That is, in fact, precisely the situation with which Marx is confronted. On the religious level, there is this one universal system; Christianity. Marx is later to encounter an analogous universal phenomenon on the economic level, namely, Capitalism. The importance of his approach to each of these phenomena is bound up with its universality. The object of his interest is not this or that religious system, but the system of religion as such. He is not in discussion with this or that theology, but with theology *per se*. He is not puzzled by man's capacity for creating gods, but by man's relationship to God, the one and only God. He is not up against this or that world, but against *the* world, the universal world in which mankind lives today. Concretely, it is in Christianity that he meets this universal religion, this universal theology, this universal God, this universal world; just as later on, on the economic level, he will face this universal world in the capitalist system.

Looking for the Archimedean point from which to move this universal world, Marx explores in vain within the boundaries of his own time, his own environment, his own world. The "country of reason", where one might escape this universal reign, is not near at hand. It may of course be found in the future; but the future can only be dreamt of or prophesied or seen in a vision. The alternative possibility is to look for this "country or reason" in the past. There is one advantage of the past as compared with the future, in that the past can be made an object of detailed study.

With this expectation in mind, Marx turns to the study of Greek philosophy. What he finds there is a complex set of phenomena which turns out, in fact, to contribute decisively to unravelling the problem he is facing in his own environment.

He discovers that the entire Greek tradition had been unable to break the magic circle of religious imagination. The struggle of Greek philosophy had been the struggle for freedom of the subjective spirit over against the objective world created by the religious imagination, a visible heaven. The substantial bond of life was too strong, the gravitation of political and religious existence proved too heavy, for Greek self-consciousness to overcome. In Socrates and Plato this struggle and its failure are exemplified. Socrates, the sage who embodies the critique of the idea over against nature, is at the same time rooted in the substantial conditions of the state and its religion; his subjectivity is unable to encroach upon the objective forces of the religious imagination. Plato turns Socrates' ideality into a mythical symbol and projects his own subjectivity as an independent realm of ideas which hovers above and beyond substantial reality. Plato's ideality is a distinct realm existing inside the philosopher's own consciousness. This ideal realm and the realm of substantial reality meet one another through the intermediary of the Platonic myths and allegories whereby the transcendent is related to the immanent.

Marx sees essential and historical relationships between Platonism and Christianity. Plato's philosophy of transcendence has religious overtones, it takes the form of a doctrine of salvation. Conversely, the Christian religion is the apex of religious evolution, it is the perfect philosophy of transcendence. Historically speaking, various Platonic elements have been absorbed by Christianity. Nevertheless, Marx has been able to distinguish sharply between the two. More important than any analogy between Socrates as personified philosophy and Christ as personified religion is the comparison between institutionalized philosophy and institutionalized religion. On this level he perceives a radical contrast between Plato and Christ. In Plato's Republic we meet the full weight of Greek substantiality. The sage, who in the person of Socrates remains rooted in the substantial soil of the religious state and the state religion, comes to represent the leading caste of Plato's state. The idea, far from breaking through the magic circle of the substantial bonds, serves to sanctify, to idealize and eternalize them. In radical contrast with Plato, it is in Christ that the principle of subjectivity is set over against the state, which is itself condemned as worldly and profane.

At this point one might have expected Marx to say something definite to the effect that in Christ he recognizes a radical break with the spirit of classical antiquity. He comes very near to such a recognition when he goes on to refer to the contrast between Plato's Republic and the Christian Church. Of course, the former has remained an ideal, whereas the latter has assumed reality. Yet this is only half the truth; for this contrast has been inverted: whereas the Platonic idea succeeded reality, the Christian idea preceded it.

The ambiguity and obscurity of this comment seem to point to an underlying ambiguity in Marx's own mind. On the one hand, he has tried to show that there is a high degree of congeniality between Platonism and Christianity; but, on the other hand, he clearly recognizes a profound contrast between Plato and Christ. This he relates to the contradistinction between a general idea and a historical individual. Whereas the Platonic state is an embodiment of the Socratic idea, the Church, conversely, is related to Christ as a historical person. However, at the same time, Marx sees Christianity in the mirror of Platonism. If this apperception of his had concerned only a number of Platonic doctrines and notions that have become deeply ingrained in the tradition of Christian theology, then the question would present no great difficulty. Any Christian theologian could settle the discussion with Marx by, on the one hand, recognizing these historical Platonic influences in Christianity, and, on the other, trying to demonstrate that, essentially, there is an unbridgeable gap between Plato and Christ.

However, nothing of that sort would meet the point, because Marx himself had already stressed the essential contrast between Plato and Christ. The heart of the matter is to be found elsewhere, namely, in the remarkable parallel betweeen the ways in which the Platonic and the Christian ideas have functioned in relation to reality. The reality of the Christian Church, which followed the coming of Christ has in fact, in the course of the Christian era, turned into a sanctification of substantial, political and religious ties, in the same way as the reality of the Greek substantial tradition came to be idealized in Plato's Republic. The transformation of the historical Socrates into a Platonic myth of love and death has been repeated in the transposition of Christ's life and death into a theological realm beyond this world.

It is this fateful continuity between the whole tradition of Greek philosophy and the Christian religion as "the perfect philosophy of transcendence" which induces Marx to look for the root of the problem inside the tradition of Greek philosophy itself. If the Christian veneration of a "written heaven", a sealed Word, is a mere continuation, on a spiritual level, of the natural adoration which the Greeks devoted to the visible heaven, has there been a point in Greek history where its inner contradictions have at least been brought to the level of consciousness; where its magnificent but fatal naïvety has been unmasked; where its essential impossibility has come very near to explosion? If such a critical turning-point did indeed occur, then this crucial moment has its relevance not only for Greek philosophy but for the Christian era which has submitted to the same historical fate as the Greeks.

It was in Epicurean philosophy that Marx discovered the turning-point, while at the same time he exposes all its contradictions. Epicurus is not transformed at his hands into a new saviour, nor is his philosophy turned into a new mythology. Epicurus failed to break open the magic circle of the religious imagination, which culminated in the Greek veneration of the visible heaven. If the adoration of the heavenly bodies was a cult celebrated by every Greek philosopher, the basic reason for that was that in the heavenly bodies Greek philosophers worshipped their own mind. Epicurus' philosophy actually rests on the same foundation. If he had drawn the logical conclusion from his own atomistic theory, he would have been obliged to join this cult of the visible heaven. For the heavenly bodies are his atoms become real.

In other words, even Epicurus did not discover, in his theoretical concept of nature, the Archimedean point from which to move the Greek substantial world. The reason was that he too remained imprisoned within the magic circle of imagination. The tautological circle which Marx exposed as the *vitium originis* of the theological proofs of God's existence, was the very circle which enclosed the Greek approach to reality. Epicurus' atomistic view of the world was as indefinite a product of the imagination as are the Christian theological concept of God, paradise, creation and salvation. If Epicurus' philosophy is the natural science of self-consciousness, then he has brought the innate spirit of Greek philosophy to its highest perfection.

Even if Epicurus had achieved no more than this, he might still have been an important Greek philosopher; yet he would not have become, in Marx's eyes, the greatest representative of Greek Enlightenment. But Epicurus was in fact more than just another Greek philosopher. He was the last of the line; his philosophy meant the end of Greek philosophy, it sounded the final chord of the Greek symphony; with it died a hero who, for century after century, had filled the stage of Greek history. In Epicurus the Greek spirit died of its own contradictions.

The crucial point in Epicurus' philosophy is located precisely where he contradicts his own presuppositions. The cult of the visible heaven, the adoration of the eternal and immutable celestial bodies, was the crown of the Greek spirit. This cult was the root, the culmination and the guarantee of the whole of the Greek substantial tradition. Greek philosophy from its very outset right up to Aristotle had projected its inmost spirit, its deepest consciousness, in this cult. And what is more, Epicurus' own view of the atoms as the immortal foundations of nature is realized in the celestial bodies. Nevertheless, in total contradiction of the whole tradition of Greek philosophy, his own included, Epicurus refuses unconditionally to defer to this cult. At this point all his efforts are designed to draw the embodiments of autonomous, immortal, sovereign nature down into earthly transitoriness, to demote the eternal to the level of mere accidentality, to profane the sanctity of the divine heaven. He breaks with the outlook of the whole Greek people and with the highest religious ideal of the philosophers, whose goal is the contemplation of the divine harmony.

Epicurus' refusal to conform is an act of apostasy. He lapses from the gravitational field of nature, and breaks the substantial ties which had held together the political and religious existence of antiquity. Moreover, he is an isolated, a lonely apostate. And worse, his act of apostasy lacks any theoretical backing; for it is in glaring opposition to his own theory. What he did was impossible; and yet he achieved it. His sole foundation, the Archimedean point from which he moves his own world, is the absolute freedom of self-consciousness which he as an individual wants to maintain against any element that threatens or derives it. But this freedom has no place within the world he is part of, it is a freedom born of exile, it obliges him to cross the frontier of his own world and to move abroad, to seek "the country of reason". In other words, in order to maintain his principle of absolute self-consciousness, he has to abandon the basis of his own theory. His freedom can be realized only in another dimension, in the dimension of praxis.

This qualitative leap from theory to practice, although made by a lonely apostate, in fact went far beyond the range of an individual action. Epicurus' philosophy is the mirror of a historical turning-point. In Aristotelian philosophy the Greek spirit reached its culmination and at the same time was confronted with its ultimate limitations. The post-Aristotelian period had either to descend into epigonism or move over to a new dimension. The post-Aristotelian philosophical schools were the typical products of such a transition. They were the result of a process of dissolution and foreshadowed an imminent catastrophe. In Epicurus' philosophy the knell is rung over the gods of antiquity. His worldless god and godless nature, consisting of a huge repulsion-process of the atoms, anticipate the collapse of the ancient harmony and the titanic struggle of the Roman period. But on the other hand, this post-Aristotelian period exhibits the first signs of a new day. Where the old gods have died, a new divinity is coming to birth.

Marx proclaims this new divinity to be the human self-consciousness, a supreme divinity without peer or rival; but that is only half the story. Shortly before he enunciated this bold creed in the preface to his dissertation, and writing in the sixth exercise-book of the preparatory studies, he had compared his own post-Hegelian situation with the transitional period of post-Aristotelian philosophy. In that connection he had described the full ambiguity of the transition; the new divinity had not so far clothed itself in the bright light of day; its features still bore the darker aspect of fate. The transition from theory to practice, the movement out of the shadowy realm of Amenthes, judge of the dead, into practical confrontation with the world, the transformation of internal thought into external will, entailed the discovery of a new continent beyond the familiar horizon.

In the mirror of Epicurus, Marx saw his own situation reflected. It is not enough to draw a parallel between Aristotle and Hegel and to point to an analogy between post-Aristotelian and post-Hegelian philosophy. Aristotelean philosophy was the culmination of the whole Greek tradition. In the same way, Hegelian philosophy summed up the Christian theological and philosophical tradition. In the mirror of Epicurus, Marx saw reflected his own departure from a Christian era whose God had died, into another country beyond the horizon, a country of the future.

8

Critique as the confessor of history

THE migration from the old Athens threatened with destruction and the founding of a new Athens upon a new
element, the sea, was not a theoretical question. There
was something prophetic about the fact that, when it came to
putting philosophy into practice, Marx finally referred to the
example of a politician, Themistocles. The proper realm for
the enactment of ideas which philosophy had prepared in a
theoretical fashion was the political realm. He had embodied
this truth in the psychological law that the theoretical spirit,
having become free within itself, is transformed into practical
energy and, appearing as will from Amenthes' shadowy realm,
turns against the earthly reality existing apart from it. The
empirical basis for the construction of this psychological law
lay nowhere else than in his own mind, not in the sense of an
inference from past experiences but solely as a prospect for the
future; this psychological "law" he had to demonstrate in
person, even to the extent of embodying it in his own life.

It was one thing to proclaim Epicurus the greatest Greek
representative of Enlightenment, and quite another to become
oneself a modern Epicurus. If post-Aristotelian philosophy had
represented the end of Greek religion, the task now lying ahead
was to show post-Hegelian philosophy to be the end of the
Christian religion. However, the language of this new philosophy had still to be deciphered. The end of Greek philosophy
had been pregnant with the Titanic struggles of the Roman
era; it had achieved the final chord, but had failed to provide

at least the rough draft of a new score. The Christian era had only served to accentuate the dilemma, since Christianity, so far from being the solution, was rather the problem to be solved. Despite his merits, Epicurus had failed to adumbrate any solution for that problem. In the first place his practical atheism had been at odds with his own philosophical presuppositions, so that a modern opposition to the Christian religion could only look in vain to antiquity for a theoretical model. Furthermore, rejecting the adoration accorded to the visible heaven was a far cry from rebellion against the written Word, the tyranny of the "written heaven". The latter was tantamount to the transition to a new dimension, the realm of the spirit.

Before we try to follow the succession of Marx's steps as explorer of a new element, we must attend to some rudimentary biographical notes. The migration from the old Athens was inextricably linked up with his practical experiences and decisions. The transformation of the theoretical spirit into practical energy left its indelible mark on his personal relationships with his environment, just as, conversely, the external situation influenced his inner transformation. It is impossible to disentangle Marx's philosophy from his practical decisions in the public realm.

The dissertation itself, to be sure, was related to the political situation. In my fourth lecture I indicated the political reasons that induced Marx to leave Berlin and take his doctor's degree at a smaller university. I need recall here only one of the measures taken by the new Minister of Cult against the influence of the Young Hegelian philosophy. I mean, the appointment of the philosopher von Schelling to the University of Berlin. A prominent representative of German idealist philosophy, Schelling had passed through several stages of development until, towards the end of his career, he was advocating a mystical vein of thought in virtue of which philosophy was crowned with a theosophical concept of revelation. A corollary of his philosophical standpoint was his unmistakable political conservatism. The combination of these two things was enough to make Schelling a chief antagonist of the Young Hegelian circle.

The reaction of the Young Hegelian students can be studied

in two articles and two pamphlets, written by Friedrich Engels, who was living in Berlin during that period, and was following Schelling's lectures. The first pamphlet was called *Schelling and Revelation. Critique of the latest reactionary attacks on free philosophy.* The second pamphlet was *Schelling, the philosopher in Christo or the elevation of worldly wisdom to divine wisdom.* Both pamphlets were published pseudonymously in 1842. The two articles, written in December 1841, give a vivid account of Schelling's lectures. Engels declares total war on Schelling in defence of Hegel's legacy, preserved by the Young Hegelian school. Although fighting now as an *ecclesia pressa*, an oppressed church, the true philosophy of self-consciousness will eventually win the great, decisive battle which is near at hand.

In the Appendix to his dissertation, Marx had launched a sharp attack on Schelling, recalling how enlightened the younger Schelling's thinking had been in 1795, and how glaring was the contrast afforded by his reactionary gnosticism in 1841. The years that followed did nothing to lessen his hostility. In a letter to Ludwig Feuerbach, written in October 1843 shortly before his leaving for Paris, Marx encourages Feuerbach to compose an attack on Schelling, to be published in Paris. He reminds Feuerbach of Schelling's political power as a member of the German federal council and as a favourite protégé of the Prussian government. The whole German police force is at Schelling's disposal, so that any hostile pamphlet published in Germany will immediately be subject to censorship. "Schelling has not only been able to conjoin philosophy with theology, but philosophy and diplomacy as well. An attack on Schelling is thus an indirect attack on our politics in general and on Prussian politics in particular. Schelling's philosophy is Prussian politics *sub specie philosophiae.*"

Marx goes on to hail Feuerbach as the exact opposite of Schelling. It is in this passage that he uses for the first time the term "opium". For the realization of the honest ideas of his youth Schelling had "no other means but imagination, no other energy but vanity, no other motive force but opium, no other organ but an irritable and effeminate receptivity". In him those ideas had always remained a fantastic youthful dream, but in Feuerbach they had become truth, reality and had attained manly stature. "Schelling is therefore your anticipated phantom *(antizipiertes Zerrbild)* and no sooner does reality confront its phantom than the latter must evaporate in a thick mist." Marx regarded Feuerbach as the necessary and natural opponent of Schelling, appointed by the twin powers of nature and history. "Your battle with Schelling is the battle between imagined philosophy and philosophy itself."

The attacks levelled independently by Engels and Marx in the period before they became close comrades derived their bitter character from the political sting hidden within the philosophical antagonism. When Marx decided to leave Berlin, he realized that this would entail the end of the academic career he had hoped for. He would have to choose a profession other than the one which his father had had in mind for him and which seemed to be in line with his evident intellectual ability. His experience could not but strengthen his conviction that defence of the established Christian religion by a semi-feudal monarchy was very much the same thing as suppression of intellectual freedom. Christianity and political reaction had proved to be twin brothers.

Switching from a career as academic philosopher to a new rôle as pressman meant that Marx was now acting on his own proposition about the necessary transition from theoretical thought to practical effort. That was in fact how he was inclined to interpret his personal experiences. Just as in earlier writings he had, as a matter of course, drawn a parallel between key points in world history and key points in his own life, so now he interpreted his change of occupation as a change consummated in the heart of philosophy itself. His reflections were embodied in an article published in the *Rheinische Zeitung* in the middle of 1842. The article was aimed at another newspaper, the *Kölnische Zeitung*, mouthpiece of the ultramontanists in the Rhineland. This newspaper had accused the *Rheinische Zeitung*, which had the support of the progressive middle-class opposition in the Rhineland, of propagating anti-Christian ideas. Inveighing against such a dangerous tendency, the *Kölnische Zeitung* had at the same time appealed for stricter censorship on the part of the government.

In his reply, Marx deployed several of the arguments already hinted at in his dissertation. The editor of the *Kölnische Zeitung* happened to be called Hermes. This fact gave Marx's ironic pen occasion to compare the politico-religious conservatism of his opponent with the servility of the Greek god Hermes. We may remember that in the preface to the dissertation Marx replied to those who were rejoicing over the apparently deteriorating social position of philosophy with a quotation from Aeschylus' tragedy *Prometheus Bound*. The quotation referred to Prometheus' retort to Hermes, the messenger of the gods, that he would rather remain the servant of the rock to which he was chained than become the submissive servant of the gods. I have already pointed out the ambiguity of the Greek word for "servitude", which has both a religious and a social reference.

There was an added element of irony in the fact that, in his reply to Herr Hermes, Marx did not quote from Aeschylus' tragedy but from Lucian's *Dialogues of the Gods*. Lucian was an outstanding Greek satirical writer of the second century. As an atheist he made a point of ridiculing various religious and philosophical ideas current in the decadent period of antiquity, especially the concepts of Christianity. The full implications of this irony are obvious from a passage in an essay written less than two years later, the *Introduction to a critique of Hegel's Philosophy of Law*. In that passage Marx exposes the anachronistic character of the contemporary German régime: "The modern *ancien régime* is only the jester of a world order whose true heroes are dead. History is meticulous and goes through many phases when carrying an old form to the grave. The last phase of a historical form is its comic aspect. The gods of Greece, already tragically and mortally wounded in Aeschylus' *Prometheus Bound,* had to die over again a comic death in Lucian's *Dialogues.* Why does history pursue such a course? So that humanity should part gaily with its past. This gay historical destiny is what we must advance in vindication of the political authorities in Germany."

Marx in fact introduces his reply to Hermes, the editor of the *Kölnische Zeitung*, with a quotation from Lucian's *Dialogues of the Gods*. The god Hermes complains of the multitude of affairs he has to attend to and the many slavish duties he has to take on. He, who is distracted by so many matters, must over and above all these attend to the whole business of the dead. This quotation serves to introduce Marx's discussion with Hermes about the proposition put forward by the latter that to spread philosophical and religious views by means of newspapers or to combat them in newspapers is equally inadmissible. Marx concludes that his opponent is advocating a further tightening of censorship in religious matters, a new police measure against the press which has hardly begun to breathe freely. "Christianity is sure of victory, but according to Mr. Hermes it is not so sure of victory that it can scorn the help of the police."

In dealing with the main question, whether philosophy should discuss religious matters even in newspaper articles, Marx develops a broad line of argument which strongly recalls certain ideas laid down in his dissertation. He begins with the proposition that the question can be answered only by criticizing it. Philosophy, above all German philosophy, has a propensity to solitude, to systematic seclusion, to dispassionate self-contemplation which opposes it from the outset in its estrangement to the slick and alert newspapers, whose only pleasure is in information. Philosophy, in accordance with its character, has never taken the first step towards replacing its ascetic priestly vestments with the light, superficial garb of the newspapers. But philosophers do not spring up like mushrooms; they are the products of their time and of their nation, whose most subtle, precious and invisible sap circulates in philosophical ideas. The same spirit that builds railways by the hands of the workers builds philosophical systems in the minds of philosophers. Philosophy does not stand outside the world any more than man's mind is outside of him because it is not in his stomach; but, of course, philosophy is in the world with its brain before it stands on the earth with its feet, whereas many another human sphere has long been rooted in the earth by its feet and plucks the fruits of the world with its hands before it has any idea that the "head" also belongs to the world or that this world is the world of the head.

Having developed this argument, Marx comes to the point at issue. Because every true philosophy is the spiritual quintessence of its time, the time must come when, not only internally by its content but externally by its appearance, philosophy comes into contact and mutual reaction with the real, contemporary world. Philosophy then ceases to be a definite system in presence of other definite systems, it becomes philosophy in general, it becomes the philosophy of the world of the present. The formal features which attest that philosophy has achieved that importance, that is the living soul of culture, that philosophy is becoming worldly and the world philosophical, have at all times been the same. Philosophy is heralded into the world by the clamour of its enemies who betray their inner malaise by their desperate appeals for help against the blazing heat of ideas. These cries of its antagonists mean as much to philosophy as the first cry of a child to the anxious ear of the mother; they are like the first cry of the ideas which have burst open the orderly, hieroglyphic husk of the system and have become citizens of the world.

Of course, the enemies first turn against the religious sector among the philosophers, partly because the public, to which the opponents of philosophy themselves belong, can feel the ideal sphere of philosophy only with their ideal, that is, their religious instincts, partly because religion is opposed not to a definite system of philosophy but generally to philosophy structured in particular systems.

The true philosophy of the present time, thus Marx's conclusion, does not differ, as far as this is concerned, from the true philosophies of the past. Indeed, this fate is a proof that history owes to the truth of philosophy. He alludes to the campaign mounted by the German papers, which for six years had been drumming against the religious trend in philosophy, calumniating, distorting, bowdlerizing it. What Marx has in mind is the series of critical attacks launched on the traditional foundations of Christianity by the Young Hegelian school, starting in 1835 with the publication of David Strauss's *Life of Jesus*; a movement which had recently, in 1841, reached its climax in Ludwig Feuerbach's *Essence of Christianity*. In spite of the charge, vociferously proclaimed by the German papers, that philosophy was not suited for public discussion, that it was the idle bragging of youth, a fashion for blasé coteries—in spite of all that, they could not be rid of it. All the papers, from the most widely read down to the local and obscure, including the *Kölnische Zeitung* were carrying on about Hegel and Schelling, Feuerbach, Bauer, and so forth. The curiosity of the public was eventually aroused; and they wanted to see the Leviathan with their own eyes, the more so when semi-official but inspired articles threatened philosophy with having a legally prescribed syllabus thrust upon it. And that was how philosophy made its appearance in the papers. Long had it kept silence, even objecting that newspapers were an inappropriate medium for it; "but in the end it had to break silence; it became a newspaper correspondent".

Marx's conclusion typifies the way in which he identified his own personal development with the inner logic of the development of philosophy generally. At the very moment he has himself been driven by the necessity of his own philosophical ideas, combined with the pressure of external reactions, to abandon a career as an academic philosopher and to move into public life, at that moment he describes his development in terms of "philosophy became a newspaper correspondent", instead of "I became a newspaper correspondent". In other words, his personal career is philosophy incarnate, philosophy immersed in the historical situation out of which it has emerged.

This was not yet the whole truth, to be sure. The question whether philosophy should discuss religious matters in newspaper articles was followed by a second question which in fact contained the heart of the matter: "Should politics be dealt with philosophically by the newspapers in a so-called Christian state?" In reply to his opponent who had defended the Christian state against the philosophical attacks made by the *Rheinische Zeitung*, Marx now goes on to tear the idea of a Christian state to pieces. The truly religious state is the theocratic state; the prince of such states must be either the God of religion, Jehovah Himself, as with the Jewish state; God's representative, the Dalai Lama, as in Tibet; or else all Christian states must submit to an infallible Church. For if, as in Protestantism, there is no supreme head of the Church, the domination of religion is nothing but the religion of domination, the cult of the will of a particular government. The dilemma cannot be resolved: either the Christian state corresponds to the concept of the state as a realization of rational freedom, or the state of rational freedom cannot be developed out of Christianity.

Therefore, Marx concludes, the state is not to be constituted on a basis of religion but of the rational character of freedom. Philosophy has done nothing in politics that physics, mathematics, medicine, every science, has not done within its own sphere. In the period immediately before and after the time of Copernicus's great discoveries regarding the solar system, the gravitational principle of the state was being discovered: the centre of gravity of the state was to be found within the state itself. Machiavelli and Campanella, followed by Hobbes, Spinoza, and Hugo Grotius on to Rousseau, Fichte and Hegel, began to contemplate the state from a truly human standpoint and to develop its natural laws on a basis of reason and experience, not of theology. Modern philosophy has simply continued a process already started by Heraclitus and Aristotle. Consequently, what ignorance yesterday, or perhaps the day before yesterday, discovered in the *Rheinische Zeitung*, is the ever-modern philosophy of reason, rather than the reason of modern philosophy.

However, if there was hardly room for his "philosophy of reason" within the sphere of academic theology and philosophy, Marx was very well aware that the prospects were even worse where the popular press was concerned. His moving into the world of the press was only a first step on a long road. It is a striking fact that the maiden article he wrote at the start of his new career, in the first months of 1842, was a sharp attack on the new instruction concerning public censorship, recently promulgated by the Prussian government. The heart of his attack is directed against what he describes as the confusion between the political and the Christian-religious principle, which had even become the official dogma of the government. Marx exposes the inner contradictions concealed in the pretensions of censorship to be defending the Christian state. A government which calls its state broadly Christian, implicitly concedes, in diplomatic terms, its unChristian character. Such a government requires of religion that it lend its support to the temporal realm, while refusing to submit the temporal realm to the verdict of religion. In that way it demonstrates what its idea of religion is: namely, the cult of its own despotism.

Small wonder that the article was suppressed by the censor, so that in the end it had to be published in a German review edited in Switzerland. It was again censorship which in March 1843 ended Marx's brief career in the service of the *Rheinische Zeitung*, just half a year after his appointment as chief editor. No sooner had the philosopher turned journalist and newspaperman, than he had to encounter the reactions aroused by a philosophy that had begun to revolt against the world.

It meant, too, leaving his family circle and abandoning his social milieu. In June 1843 he married Jenny von Westphalen, the daughter of an aristocratic family. Not long before, he wrote in a letter to his friend, Arnold Ruge: "For more than seven years our engagement has continued, and my fiancée has, on my behalf, fought some very severe battles which have almost undermined her health, contesting partly against her own pietistic-cum-aristocratic relatives who adore both 'the sovereign in Heaven' and 'the sovereign in Berlin' as cultic objects, partly against my own family, which has been intruded upon by some clerics and other enemies of mine. I and my fiancée have struggled during these years through more unnecessary and emotional conflicts than many others who, three times as old as we, boast of their wisdom and experience." The conflict with his family deprived Marx of any financial support from that side.

Last but not least, this loss of family and social milieu also meant geographical emigration. From now on Marx and his family were doomed to share the wandering life of so many exiles. At the same time, his exile enabled him to break out of the confines of a narrow German provincialism and to evolve into a European, a citizen of the world. In co-operation with Arnold Ruge he decided to move to Paris as editor of the new periodical *Deutsch-Französische Jahrbücher*. The design behind this international review had had its sad prehistory in Germany itself. Five years earlier, the Young Hegelian group had launched a review *Hallische Jahrbücher für Wissenschaft und Kunst*. Anticipating some action on the part of the Prussian censor, the editorial committee had moved after three years to Leipzig in Saxony and renamed their publication *Deutsche Jahrbücher für Wissenschaft und Kunst*. This move brought no more than a brief respite; for one and a half years later, in January 1843, the review was prohibited by the government of Saxony, whose decision the German Federal Council extended and applied to the whole of Germany. Thus it came about that its editor, Arnold Ruge, was faced at the same time as Marx with the necessity to move his 'editorial activities abroad. The idea of an international review that should be jointly edited by the

German and French *avant-garde*, was inspired by Ludwig Feuerbach's proclamation of the Gallo-German principle that the true philosopher, that is, the man whose philosophy is in harmony with life and humanity, should be of Gallo-German origin. His heart had to be French, and his head German. The head must reform, the heart revolutionize.

In Paris, Marx had excellent opportunity to study the prehistory and history of the French Revolution; he read the works of French and British socialist thinkers and made contact with a number of French socialists. At the same time he began his study of political economy, which for the rest of his life, spent in London, was to engage most of his attention and energy.

The *Deutsch-Französiche Jahrbücher* was fated to have an even shorter life than its German predecessors. Only one double issue was published before the various setbacks and obstacles to distribution in Germany, along with financial problems and a conflict of opinion between Marx and Ruge, brought this promising international project to a premature end. A month later, in April 1844, Marx's articles published in this review prompted an accusation of "high treason and lese-majesty" from the Prussian government, which then issued a warrant for Marx's arrest, if at any time he should enter Germany. In the early part of 1845, the Prussians successfully put pressure on the French government to have Marx expelled from France. Exiled from Paris, he moved to Brussels. When the Prussian government kept up its pressure on the Belgian government, Marx decided, at the end of the same year, to renounce his Prussian citizenship. He never afterwards acquired any other nationality. The revolutionary year of 1848 drove him via Paris to Cologne whence, expelled once more by the Prussian government, he returned in July 1849 to Paris. The next month saw his third period of exile followed; this time he sought refuge for himself and his family in London, where he was to remain for the rest of his life, a victim of the direst poverty, yet absorbed in his study and writing, and maintaining, as he expressed it in a letter to his friend Engels, a position of authentic isolation. The philosopher whom his own philosophy had thrust into the midst of world affairs, could not realize that philosophy save as an exile, nor live his exile except as a philosopher.

Against this background of a personal migration—viewed under the triple aspect of philosophy, social milieu and nationality—we have to interpret Marx's critique of heaven and earth. His life embodied his critical philosophy, just as his philosophy was rendered critical by his life. An adequate introduction to Marx's critique as it took shape in the crucial years between his departure from his fatherland and his arrival in London, is afforded by his letters to Ruge, written in 1843 between his resignation as chief-editor of the *Rheinische Zeitung* and his removal to Paris. The letters were published in the *Deutsch-Französische Jahrbücher*, edited in 1844. The first letter was written while Marx was travelling by barge in Holland. He confesses his feelings of shame and despair regarding the political situation of his fatherland, where the fine apparel of liberalism had fallen away to reveal a hideous despotism, exposed to the world in all its nakedness. That is also a revelation, although a perverted one. Shame is in itself a revolution, the real victory won by the French Revolution over the German patriotism which had defeated it in 1813. Shame is a kind of rage, turned inward upon itself. If a whole nation were really to feel ashamed, it would become like a lion crouched and poised ready to spring. In fact, there is still no shame in Germany. On the contrary, the wretched Germans are still patriots. But the comedy of despotism being enacted by the present king is no less dangerous for him than a fatally tragic despotism had once been for the Stuarts and the Bourbons. Even if that comedy should for a time succeed in concealing its true colours, it would still mean a revolution. The state is much too weighty a matter to be dragged down to the level of a charade. A ship of fools might well drift before the wind for quite a time before anything disastrous happened; but it would finally meet its doom, simply because the fools refused to believe it. That doom is the revolution now near at hand.

Replying in May to Ruge's answer, which contains a long jeremiad on the hopeless situation of their fatherland, Marx sends a second letter, from Cologne. He calls Ruge's letter a fine elegy, a breath-taking lament; but it is not in the least political. No doubt the old world belongs to the Philistines. However, let us leave the dead to bury their dead. It is on the other hand a privilege to be the first to enter into the new life;

that should be our destiny! Human self-respect, a sense of
freedom, should be revived in these people. This feeling for
freedom disappeared from the world with the Greek; and with
Christianity it vanished into the blue haze of heaven. But only
with the aid of this feeling can society be renewed as a community which serves the supreme human goal, a democratic
state. The Philistine world is a world of political animals, a dehumanized world. Germany, the culmination of the Philistine
world, cannot but lag behind the French Revolution, which
restored man as a human being. For the principle of the
monarchy generally is man as a despised, dehumanized being;
and the Prussian king will remain typical of all the rest of his
people, so long as the perverted world is the real world. Therefore, the task ahead of us is to expose the old world in its totality
to the daylight and to shape the new. The longer the time
thinking men have in order to come to their senses, and suffering mankind is granted for concentration, the more mature,
when finally brought to birth, will be the product now growing
in the womb of the present.

The third letter was sent from Kreuznach where, since his
marriage in June, Marx had been staying at his mother-in-
law's house, waiting to set out for Paris. He is looking forward
to the new project, the review *Deutsch-Französische Jahrbücher*,
which he is to edit in collaboration with Ruge; and he is longing to escape from the tyrannical atmosphere of his fatherland
into the free air of the new Capital of the new world. He then
begins to consider the internal difficulties inherent in the new
enterprise. General anarchy has broken out among the re-
formers; and they would all be compelled to admit that they
have no precise idea about the future. However, it is precisely
the advantage of the new movement that we do not seek to
anticipate the new world dogmatically, but rather to discover
it in the critique of the old. Up to now the philosophers have
always had the solution to the riddle lying in their writing
desks; and all the stupid outside world had to do was to close
its eyes and open its mouth to receive the ready-baked pie of
absolute science. Philosophy has become worldly; and the
most striking proof of this is that the philosophical consciousness itself has been drawn into the heat of the fray, not just
superficially, but completely. "It is certainly not our task to

construct the future in advance and to settle all problems for all time; but it just as certainly is our task to criticize the existing world ruthlessly. I mean ruthlessly in the sense that we must be unafraid of our own conclusions and equally unafraid of coming into conflict with the prevailing powers."

Marx continues his letter with an exposition of the contrast between critique and dogmatism. The function of critique is to force the dogmatic thinkers to clarify the meaning of their propositions. He has no desire to unfurl any dogmatical standard; and communism as advocated by Cabet, Dezamy and Weitling he regards as a dogmatic abstraction. Whether one likes it or not, the chief interest of contemporary Germany is in religion and only secondarily in politics. It is no use presenting them with a ready-made system like that contained in "The journey to Icaria".

Reason has always existed, albeit not always in a rational guise. Critique can begin, therefore, with any form of theoretical and practical consciousness; and out of the specific forms of existing reality it can develop the true reality as its "ought" *(Sollen)* and its ultimate goal. Social truth can be arrived at everywhere from the contradiction in the political state, from the conflict between its ideal goal and its practical assumptions. Just as religion is the summation of the theoretical battles of mankind, so the political State is the summation of its practical battles. Thus, the political State in its specific form, i.e. *sub specie rei publicae* (considered from the political point of view), is the expression of all social struggles, needs, truths. There is therefore nothing to prevent our beginning our critique with a critique of politics, taking part in politics, that is to say, in real struggles. In this way, we would avoid presenting ourselves to the world in doctrinaire fashion and with a new principle, declaring: here is truth, bow down and worship it. We should develop new principles for the world out of its old ones. We must not say to the world: stop your quarrels, they are foolish, and listen to us; we possess the real truth. Instead we must show the world why it struggles; and this consciousness is something it must acquire, whether it likes it or not. The reform of consciousness simply consists in helping the world to take possession of its own consciousness; it means awakening the world from its dream about itself, explaining to the world its own actions.

At this point Marx mentions the work of Feuerbach, but with a crucial addition. As Feuerbach's critique had done at the religious level, so now it is necessary to cast religious and political questions in the form of human self-consciousness. Our programme should be the reform of consciousness, not by means of dogmas, but by analysing the nebulous, mystical consciousness both in its religious and in its political manifestations. It will then become evident that in order to possess it in reality, the world must possess a thing consciously which it has long been dreaming of. It will also become evident that the point at issue is not a caesura between past and present, but the realization of the ideas of the past. Finally, it will become evident that mankind is not embarking on a new task but is setting out to complete an old one.

Marx then summarizes his argument in a succinct editorial formula for the new review about to be launched in Paris: to help the age to come towards a realization of its struggles and its yearnings *(Selbst-verständigung)*—in a word, critical philosophy. This, he concludes, is a task designed to benefit the world and ourselves. It calls for unanimity. "The heart of the matter is a confession, that is all. In order to receive forgiveness of its sins, mankind need only explain them in their true reality."

With these triumphant words Marx ends his last letter to Arnold Ruge, written on the eve of his departure for Paris, "the new capital of the new world", chosen to be the centre for the realization of this programme. In these three letters, and especially in the third one, are contained the germs of the philosophy which in the following years was to be brought to theoretical and practical fruition. It is useful, therefore, to summarize its main points.

The closing sentence of Marx's third letter sums up his whole programme as the realization of the forgiveness of sins. We are strongly reminded here of the comparison between Socrates and Christ which Marx had elaborated in the preparatory studies for his dissertation. There he had pointed to a radical contrast between Socrates' skill as a midwife of philosophy and Christ's religious work as saviour from sin. In other words, whereas Socrates is the perfect philosopher of immanence, Christianity is the perfect philosophy of transcendence. Now, only a few years later, Marx has in fact transferred the issue from the individual realm to that of mankind generally; and at the same time the scene has shifted from within the human mind on to the stage of world history in its full dimensions. The sins which need to be confessed in order to be forgiven are more than personal aberrations; they are collective sins, the sins of the world, of mankind as a whole; and they have been committed by countless generations. They constitute in fact the cumulative sin of world history.

This is obviously to transmute critical philosophy into something Socrates could never have dreamt of. In the preparatory studies for his dissertation Marx had hinted at two further implications of Socrates' philosophy, one in the religious and one in the political sphere. In the religious sphere, Socrates' historical personality had been turned by Plato into a myth, the myth of the negative dialectics of death and love, which found its final consummation in Plotinus' ecstatic contemplation. Marx suggested that there was a deeper congeniality between Platonic mythology, which turns philosophy into religion, and a Christian religion which is the perfect philosophy of transcendence. In other words Socrates' critical philosophy had finished up in the blind alley of religion, either neoplatonic or Christian.

As far as the political aspect is concerned, Marx had analysed the contradictory character of Socrates' philosophy, which on the one hand was profoundly critical, and at the same time was incapable of breaking through the substantial limitations of Greek life and thought. In Plato's Republic the balance came down on the side of substantiality, which overrode and absorbed the Socratic element of critical subjectivity. In that connection, Marx had noted the radical contrast between Plato and Christ, in that Christ had championed the subjective element against the existing State. Marx's tacit conclusion was that, unfortunately, this subjective critique of the State had gone astray, had been sidetracked by religion. If we try to express the conclusion implicit in Marx's reasoning, then we come to something like the following argument. The close affinity between Platonism and Christianity on the religious level is counterbalanced by the sharp contrast between Plato and Christ in the political realm. Nevertheless, Christianity failed in this respect no less fatally than Platonism, though for opposite reasons. Whereas Socrates and, *a fortiori*, his pupil

Plato succumbed to the substantiality of Greek life and thought as embodied in the unity of religion and politics, Christ and the Christian Church on the other hand opposed their subjective religiosity to the profane political realm, and in so doing transposed the subjective spirit into an otherworldly region. This conclusion seems to be implicit in a remark made in Marx's first letter to Arnold Ruge, that the feeling for freedom vanished from the world with the Greeks, and with Christianity disappeared into the heavenly blue. Here then was double proof of the fatal influence of religion, whether of the substantial or the subjective variety, when it came to involvement in the political realm.

The point at issue now, therefore, was how to revive this vanished feeling for freedom, which alone is capable of transforming society into a community of men fitted to serve their highest destiny, that is, a democratic state. This was the task outlined by Marx for critical philosophy. Enthusiasm for freedom might seem to have vanished. Actually, it was still present, but in a perverted form; for it had disappeared into a dream-world. The function assigned by Marx to critical philosophy is comparable to the function which, half a century later, Siegmund Freud proposed for psycho-analysis. An inverted consciousness has to be restored through analysis of its unreal, its dreamlike, manifestations. But whereas Freud, in spite of the revolutionary implications of his approach, was, like Socrates, to keep his critical analysis strictly within the confines of the prevailing political system, Marx, on the contrary, wielded his critical armoury against the political system itself. And whereas Freud, like Socrates, took as his viewpoint the individual consciousness, the viewpoint of Marx was the consciousness of mankind as a whole, of mankind throughout the course of its history. Therefore, when Marx came to interpret the confession of sins needed for man's self-liberation, he did not relate this to man's individual errors, but to his false consciousness as embodied in the collective structures of religion and politics.

In other words, Marx transmuted Socrates' critique into a profoundly historical action. Philosophy had become involved with the world, had been drawn into the front line of the battles of contemporary history. That was where philosophy was called upon to apply its critique and so to bring about the reform of consciousness. The reform of consciousness could not be achieved without a revolution. Revolution is conceived in the head of philosophy, just as philosophy is born in the midst of world affairs.

We have already heard one part of Marx's attack on Herr Hermes, editor of the *Kölnische Zeitung*, a passage comparing the introduction of philosophy into the world with the birth of a child. The cries of its enemies mean as much to philosophy as the first cry of a child to the anxious ear of the mother. This strange comparison is only understandable in terms of its mythological origin. Marx is thinking of the ancient Greek story about the birth of the god Zeus, which was announced by a roll of drums performed by the Corybantes and the Cabiri, the priests of the goddess Cybele.

This is reminiscent of a passage in the preparatory studies of Marx's dissertation which deals with the Epicurean idea of the declination of the atom from the straight line. The declination of the atom is the principle of its absolute autonomy, it is the soul of the atom. Epicurus' atomic world is a world in which independent atoms engage in a process of reciprocal repulsion. Marx illustrates this with a reference to the ancient Greek story about the birth of the god Zeus: "Just as Zeus grew up amid the furious war-dances of the Curetes, so in Epicurus' view the world originates amid the clanging war-dances of the atoms."

This present reference has to do with a parallel version of the same story. The Corybantes and Cabiri were identified in Asia Minor with the Curetes, priests of the goddess Rhea, mother of Zeus. According to the myth, the Curetes drowned the voice of the new-born Zeus by striking upon their shields with their swords.

Marx envisages the birth of philosophy as the creation of a world. The world, that is, the world of man, the war-like world of modern society. Philosophy does not spring out of pure thought, but grows up in the midst of history.

9

The realization of philosophy

MARX'S critique of religion is an essential part of his critical philosophy; or, to put it another way, his critique of religion has to be understood as the culmination of his critique of philosophy. Since throughout the development of Marx's thinking the philosophy of Hegel was the culmination of all philosophy, Marx's critique of philosophy is, in fact, the story of his critical relationship to Hegel. In short, Marx's critique of religion is the culmination of his critique of Hegel.

In an earlier lecture I examined the ambiguous relationship in which Marx was involved from the moment he began to realize the significance of Hegel's philosophy. In his *Critique of Hegel's dialectic and philosophy as a whole*, written in 1844, Marx stressed the necessity for true philosophy of a critical confrontation "with its mother, Hegel's dialectic". He blamed members of the Young Hegelian school like Bruno Bauer for being incapable of this critical distancing. From the very outset Marx had had an ambivalent relationship to Hegel, compounded of admiration and aversion, love and resentment, dependence and independence, identification and dissatisfaction. The gods which he had now begun to look for in the very midst of the world still remained gods. The idea which he tried to find in reality itself continued to be an idea. Hegel's "grotesque melody of the rock" disquieted his mind because of the contradictory elements it was composed of. On the one hand, Hegel's absolute spirit was inaccessible to him, shrouded in darkness like a god; and he felt as though he were swept off his feet in the demonic torrent of Hegel's dialectic. On the other hand, Hegel promised him the understanding of concrete, down-to-earth reality, in contrast with an earlier German idealism which was given to flying off into the stratosphere.

In consequence, the dissertation offered Marx an excellent practice-ground for clarifying his ambivalent feelings. In fact the dissertation already contains, in principle, the essential critique which in subsequent years Marx was to develop and direct against Hegel's philosophy. At the same time Marx recognized the importance of the admirably bold plan of Hegel's history of philosophy, which he regarded as the very foundation of the history of philosophy. However, both the strength of Hegel's position as an *historian* of philosophy and his weakness as a *philosopher* of history induced Marx to take the necessary steps whereby he could transcend Hegel's position.

In the foreword to the dissertation the three main elements of Marx's critique are already implicitly formulated. His first objection is to Hegel's neglect of detail—a defect which he explains as an inevitable corollary of the stupendous sweep of Hegel's enterprise. This objection in itself might have been of no very great importance; for it is usual enough for a scholar to offer some correction of his mentor and predecessor. But the detail which Hegel had overlooked and which Marx claimed to have discovered turned out to be of overriding significance. Its neglect therefore had far-reaching consequences. Its discovery was precisely the discovery of "the key to the true history of Greek philosophy", as Marx triumphantly describes the result of his study. In other words, for all his merit as a systematic historian of Greek philosophy within the larger historical setting of philosophy in general, Hegel is alleged to have missed the key. The door giving access to the truth of Greek philosophy did not open for him.

But the stone which the builders rejected became the chief cornerstone for the new building that Marx was beginning to design. His discovery and the method which led him to it bear a striking resemblance to Kepler's revolutionary discovery in the astronomical field.

Introducing the first chapter of his dissertation, Marx describes how he has succeeded in parting company with the well-established prejudice that saw in Epicurean physics only certain arbitrary modifications of Democritean physics and regarded the two systems as, in effect, identical. Precisely because this prejudice is as old as the history of philosophy, Marx was obliged to go into the minutest detail. The differences are so concealed that it takes a microscope, so to speak, to detect them. But, Marx argues, the outcome will be all the more important, since what can be demonstrated on a small scale can be demonstrated better still where the relationships are envisaged in larger dimensions. The result was, in fact, important; for the detail which Marx discovered to be crucial, namely, Epicurus' view of the declination of atoms from a straight line, was, as it turned out, the key to the radical departure of Epicurean philosophy, evident in his theory of the celestial bodies, its departure from the whole religious tradition of Greek philosophy.

Marx's discovery parallels that which in the first decade of the seventeenth century obliged Johannes Kepler to overturn the traditional view of the celestial bodies and their motions. The parallel is noteworthy in various respects; but for the moment it will suffice to concentrate on one particular aspect. Kepler had been assistant to the great Danish astronomer, Tycho Brahe, who by means of considerably improved technical instruments had been able to refine astronomical observations and to reduce the margin of error in measurement to less than two minutes of a degree. After Tycho Brahe's death, his detailed measurements of the motion of the planet Mars were placed at Kepler's disposal. When he compared the result of the measurements in every detail with the movements as they ought to be according to his conception of the celestial movements, he discovered a difference of eight arc-minutes. More essential even than his discovery was the fact that he made it and the consequences he drew from it. The fact of Kepler's discovery resulted from his principle concerning the necessity of perfect agreement between measurement and concept, between observation and hypothesis. Whereas Ptolemy and even Copernicus would have ignored the slight difference which Kepler had observed—so that they would have considered his observation to confirm their hypothesis—Kepler made the opposite choice. In order to justify the observation, he rejected the hypothesis. In the closing sentence of the nineteenth chapter of his book *Astronomia Nova* Kepler speaks of his revolutionary discovery: "Solely by these eight arc-minutes I have been guided towards the total reformation of astronomy; they have become the material for a great part of this book."

Marx, like Kepler, was guided towards a radically new concept by a detail, only discoverable by refined measurements or, as Marx puts it, by a microscope. A detail, neglected by the whole history of philosophy, forced him to adopt a new approach to philosophy and, more especially, to part company with Hegel.

The stupendous sweep of Hegel's history of philosophy, which made him overlook certain crucial details, was connected with a second aspect to which Marx objected, namely, Hegel's speculative view. What Hegel called the speculative idea *par excellence* hindered him from recognizing in the post-Aristotelian systems the great importance that they have for the history of Greek philosophy and for the Greek mind in general. Marx does not precisely explain what he means by Hegel's view of the speculative idea or what his fundamental objections to this view are; but he several times uses the term "speculation" with reference to the history of Greek philosophy also. When he tries to define the wider subject to which his dissertation is only preliminary, he uses two alternative expressions. When referring to the cycle of post-Aristotelian philosophy, he several times uses an expression like "in relation to previous Greek philosophy"; but other phrases, obviously with an identical meaning, are: "in relation to all Greek speculation" and "in relation to earlier speculation".

Evidently, what he intends is a contrast between non-speculative and speculative Greek philosophy. A further indication of this is to be found in the second draft of a foreword for his dissertation, which Marx wrote at the end of 1841 or the beginning of 1842, that is, in the period when he had just abandoned his planned academic career but had not yet given up wanting to have his dissertation printed and published. Marx introduces his dissertation as an earlier work, designed as part of a presentation of Epicurean, Stoic and Sceptic philosophy as a whole, a project which at this moment cannot be realized, being interrupted by political and philosophical concerns of a totally different character. Now, at last, the time has arrived for real understanding of these philosophical systems. Their authors are the philosophers of self-consciousness. This last sentence is substituted for another which he has crossed out, but which had begun with the statement that hitherto all philosophers have slighted these three philosophies, the philosophies of self-consciousness, on account of their non-speculative character.

The term "non-speculative" is obviously taken by Marx to be synonymous with "subjective". In the introduction to the first chapter he opposes the subjective form of Greek philosophy to its content. If the preceding systems are more significant and more interesting in virtue of their content, the post-Aristotelian ones, and particularly the cycle of Epicurean, Stoic and Sceptic schools, are important because of the subjective form, the character of Greek philosophy. It is precisely the subjective form, the mental vehicle of philosophical systems, which we have until now almost entirely ignored in considering only their metaphysical pronouncements.

In other words, the characterization of Hegel as a speculative philosopher applies also to the earlier philosophers, all of whom have disdained these post-Aristotelian systems and have one-sidedly preferred the preceding tradition of Greek Speculation. The parallel between Hegel and Aristotle has to be understood, therefore, as indicating that both philosophers consummated the tradition of speculative philosophy, that is, of a philosophy which presents a metaphysical content. By way of contrast, Marx wants to display the subjective form of philosophy; he is concerned with its mental vehicle, with its character.

At the time he was preparing his dissertation, Marx did not yet fully realize that his departure from Hegel had even more far-reaching consequences. They are, however, implicit in his conclusions. His critique of Plutarch had a wider significance. In his foreword, Marx stresses the importance of his critique as being aimed at a typical representative of a species: Plutarch's attack on Epicurus' theology strikingly represents the relation of the theologizing intellect to philosophy. Of course, the term "philosophy" is used here in a special sense, namely, as the true philosophy exhibited in Epicurus' radical break with the whole theologizing tradition of Greek philosophy.

This is precisely what Marx elsewhere describes as Greek Speculation. The basic reason for Hegel's misunderstanding of Epicurus' importance lies, therefore, in the speculative trend of Hegel's philosophy which, far from overcoming the theologizing intellect, tended rather to confirm and sanction it. In the years that ensued, it was to become obvious that Marx's critique of Plutarch as representative of the religious tradition in itself entailed, implicitly at any rate, a critique of Hegel.

These features of Marx's critique *vis-à-vis* Hegel's philosophy are only aspects of the crucial problem of how to live in a post-Hegelian era. It was this which impelled Marx to choose Epicurean philosophy as the subject of his dissertation. After a total philosophy such as Hegel's, has life lost its meaning? How is it possible to live in such an aftermath? The question was anything but theoretical, since philosophy was anything but a theoretical issue. In Hegel's philosophy, Marx had faced the totality of contemporary history, the conscious expression of the total context in which he had been born. To come to grips with Hegel therefore involved a decisive struggle with his own historical situation. Hegel's thinking had, as it were, absorbed the world into the totality of his speculation. And so after the death of the master it was simply impossible to continue along the same lines; Hegel's death spelt the end of an era, an end to the possibility of identifying oneself with the world in a philosophical manner. From now on, man's relationship to his own world had radically changed.

The historical analogy helped Marx to come to grips with his own situation. As post-Aristotelian philosophy had revealed the inner dissolution of the Greek era and had anticipated the Titanic struggle of the Roman period, so post-Hegelian philosophy had contained the germ of a gigantic schism which was to disrupt the coming era. Any attempt by Hegelian philosophers to follow in their master's footsteps could only produce pathetic examples of impotent epigonism. Hegel's philosophy resembled Aeolus' harp, from which only the tempest could conjure music. The true import of this philosophy was for the future to demonstrate. The mature plant had to die for the seeds to come to fruition.

In this way Marx tried to clarify his own ambivalent relationship to Hegel as the necessary corollary of his historical situation. The paradoxical nature of his own consciousness sprang logically out of his attachment to the master; for the conscious realization of the inner contradictions of history was the essence of Hegel's thinking. Thus it was possible for Marx to explain Hegel's increasing conservatism in terms of the maturation of a total philosophy. He defended Hegel against the suggestion made by some Young Hegelian thinkers that certain aspects of their master's system were to be explained by his accommodating himself to the authorities. These critics overlooked the essential difference between Hegel's position and their own. The disciples had received the system ready-made from the master's hands; their relationship to it had the character of reflection. Conversely, for the teacher himself philosophy was in process of being created, so that his spiritual energy pulsated to its farthest periphery; his relationship to his own system was immediate, substantial.

This explanation did not, however, emerge from any attempt on Marx's part to take Hegel's increasing conservatism for granted. He even reckoned with the possibility that Hegel's accommodation to the established political powers had been deliberate. However, discussion of the moral implications of Hegel's attitude was pointless. The point at issue was whether this was rooted in a fundamental defect, inherent in Hegel's system as such. The master himself could not have been in the least aware that this external attitude resulted from a basic error. Therefore, it was the task of his pupils, instead of casting aspersions on the master's private conscience, to construe the essential form of his consciousness. In so doing they would really succeed in transcending the master's system.

On the same grounds, Marx rebutted the suggestion of an analogy between Socrates and Hegel, resulting in the conclusion that, since Socrates' philosophy had been condemned by the official authorities of his time, Hegel's philosophy was likewise bound to be condemned. This suggestion completely ignored the essential difference between the respective historical situations of the two philosophers. Socrates was still imprisoned within the substantial circle enclosing Greek political and religious existence; and so his condemnation was an inevitable corollary of his own intrinsic limitations. But in our time the struggle is no longer one between spirit and nature; both sides have now become spirit and want to be recognized as such. Hegel was no longer a lonely apostate, fallen away from the gravitational field of nature; but in his total philosophy the development of world history from nature to spirit had been raised to the level of consciousness.

The fate of Hegel's philosophy was therefore different from that which condemned Socrates to drink the poisoned cup—different too from the fate which forced Giordano Bruno to pay for his fieriness of spirit at the stake. Hegel's system is not condemned by a hostile world, nor indeed was Hegel destined for martyrdom; but his philosophy is disintegrating at the very moment of its realization. For the realization of his philosophy is through and through contradictory; and the contradictions become manifest in the process of realization.

Marx, then, elucidates three aspects of this process whereby Hegel's philosophy changes from a speculative system into praxis, from theoretical spirit into the practical energy of the will.

First, when philosophy turns outward and opposes the phenomenal world, the philosophical system begins to solidify into an abstract totality. It becomes one side of the world in contradiction with another side. In the very process whereby the world becomes philosophical, philosophy becomes worldly, so that the realization of philosophy is at the same time its overthrow. In combating the world, philosophy fights against its own inner defect. Its antagonist is its own self, albeit with the factors inverted.

Besides this objective aspect, the realization of philosophy has a subjective aspect too. This latter concerns the relationship of the philosophical system which is being realized to its mental vehicles, its relationship to the individual self-consciousness. Parallel to the contradictions inherent in the objective aspect, this subjective aspect has its own contradictory implications. The individual self-consciousness is like a two-edged sword, one side of which is turned against the world, the other side against philosophy. For what from the objective viewpoint appears as an inverted relationship between philosophy and world, appears on the subjective view as a two-sided, contradictory purpose and act. When the individual self-consciousness liberates the world from perverted philosophy, non-philosophy (*Unphilosophie*), at the same time it liberates itself from the philosophy which by changing into a complete system also turned into a straitjacket. However, because this movement is still only beginning, the individual self-consciousness is still absorbed in the immediate activity of self-liberation; it has not had the time to transcend the system from a theoretical viewpoint. For this reason, the self-liberating consciousness is still involved in its opposition to the immutability of the system, it is still ignorant of the hidden fact that, in combating the system, it is engaged in realizing its several elements.

Thirdly, this double-edged character of philosophical self-consciousness presents itself in the form of a duality of philosophical schools, involved in a radical, mutual opposition. One school, the liberal or Young Hegelian party, clings to the concept and principle of philosophy, whereas the other party, the Old Hegelian school of positive philosophers, stresses the aspect of reality, the non-conceptual aspect of philosophy. The critical activity of the first school is philosophy turning outward; the second school tries to philosophize, that is to say, philosophy turns inward. Whereas the second school looks for the defect in the very heart of philosophy, the first school sees the defect as a defect of the world, so that it is its task to render the world philosophical.

It is strange that each party is doing the very thing which the other party wants to do and which itself alone does not want to do. However, the first party, despite its inner contradiction, is in general conscious of the principle and of its purpose. In the second school the perversity, the foolishness, becomes evident. Whereas the first party is capable of really progressive activities, the second party is only capable of defining purposes and tendencies, the form of which is in contradiction with their import.

To sum up, the inner contradictions inherent in the realization of Hegel's philosophy become manifest in three different modes or aspects. First, they appear as an inverted relationship and antagonistic rift between philosophy and the world; secondly, they appear as an internal schism inside the individual philosophical self-consciousness; and, finally, they appear as an external bifurcation and duality of philosophy, as two mutually antagonistic philosophical schools.

In this outline, written as a note to his dissertation, Marx summarized in essence the programme which lay ahead. The development of his thinking over the ensuing years is like the elaboration of a theme in music, being based on this initial pattern. There is only one point on which in the years that followed Marx materially transcended the confines of this outline. He stresses the fact that the very transformation of philosophy from theoretical spirit into practical energy has a theoretical character. The very praxis of philosophy is still theoretical; for it is the critique which measures the individual existence against the essence, the particular reality against the idea.

The fact is that as long as the shift from theory to praxis remained a shift inside the realm of philosophical reflection, the decisive step had not yet been taken. That step would mean proceeding from theoretical praxis to practical praxis, from philosophical action to real action, from a world illuminated by critical reflection to a world obscured by uncritical instinct. On the other hand, Marx would not have felt impelled to take that essential step beyond the philosophical realm, if its necessity had not been forced upon his mind during his explorations inside the philosophical realm. It was not until he had probed the final boundaries of philosophical reflection that he perceived the possibility and necessity of a leap beyond.

If we bear this fundamental limitation in mind, then the way Marx describes the threefold contradictions inherent in the realization of Hegel's philosophy does indeed contain the essential elements of his subsequent development. The interdependence of the three aspects is crucial. The unbearable contradiction between a total philosophy and a world which was its very counterpart emerged from the same source that produces the awareness of being imprisoned within a speculative, ready-made philosophical system. Likewise, the internal schism which had divided Hegel's legacy between two irreconcilable groups of inheritors was connected with the same background. Therefore, Marx's confrontation which took place in the following years with both schools of Hegelianism was only one prominent aspect of his attempt to overcome the contradictions which divided his own mind, as well as those inherent in the transformation of a theoretical philosophy into the dimension of practical reality. When we look at Marx's writings of the next few years, that is, up to 1845, it is evident that what he called his work of "self-explanation" (*Selbstverständigung*) went hand in hand with a critique, direct and indirect, of Hegel, intertwined with actions which translated this critique into practice. The indirect critique found expression in writings which enshrined his confrontation with the Hegelian Right and the Hegelian Left. In three other writings he tried to get to grips with the master himself.

Let us glance first of all at the evidences for his indirect critique. Small wonder that Marx first turned his critical reflection against the Hegelian Right. This was the second school mentioned in his outline, the school of so-called "Positive Philosophy". In a letter to Arnold Ruge of April 1842, Marx promises to send him four different treatises: 1. "On religious art"; 2. "On the romanticists"; 3. "The philosophical manifest of the Historical School of Jurisprudence"; 4. "The positive philosophers". Of these four treatises, only the third, a critical analysis of the Historical School of Jurisprudence, has been published, as an article in the *Rheinische Zeitung*. The others were never published, partly owing to repressive measures taken against the reviews in which they might have appeared. They have not even been preserved among Marx's manuscripts. But, in his letters to Ruge, Marx made some allusions to their content. The treatise on religious art originated as a treatise on Christian art, to be published as the second volume of the so-called *Trumpet*. The year before, the leader of the Young Hegelian school Bruno Bauer, had published an anonymous pamphlet with the title *The Trumpet of the Last Judgment on Hegel the atheist and antichrist. An ultimatum.* Affecting the standpoint of an orthodox Lutheran dismayed by the official approbation of Hegelianism, the pamphlet presented a series of quotations from Hegel, designed to show that he was not at all a pious conservative but a dangerous radical and atheist. Bauer had planned, in co-operation with Marx, to expand this pamphlet into a series of pamphlets under the same title, presenting a systematic exposition of Hegel's Aesthetics, Philosophy of Law, and so forth, in order to demonstrate that the Young Hegelian, not the Old Hegelian, school was truly loyal to the master's legacy. When censorship had frustrated this design, Marx rewrote his treatise under the title: "On religion and art, with particular reference to Christian art"; this new fashion, as he explains, had been liberated from the trumpet-like tone of the biblical prophetic style as with "The Lord roars from Zion", as well as from the cumbersome restrictiveness of Hegel's presentation, which he had replaced with a more fundamental and freer presentation. The treatise had impelled him to discuss the general essence of religion, a theme which had brought him slightly into collision with Feuerbach, over the form, not the principle, of Feuerbach's approach. At all events, he concluded, so much the worse for religion.

Although the treatise itself has not been preserved, these clues are instructive enough. They inform us, first, about the intense interest Marx was showing, at this time, in the question of the essence of Christianity and of religion in general, which question he approached from the artistic viewpoint. For him this particular viewpoint was only one element of a larger whole, of which the political viewpoint was another aspect. In the same letter he comments on a recent declaration of the Prussian government regarding the scope of the law concerning crimes against the State and its officials. This leads Marx to make the biting observation that "a transcendental State and a positive religion belong together like a pocket-god and a pickpocket". Furthermore, there would seem to be a close connection between his relationship to the Christian religion and his relationship to Hegel's philosophy. He begins to liberate himself from the pressure of the Christian tradition and, along with that, from the shackles of Hegel's system. The year before, Marx had read Feuerbach's recently published book, *The Essence of Christianity*; but in spite of his enthusiasm, he felt even at this early stage that his own approach was different.

The second of the four treatises mentioned by Marx in his letter to Ruge dealt with Romanticism. The title suggests a critical confrontation with an influential movement which, as we know from the poetry produced in his early academic years, had once fascinated him. In having it out with the Christian religion and with religion in general, he attempts at the same time to dispose of his own romanticist past. The fourth treatise is described by Marx as being directed against the "positive philosophers" whom, as he says with a touch of irony, "I have tickled a little". We may infer from the title that this treatise contained a direct attack on the Old Hegelian school, which saw in Hegel's philosophy the mysteries of divine revelation confirmed and glorified.

The third treatise—the only one to have been preserved—contains a sharp attack on the so-called Historical School of Jurisprudence which Marx considered to be the culmination of reactionary political and juridical theory.

He stresses the fact that as far as their content is concerned these four treatises belong together. This is worth noting, since their paths lead in very different directions. The subjects cover a wide spectrum, ranging from romanticism, aesthetics, religious art and religion in general, via Hegel's philosophy, to the theory of law and State. Obviously, Marx views his arguments on all these divergent fronts in a single perspective.

However, Marx's confrontation with religious and political conservatism and more particularly with the Old Hegelian school, although important in itself, was less characteristic of his development than the encounter with his own confrères. Without this confrontation with others on the left, Marx would have been no more than a brilliant member of the Young Hegelian school; and his critique of religion would merely have added some literary touches to the already considerable amount of radically atheist polemics against the Christian religion and its established tradition. It is in his dialogue with the Young Hegelian school that the roots of Marx's critique of religion become visible. His critique proves to be directed not against religion as such but against an underlying tendency that can also be concealed in irreligious and atheistic theories. It is the tendency described in the preface to his dissertation as "speculation". By introducing this term he succeeds in transposing the debate with religion to the general level of anthropology. At the same time, the term helps him to clarify his ambivalent relationship with Hegel's philosophy, since it is the speculative character of Hegel's thought which arouses his antagonism.

Marx's writings during the years 1843–47 witness to an ever more radical confrontation with the tendency to speculation wherever he meets it. It is noteworthy that even apart from those of his writings which contain his explicit and direct dealing with Hegel's philosophy, all his writings during these years are indirect attempts to settle accounts with speculation in its most perfect, that is, its Hegelian form. The article *On the Jewish question* was aimed at Bruno Bauer, the leader of the Young Hegelian school. It exposed Bauer's one-sided theological approach to the question of Jewish emancipation, which prevented him from getting down to the real point at issue, namely, a critique of politics. The content of this article was closely akin to that of another one published in the *Deutsch-Französische Jahrbücher* of 1844, the *Introduction to a critique of Hegel's Philosophy of Law*.

The argument was continued and enormously expanded in the book Marx wrote in co-operation with Engels during the autumn of the same year. The *Critique of Critical Critique*, directed at Bruno Bauer, his two brothers and their Young Hegelian colleagues—a group nicknamed "The Holy Family"—contained a series of devastating attacks on this post-Hegelian philosophy, which had turned the master's speculation into something like caricature. "The worst enemy of real humanism to be found in Germany," runs the authors' opening broadside in the Foreword, "is Spiritualism or speculative Idealism, which substitutes 'self-consciousness' or the 'Spirit' for real, individual man. It follows the teaching of the Gospel according to John: 'It is the spirit that gives life, the flesh is of no avail.' Self-evidently, this fleshless spirit is only spirit in the imagination of this spiritualism. It is the complete caricature of speculation that we are combating in Bauer's critique. We consider it the most perfect expression of the Christian-German principle in its final attempt to assert itself by transforming 'Critique' into a transcendental power." This book still presents Feuerbach's critique of Hegel as the true expression of "real humanism", which had substituted "man" for the "old toggery" (*an die Stelle des alten Plunders*) of the "infinite self-consciousness". It praises Feuerbach as the thinker who "completed and criticized Hegel from the Hegelian viewpoint, in that he dissolved the metaphysical absolute Spirit in the 'real man based on nature' ". It was Feuerbach who "completed the critique of religion at the very moment he designed the great, nay, masterly, blueprint of a critique of Hegel's speculation, in a word, of all metaphysics".

176

As a matter of fact, Feuerbach had criticized Hegel, but he did so from a Hegelian viewpoint. Feuerbach's real humanism was, in itself, a decisive step beyond Young Hegelian speculation, which remained imprisoned within the three elements of Hegel's philosophy: Spinoza's substance, Fichte's self-consciousness and the Hegelian absolute spirit as necessary-contradictory unity of substance and self-consciousness. Feuerbach had unmasked these elements as metaphysical travesties: substance is the metaphysical travesty of nature in its isolation from man: self-consciousness is the travesty of spirit in its isolation from nature; the absolute spirit is the metaphysically travestied unity of nature and spirit, that is, real man and the real human species.

Yet underneath the surface of this apparent agreement with Feuerbach's "real humanism", Marx's crucial problem remained unanswered. No sooner had Marx, the exile from Paris, arrived in Brussels than, once again in co-operation with Engels, he was preparing a new book which contained a definitive confrontation with the diverse offshoots of the Young Hegelian school, including both Feuerbach and the so-called "true socialist" philosophers. This polemic, compiled little more than six months after "The Holy Family", lumped them all together as representatives of "The German ideology". Feuerbach's humanism, which in "The Holy Family" had still been approved as revealing the real basis of Hegelian speculation, was now in its turn unmasked as being merely a continuation of Hegelian speculation in a new form. Whereas Strauss and Bauer had worked with pure Hegelian categories, such as substance and self-consciousness, more recently Feuerbach and Max Stirmer had simply replaced these with mundane-sounding terms like man, human species and the individual. In other words, what until recently Marx had regarded as Feuerbach's *exposé* of Hegelian metaphysical speculation was now, conversely, unveiled as Feuerbach's profanation of Hegel, a secular translation of Hegelian speculation. Feuerbach turned out to have been incapable either of radically criticizing Hegel or of constructing a radical critique of religion.

The heart of the matter was a general failure of all German philosophical critique after Hegel. Basing itself on the foundation of the Hegelian system, it had reduced its critique to one of religious imaginings, it had remained a theological critique. The Young Hegelian school stood on the same ground as the Old Hegelian school, in that both believed in the dominance of religion, of concepts, of general ideas, over the existing world. The two schools parted company, in that this religious dominance was justified and sanctified by the Old Hegelian school, whereas it was assailed as usurpation by the Young Hegelians. This latter school was even arraigned by Marx as the main conservative force. Its critique fielded a recognition of the existing world. The result, that is to say, was the same; only the means, the interpretation, differed. Its revolution was carried out in the imaginary world of pure thought. To none of these critical philosophers has it occurred to question the relationship of their critique to their own material environment. Their German ideology turned out to be no more than a miserable reflection of the German situation. Or as Marx put it in his aphoristic comment on Feuerbach, written in the same year: "the philosophers have merely interpreted the world in various ways; the point, however, is to change it."

This radical attack on Hegelian speculation and its offshoots was at the same time Marx's definitive critique of what had initially been his own approach, as represented by his dissertation. Typically enough, Marx himself never explicitly acknowledged to what extent, in the years following upon his dissertation, his development had involved a departure from his original standpoint. In the years after 1848, his earlier writings seemed to him to be mere exercises, stages on the road which had led him to the final critique of political economy. For the observer trying, after the passage of a century, to survey Marx's career as a whole, the case is different. On closer analysis, the dilemma which had puzzled Marx when he was preparing and writing his dissertation proves to have been the crux which finally compelled him to look for a solution beyond the philosophical realm. It was the question of finding the Archimedean standpoint for a true critique of heaven, of theology, of religion.

Marx had chosen Epicurean philosophy as the perfect Greek example of the philosophy of self-consciousness. The choice expressed his acknowledgement of human self-consciousness as the highest divinity, impatient of any rival. It was an affirmation generally accepted by the Young Hegelian school at the time. However, it very soon appeared that although Marx might subscribe to the same creed, his perspective was fundamentally different from anything that his colleagues had in view. Less than four years later he rejected this philosophy of self-consciousness as merely a form of Hegelian speculation or, in other words, as an instance of German ideology. He concluded that no forms and products of consciousness can be overcome by theoretical critique, by resolution into "self-consciousness", but only by the overthrow, in practice, of the actual social relations giving rise to this idealistic humbug; that not critique but revolution is the driving force of history, as also of religion, of philosophy, and of all other types of theory.

The pseudo-revolutionary idealism of this Young Hegelian philosophy was in Marx's view much like the self-deception of the eccentric who fought a life-long battle against the very idea of gravitation which, in his unbending opinion, was the cause of man's drowning in water. This comparison recalls the reference, in the preparatory studies for Marx's dissertation, to Epicurus as a lonely apostate from the gravitational field of nature, or, in other words, an apostate from the gravitational field of political and religious existence, the substantial bond which served to consolidate Greek life.

Marx refers in this passage to the substantial bond of Greek political and religious existence. Although, as we have observed in earlier lectures, in the preparatory studies, particularly in connection with the position of Socrates and Plato, the political aspect of this substantial dependence is explicitly discussed, the dissertation itself focuses attention exclusively on the religious side of Epicurus' relationship to Greek life and thought. For the sake of our present argument, it may be useful to summarize the essential points of Marx's analysis. Epicurus' original concept consisted in the notion of the declination of atoms from the straight line. The fall in a straight line, that is, the motion of gravity, reduces the atom to dependence upon the blind necessity of nature; its existence is purely material. The motion of declination from the straight line, therefore, constitutes the independence and freedom of the atom. In virtue of this deviation the atoms are purely autonomous bodies, or rather are bodies conceived in an absolute autonomy.

In declination the real soul of the atom, the concept of abstract individuality, is represented.

Epicurus had in fact designed this concept by analogy with the motion of the heavenly bodies, which move not in straight but in oblique lines. The heavenly bodies are the highest representation of autonomy, of individuality, of weight. They are eternal and unchanging; they have their centre of gravity in themselves, not outside themselves. Separated by empty space, they deviate from the straight line, thus forming a system of repulsion and attraction in which they retain all their autonomy. Thus the heavenly bodies are atoms become real. In them matter has acquired individuality. Epicurus must have seen in this the highest existence of his principle element, the apex of his system. Nevertheless, he rebelled at this point against the consequence of his own philosophy and turned zealously against the worship of the heavenly bodies. This was his greatest inconsistency; and it was the deepest wisdom of his system that he should feel this and should express it consciously. Epicurus refused to follow the tradition of Greek philosophy which worshipped its own mind in autonomous nature, in the heavenly bodies. He opposed the view accepted by the Greeks as a whole, and so became the greatest Greek representative of Enlightenment.

This contradiction was rooted in the way Epicurus had designed his atomistic philosophy. The atom is a pure product of thought, its existence is a world of pure thought, empty space, annihilated nature. In so far as it comes into real existence it descends to a material basis which, as the vehicle of a world of multitudinous relations, never exists except in its external form. The atom, conceived as an abstract and complete particular substance, cannot affirm itself as an idealizing and dominating power over that multiplicity. Abstract particularity is freedom from being, not freedom in being. Therefore, the atom does not manifest itself in the light of appearance; or it descends to a material basis when it does enter it. The atom as such exists only in the void. Thus the death of nature has become its immortal substance.

The crucial point is that not only the atom but also the totality of atoms, the atomistic world, exists as pure ideality. It is owing to the declination of atoms from the straight line, that is, by the negation of the natural necessity of gravitation, that the atoms encounter one another. If the atoms were not accustomed to decline, neither repulsion nor encounter would have arisen, and the world would never have been created. For the atoms are their own unique object and have reference only to themselves. Consequently, expressed in terms of space, they meet one another only when every relative aspect of their being, in which they are related to something else, is negated. This relative existence is their original motion, that of falling in a straight line. Thus they meet only through their declination. The immediate existing individual is realized according to its concept only in so far as it refers to another which is itself, even if the other thing appears as its opposite, in the form of immediate existence. Thus it is that man ceases to be a product of nature only if the other thing, to which he is related, is not a different existence but rather itself an individual human being. But in order for man to become his only true object, he must have crushed within himself his relative mode of being, the force of passion and of mere nature. Repulsion is the first form of self-consciousness; it corresponds therefore to the self-consciousness which comprehends itself as an immediately existing entity, an abstractly individual thing.

It is obvious from this summary that already in his dissertation Marx has drawn a parallel between the world of atoms, as conceived by Epicurus in his philosophy of nature, on the one hand, and the world of man, on the other. He even finished this chapter with an explicit reference to more concrete forms of repulsion instanced by Epicurus: "in the political sphere it is the contract, in the social sphere friendship, which is praised as the highest." Marx did not, however, elaborate or explain this analogy. The theme of his dissertation was Epicurus' act of rebellion against the religious tradition of Greek philosophy, a rebellion which went completely against the logic of Epicurus' own atomistic philosophy. The political aspect of Greek life was passed over in silence in the dissertation; but in the preparatory studies Marx made a memorable reference to the political implications. Analysing the way in which Epicurus' concept of the declination and repulsion of the atoms has been dramatized in Lucretius' famous poem, Marx extols Lucretius as the true Roman epic poet who celebrates the substance of the Roman spirit. This Epicurean world, created by the mutual repulsion of completely autonomous atoms, reflects the *bellum omnium contra omnes*, the war of all men against all men, the rigid form of self-sufficiency, in a word, a nature become godless and a God become worldless.

The congeniality to which Marx refers between Epicurus' world of atoms and the Roman view of society as a world of self-sufficient individuals is the hidden link between his dissertation and the writings and activities of his later years, in fact, of the remainder of his life. The fundamental issue, discussed in his dissertation in relation to the religious sphere, is in later years transposed to the political and economic realm. But the issue remains essentially the same. Remarkable evidence of this essential continuity is provided by a passage in the book *The Holy Family*.

The passage contains an attack on Bruno Bauer's political philosophy, notably on Bauer's thesis that the state is necessary in order to hold together the individual, egoistic atoms of civil society. Marx refutes this thesis by analysing the difference between civil society and the world of atoms. Without mentioning Epicurus, he takes up, in fact, the theme of his dissertation. He begins by demonstrating that, in the exact and prosaic sense of the word, the members of civil society are not atoms. Characteristic of atoms is the very quality of having no qualities at all, so that they have no relationship to other entities conditioned by natural necessity. The atom has no needs, is self-sufficient; the world outside the atom is the absolute void, is without content, meaningless; for the atom possesses in itself the fullness of its totality.

Marx then goes on to admit that in fact this atomic world does bear a resemblance to the structure of civil society. The egoistic individual within civil society may indeed believe himself to be an atom, that is to say, a relationless, self-sufficient, absolutely satiated, blissful being which does not need anything outside itself. But this belief is completely illusory. It consists in an unsensuous imagination, a lifeless abstraction whereby man inflates himself to the magnitude of an atom. This delusion is in total conflict with the joyless reality conveyed by the senses, which is not at all concerned with man's imagination. Man is forced by each of his senses to acknowledge the reality of the world and of the individuals outside himself; and even by his profane stomach he is reminded every day of the fact that the world outside himself is not empty but is the very source of fullness. Every activity and quality of man, every passion, becomes a dependence, a need whereby his egocentricity is turned into a desire for other things and other human beings outside himself. However, the egoistic individual has no self-evident awareness that he needs another egoistic individual in order to satisfy his needs. This relationship has therefore to be created by every individual, in that he becomes a procurer, as it were, between the alien need and the object of this need. Consequently, it is by sheer natural necessity, that is, by those human qualities which men apprehend as alienated from their own essence, in other words, by interests (*Interesse*) that the fellow members of civil society are held together. Their real bond is civil life, not political life. It is not by the state that atoms of civil society are held together, but by the fact that they are atoms merely in their own imagination, in the heaven of their fantasy, whilst in reality they are vastly different from atoms, being not divine egoists, but egoistic human beings. Today only crass political ignorance could lead us to suppose that civil life must be held together by the state. The truth is that the state is held together by civil life.

Here, at last, Marx applies his analysis of Epicurean philosophy to the political domain. The inner contradictions of Epicurus' theoretical philosophy of self-consciousness had induced him to turn his back upon Greek religion; but those contradictions proved insoluble in the philosophical dimension. The practical solution which he found in the wisdom of perfect self-sufficiency was in line with his theoretical philosophy; but it offered a solution to its inner contradiction only in his imagination. While it was his greatness to have rebelled against the Greek concept of the *cosmos*, at the same time he rang down the curtain on the Greek *polis* and anticipated the Roman era. Marx completed for the modern era the task which had been accomplished by Epicurus for the Roman era. He turned the critique of heaven into a critique of earth, the critique of theology into a critique of politics.

10

From the critique of religion to the critique of law

AT the root of Marx's critique of religion, as this took shape during his ten formative years between 1836 and 1846, there is a fundamental paradox. It would be unfair and beside the point to suggest that Marx himself was not conscious of this paradox, or that he was only dimly aware of it, or even that he must have banished his awareness of it to the region of the subconscious. This last suggestion only dissolves the problem into vague psycho-analytic generalities, whereas the first overlooks the specific way in which Marx wrestled with the paradox. The second suggestion, that some hazy notion of the problem might have lingered in his mind, is no more than a combination of the two other ways of evading the real issue.

The paradox becomes evident in Marx's development during these years, which impelled him to start out on his critique of religion just when he had come to regard it as already completed. The contrast between these two insights may be illustrated by two remarks, the first made in 1842, the second dating from two years later. In a letter of November 1842 to Arnold Ruge, Marx opens his attack on the merely philosophical atheism and communism of Bruno Bauer and his Young Hegelian colleagues. Being at this time editor of the *Rheinische Zeitung*, Marx has become convinced of the need to come to grips with the political situation at a very concrete and practical level. He wants "to criticize religion by criticizing political

184

conditions rather than the other way round". His first reason for this is that it would be more in accordance with the character of a newspaper and the necessity of educating the public. Secondly, it is "because religion, quite vacuous in itself, draws its life from this earth and not from heaven and will disappear of its own accord, once the perverted reality whose theory it represents is dissolved". Finally, if one wants to deal with philosophy, one should flirt less with the idea of atheism (which is reminiscent of those children who loudly inform anyone who cares to listen that they are not afraid of the bogeyman) and do more to acquaint people with its meaning. These remarks might well be taken to indicate that Marx regarded the critique of religion as tilting at windmills, and so turned once and for all to the critique of politics.

However, two years later, in *The Holy Family*, Marx praises Feuerbach for having completed the critique of religion by, in effect, providing a blueprint for the critique of Hegelian speculation, in a word, of all metaphysics. This time Marx recognizes that the critique of religion can only be realized by means of a critique of Hegelian speculation; he takes religion, in its philosophical guise, in deadly earnest. The clue to this differentiation is to be found in two comments on Feuerbach, made in letters written during the intervening period. In a letter to Arnold Ruge of March 1843, in which Marx welcomes the idea of starting the *Deutsch-Französische Jahrbücher* (German-French Annals), he comments on Feuerbach's recently published *Preliminary Theses on the Reform of Philosophy*. His criticism concerns the one-sidedness of Feuerbach's aphorisms, which concern themselves too much with nature and too little with politics. Marx is convinced that an alliance with politics is the only way for contemporary philosophy to become a reality. But he adds that it will probably turn out as it did in the sixteenth century, when the champions of nature were confronted with another set of enthusiasts, the champions of the State. One and a half years later, in August 1844, Marx writes a letter to Feuerbach himself, in which he promises to send him his own recently published article *Introduction to a Critique of Hegel's Philosophy of Law*. Marx takes the opportunity to comment on two of Feuerbach's recent books, namely, *Grundsätze der Philosophie der Zukunft* (Principles of a Philosophy of the Future)

(1843), and *Das Wesen des Glaubens im Sinne Luther's. Ein Beitrag zum "Wesen des Christentums"* (The Essence of Faith according to Luther's doctrine. A contribution to "The Essence of Christianity") (1844). He commends these books for having— perhaps involuntarily—laid a philosophical foundation for socialism. Feuerbach has drawn the notion of the human species from the heaven of abstraction down to the real earth. And, Marx adds, is not this notion exactly the same as the notion of society?

This casual addition enshrined a basic difference between Marx and Feuerbach. For by interpreting Feuerbach's concept of man as identical with his own concept of society Marx was, in fact, bridging the gap between Feuerbach's concern with an abstract concept of nature and his own interest in the concrete realm of politics. In the "German Ideology" it was soon to become evident that Marx's "real earth" was something fundamentally different from the "real earth" of Feuerbach. The crucial point of difference was that Feuerbach, in pulling his concept from the heaven of abstraction down to earth, had merely substituted an abstract earth for an abstract heaven. The real critique of heaven had not been completed by Feuerbach at all; it had still to be accomplished, not by replacing heaven with earth, but by criticizing heaven in its earthly manifestations or, to put it the other way round, by criticizing the earth in its heavenly manifestations. This paradox is the key to Marx's development during his ten formative years. Having turned from the theoretical and philosophical to the practical and political realm, it was his initial belief that religion would disappear of its own accord, once the perverted reality whose theory it represents had been dissolved. At the same time he discovered that the critique of earth itself consists in a critique of the heavenly manifestation of the earth. His critique was, in essence, a radical critique of Hegel.

It seems that, initially, Marx had it in mind to publish the articles he intended to write about various parts of Hegel's philosophy, in the series of pamphlets designed to continue Bruno Bauer's anonymously published pamphlet, *The Trumpet of the last judgment on Hegel the atheist and antichrist.* By the time when, in a letter to Ruge of March 1842, he gave notice of an article containing a critique of Hegel's theory of natural law, censorship had already succeeded in putting a stop to this initial series of pamphlets. The article was not, in fact, published in any of the other reviews edited by Ruge. According to Marx's account of it, it contained an attack on Hegel's theory of constitutional monarchy, which Marx regarded as a thoroughly self-contradictory and inconsistent hybrid. In the next letter, written a fortnight later, he describes his article as "the critique of Hegel's Philosophy of Law"; and he apologizes for the delay in sending it off, which, he says, was owing to unforeseen circumstances. As a matter of fact, something more than a year later, during the summer of 1843 which Marx spent in Kreuznach, he wrote an extensive article with the same title. This was obviously a new and more elaborate version of his earlier attempt. It is his intention, he says, to publish it in the *German-French Annals*, to be launched before very long in Paris. In the last months of 1843, Marx wrote an introduction to the article; which introduction was indeed published. The publication of the article itself was plainly adumbrated in this introduction. Of course, the collapse of the *German-French Annals* frustrated this project; but that was certainly not the only, nor even the most important, reason for the fact that it was never published—and for that matter never even completed. In his letter to Feuerbach of August 1844 Marx describes his "Introduction" as "referring to some elements of my critical philosophy of law, which I had already once completed but subsequently subjected to revision, with a view to making it generally understandable".

The year 1844 finds Marx at work on the so-called Parisian manuscripts, which remained unpublished until 1932, when they appeared under the title *Economic and Philosophical Manuscripts of the Year 1844.* In the draft preface Marx explains the basic reasons that have so far prevented him from publishing his *Critique of Hegel's Philosophy of Law.* When he was preparing the work for publication, it became apparent that a combination of the critique directed solely against the speculative theory with the critique of the various subjects would be quite unmanageable; it would hamper the development of the argument and make it more difficult to follow. Moreover, he could only have compressed such a wealth of diverse subjects into a single work by writing in an aphoristic style; and that would have given an impression of arbitrary systematization. It was therefore his intention to publish his critique of law, morals, politics, and so forth, in a number of separate brochures. Finally, he would attempt, in a separate work, to present the interconnected whole, to show the relationships between the parts, and to provide a critique of the speculative treatment of this material.

In the same draft preface Marx refers to the final chapter of the present work, a critique of Hegel's dialectic and general philosophy. He calls this "the necessary confrontation of the critique with its place of origin, Hegel's dialectic and German philosophy as a whole". Unlike the critical theologians such as Bruno Bauer and his fellow Young Hegelians, he considers such a critical approach to be absolutely essential; for the real task has not yet been accomplished. This lack of thoroughness is not accidental; for the critical theologian remains a theologian. Looked at more closely, theological critique, which at the beginning of the movement was a genuinely progressive factor, is seen in the last analysis to be no more than the culmination and consequence of the old philosophical, and especially Hegelian, transcendentalism, twisted into a theological caricature. He praises Feuerbach as the founder of a positive, humanistic and naturalistic critique. His writings are the only since Hegel's *Phenomenology and Logic* that contain a genuinely theoretical revolution.

Obviously, this concluding *Critique of the Hegelian dialectic and philosophy as a whole,* was designed by Marx as a first attempt to complete the critique of religion which, as he explained a year later in *The Holy Family,* had been provided with a blueprint in Feuerbach's critique of Hegelian speculation, in a word, of all metaphysics. Thus the three articles enshrining Marx's direct confrontation with Hegel, afford us an insight into the total context of his approach. First, it is noteworthy that of these only one has been published, namely, the *Introduction,* which in Marx's own opinion did little more than allude to some elements of his *Critique of Hegel's Philosophy of Law,* which article was never published in his lifetime, and was never even completed. The third treatise, which contains at least a first attempt to settle accounts with Hegelian speculation as a whole, not only remained unpublished and unfinished but, being one of the 1844 Parisian Manuscripts, was even lost to view until it was recovered in the present century. These facts not only mirror a typical feature of Marx's character, I mean, his endless self-criticism and restless creativity of mind; they also show how intense was his relationship to what he considered to be the womb and progenitor of his own thinking, the philosophy of Hegel. His relationship to Hegel's thinking was so much a part of the inner recesses of his mind and was so intimately involved in his most personal reflections that only with the most painful effort was he able to produce a few pages which he considered it worthwhile for a larger public to read.

Apart from that, the three articles on Hegel's philosophy also illuminate another important characteristic. The admixture of pure critique of Hegel's speculation as such and a critique of specific subjects treated by Hegel—an amalgam which Marx earnestly deplored in his *Critique of Hegel's Philosophy of Law*— was not an accidental, merely stylistic error. On the contrary, this strange mixture reflected an essential feature of Marx's approach. What he dreaded most of all was abstraction. It was on these grounds that he took exception to Bauer's critique. It was the ability to reject abstraction which, initially, fascinated him in Feuerbach's critique; and it was Feuerbach's inability really to overcome abstraction which in the end made him opposed to Feuerbach. It was the magic spell of Hegel's approach to concrete reality which, initially, captivated his mind; and it was Hegel's falling victim to the spell of his own abstractions that ultimately aroused the deepest resistance on Marx's part. But with Hegel philosophy had absorbed the world; and so it was impossible to criticize the world without at the same time criticizing philosophy. On the other hand, it proved impossible to criticize Hegel's speculation without at the same time criticizing the world which had fallen under Hegel's spell and had become part of his speculation. Marx was never able, therefore, to separate his critique of Hegel's speculation from his critical analysis of political reality. The Parisian Manuscripts of 1844 are an impressive illustration of this essential admixture. The *Critique of Hegelian dialectic and philosophy as a whole* is not only part of a manuscript which itself contains a unique mixture of political economy and philosophical anthropology but, although it was designed to be a concluding chapter, its content is strangely dispersed and disseminated among other passages in the Parisian Manuscripts. The Manuscripts as a whole are a challenge and a source of bewilderment to the analytic interpreter who tries to create a reasonable order out of the jigsaw puzzle Marx has left behind.

Recognition of the indissoluble unity of Marx's critique is an indispensable premise to any understanding of the relationship between its two dimensions. In this concluding lecture, which links up my first series on the critique of heaven with the second series dealing with the critique of earth, I must be content to illustrate this essential unity with some references to Marx's direct confrontation with Hegel. A closer analysis of Marx's writings of 1843 and 1844, which contain his direct critique of Hegel's philosophy, would go beyond the limited goal of this first series. The essential mixture of Marx's formal confrontation with Hegel's speculation and his material critique of Hegel's political philosophy forces the student of Marx's critique to move for an adequate analysis to the other dimension, the critique of earth. And so a rough sketch of the general context of Marx's critique of Hegel must suffice to conclude my first series of lectures.

We take as our starting-point the *Introduction to the critique of Hegel's Philosophy of Law*. Other documents—in the first instance the other two articles on Hegel's philosophy and, additionally, the writings of the two subsequent years—in so far as they can contribute to a better understanding, will be used as sources of interpretation.

The *Introduction* starts with a definition of the critique of religion. Its basic postulate is that man makes religion. Man here means the world of man, the state, society. This state, this society, produce religion, a perverted world-consciousness, because they constitute a perverted world. Marx then proceeds to enumerate various characteristic ways in which religion is the perverted world-consciousness of a perverted world. Religion is the general theory of that world, its encyclopaedic compendium, its logic in a popular form, its spiritual *point d'honneur*, and so forth. The passage finally reaches the conclusion that the struggle against religion is therefore indirectly the fight against that world, a world of which religion is the spiritual aroma.

The list of characteristics of religion enumerated by Marx is twice as long; but I have deliberately mentioned only the first half. For the description of religion as the general theory of a perverted world, its encyclopaedic compendium, its logic, contains a direct and unmistakable reference to Hegel's philosophy. The further remark that it is logic in a popular form is an allusion to Hegel's view of religion as a representation of absolute philosophical truth in a popular imaginative form. The fourth characteristic, that is, religion as the spiritual *point d'honneur*, is the link between the first run of characteristics, stressing the theoretical, philosophical aspect, and the second part of the list which summarizes the ethical and emotive elements in religion: religion as the enthusiasm of a perverted world, its moral sanction, its solemn completion, its universal ground for consolation and justification. The two distinct aspects are defined in an ensuing passage as spirit and heart: religion is the heart of a heartless world, just as it is the spirit of a spiritless situation. The latter expression recalls the central principle of Hegel's philosophy, whereas the former describes the emotive function of religion.

An essential element in Marx's description is that from the very outset his concern is focused on the relationship of religion and the world of man, state, society. This is the only relationship in which he is interested. Any other explanation of, for instance, religion as a psychological phenomenon, a process inside the human soul, a form of transempirical self-projection, is beside the specific point under discussion. In so far as religion has reality, albeit a perverted reality, it owes its reality to this world. Marx does not write a psychological or phenomenological treatise about the import of religion; but his description forms part of the *Introduction to a critique of Hegel's Philosophy of Law*. That implies two things. First, it means that the theme is the world of man, state and society. The second implication is that the subject of Marx's critique is the philosophy which claims to represent the spiritual completion of that world of man, its universal ground of justification. Hegel's philosophy claims to be the summary, the comprehension of the world. His *Logic,* far from being merely an analysis of the laws of human reason, is the logic of the world, just as his *Encyclopaedia* is the encyclopaedic compendium of that world.

An adequate understanding of Marx's critique of religion must start, therefore, from his critique of Hegel's philosophy as a whole. Marx's analysis can be summarized as follows. Hegel's *Encyclopaedia* begins with logic, with pure speculative thought, and ends with absolute knowledge, self-conscious and self-conceiving philosophical or absolute mind, that is to say, superhuman, abstract mind. The whole of the Encyclopaedia is nothing but the extended being of the philosophical mind, its self-objectification; and the philosophical mind is nothing but the mind of the alienated world, thinking within the confines of its self-alienation, that is, conceiving itself in an abstract manner. Likewise, Hegel's Logic is the currency of the mind, the speculative thought-value of man and of nature, their essence, unrelated to any real, determinate character, and thus unreal; thought which is alienated and abstract and ignores real nature and man. Finally, Hegel's spirit, this thought which returns to its own origin and which, as anthropological, phenomenological, psychological, customary, artistic-religious spirit, is not valid for itself until it discovers itself and relates itself to itself as absolute knowledge in the absolute (i.e. abstract) spirit, and so receives its conscious and fitting existence. For its real mode of existence is abstraction.

Marx tries to demonstrate that the way religion is absorbed in this concept is only one aspect of Hegel's spiritual comprehension of the total world of man. Feuerbach had shown that philosophy is nothing more than religion translated into thought and developed by thought, and that it is equally to be condemned as another form and mode of existence of human alienation. Hegel's dialectic begins from the infinite, the absolute and fixed abstraction, which is to say in ordinary language, from religion and theology. Secondly, he supersedes the infinite and posits the real, the perceptible, the finite and the particular; in other words, philosophy is posited as the supersession of religion and theology. Thirdly, he then supersedes the positive and re-establishes the abstraction, the infinite; in other words, the re-establishment of religion and theology. Thus self-conscious man, after superseding religion, when he has recognized religion as a product of self-alienation, then finds a confirmation of himself in religion as religion.

Marx calls this the root of Hegel's false positivism, or of his merely apparent critique. Whereas Feuerbach had launched his attack on Hegel's dialectic of positing, negating and re-establishing merely in so far as this concerned religion and theology, Marx looks at this in a more general way. In Hegel's philosophy, the same man, who has recognized that he leads an alienated life in law, politics, and so forth, leads his true human life in this alienated life as such. Reason is at home in unreason as such. Self-affirmation, in conflict with itself, in conflict with the knowledge and the nature of the object, is thus the true knowledge and life. In other words, the suggestion raised in Marx's dissertation that Hegel's so-called accommodation to the established situation is rooted in the nature of his philo-sophy, is found to be confirmed. There can no longer be any question about Hegel's compromise with religion, the state, and so on; for this error is the error of his whole argument.

In Hegel's dialectic the act of supersession plays a strange part, in that denial and preservation, denial and affirmation, are linked together. Marx illustrates this procedure with Hegel's Philosophy of Law: private law superseded equals morality, morality superseded equals the family, the family superseded equals civil society, civil society superseded equals the state and the state superseded equals world history. But in actuality private law, morality, the family, civil society, the state, etc. remain; only they have become "moments", modes of man's existence, which have no validity in isolation but which mutually dissolve and engender one another. They are moments of the movement. In their actual, existence this mobile nature is concealed. It is first revealed in thought, in philosophy; consequently, my true religious existence is my existence in the philosophy of religion, my true political exist-ence is my existence in the philosophy of law, and so on. In the one aspect, the existence which Hegel supersedes in philosophy is not therefore the actual religion, state, or nature, but religion itself as an object of knowledge, that is, dogmatics, and simi-larly with jurisprudence, political science, and natural science. From the other aspect, the religious man, for instance, can find in Hegel his ultimate confirmation.

The key to the mystery of Hegel's philosophy had already been found by Marx in the course of preparing for his dis-sertation. Discussing Plutarch's polemic aimed at Epicurus' sensualist philosophy, he accuses Plutarch of turning being and non-being into fixed predicates. Thus Plutarch tries to separate qualities which in the actuality of the senses are not separated. Marx concludes that the common way of thinking always has abstract predicates to hand, predicates which it separates from the subject. "All philosophers have turned the very predicates into subjects."

This discovery, at the moment of its formulation, was applied to Plutarch's misunderstanding of Epicurus which in Marx's view strikingly presented the relation of the theologizing intellect to philosophy. None the less, the formula is remarkable in two respects. First, it expresses the conviction that this particular case is more than an accidental feature of a thinker of the remote past; Marx's intuition claims to have traced a general characteristic. Secondly, though Plutarch is treated as a typical representative of theology as opposed to philosophy, it is not the theologians but the philosophers who are the subject of Marx's critique. Plutarch's theological relation to philosophy, which seemed to consist merely in a contrast between opposites, is revealed as bearing the seed of a profound congeniality. On closer analysis, philosophy turns out to conceal a theological kernel.

In this way, a fortuitous critique relating to a Greek theologian developed into a fundamental thesis that can be regarded as the cornerstone of Marx's critique of Hegel's philosophy and of metaphysics as a whole. It is this thesis which lies at the root of Marx's definition of religion as the general theory of a perverted world, its logic in a popular form. Religious man can find in Hegel his ultimate confirmation. Hegel's dialectic turns real man and real nature into mere predicates of a divine process which man's abstract, pure, absolute being, as distinguished from himself, traverses. Subject and object therefore have an inverted relation to each other. Hegel's Logic is the endless movement of a mystical subject-object; pure, unceasingly revolving upon itself; forms of thought, logical forms, which are detached from real spirit and real nature. Man alienated from himself is also the thinker alienated from his being, that is, from his natural and human life. Consequently, his thoughts are spirits existing outside nature and man. In his Logic Hegel has imprisoned all these spirits together. Just as Marx finds in Hegel's philosophy the culmination and final confirmation of religion, he is continually using a religious terminology for purposes of qualification. In his *Critique of Hegel's Philosophy of Law*, Marx even goes to the extreme of labelling Hegel's Logic a *Santa Casa*. This was the terrible name (*Santa Casa* means "Holy House") by which the Roman Catholic Inquisition in Madrid sanctified its prison as the place of its holy terrorism. The whole of Hegel's philosophy of law is exposed by Marx as an instance of logical, pantheistic mysticism, or in other words as a mere parenthesis of Hegel's Logic. The state serves as a test of the Logic.

This is demonstrated by Marx in various ways. First, Hegel's concept of the sovereignty of the state, embodied in the monarchy, is unmasked as a mystification. Hegel turns predicates into independent entities, and then allows them to be turned mystically into their own subjects. The sovereignty of the state exists as an abstract idea and is thereupon embodied in the monarch as the actual "God-man" (*Gott-mensch*). Hegel had compared this realization of the absolute concept of sovereignty in the corporeal existence of the monarch with the ontological proof of God's existence. Marx exposes it as the product of imagination, comparable to the dogma of the Immaculate Conception of the Virgin Mary. Secondly, Hegel's view of the relationship between the state and civil society is analysed as an outcome of his Logic. Hegel's concept of the state is a phantasmal abstraction which he turns into a mystical, absolute entity. Proceeding from this idea, which is in reality the predicate, Hegel changes the real subject, man, into the predicate of the state. Man is turned into the subjectified state. By the inversion of subject and predicate, therefore, Hegel turns the real relationship upside down. Marx launches against this procedure exactly the same critique as against religion. Man makes religion, religion does not make man; likewise, the people make the political constitution, that constitution does not make the people. As a matter of fact, during the Middle Ages the political constitution was the religious sphere, the religion of the ordinary life of the people, the heaven of its general essence, as contrasted with the earthly existence of its reality. Whereas, during the Middle Ages, this dualism was a real dualism, in modern times it has turned into an abstract dualism. Politics, once the religion of the ordinary life of the people, has changed to become the scholasticism of their life: for the political state has become an abstraction. Just as Christians are equal in heaven, unequal upon earth, so the individuals who make up the people are equal in the heaven of their political world, unequal in the earthly existence of civil society.

Hegel's recognition of the separation, in modern times, between state and civil society, was right: but he was misled by the theological structure of his philosophy and so mistook mere abstractions for realities. He described civil society as a *bellum omnium contra omnes*, as a "battlefield where everyone's individual, private interest clashes with everyone else's"; but he did not recognize that this applies merely to the abstract construct of a civil society, as distinct from an abstract political state. Therefore, like his philosophy of religion, Hegel's philosophy of law does not solve the problem but only dissolves it into a mystifying solution.

Thus Marx's thesis that religion is the logic of a perverted world is demonstrated in the political sphere, in that Hegel's concept of state and society turns out to be a direct result of his Logic. The thesis applies to the economic sphere as well. I have already mentioned Marx's description of Hegel's Logic as "the currency of the mind, the speculative thought-value of man and nature, their essence, unrelated to any real, determinate character, and thus unreal". This comparison between logic and money is more than an artistic metaphor; it has a fundamental bearing on Marx's concept of modern economic life. The phrase which associates logic with money is part of Marx's *Critique of Hegel's dialectic and philosophy as a whole* and can be regarded as a natural conclusion from the argument presented in the preceding pages of the *Economic and Philosophical Manuscripts*, of which this critique forms the concluding chapter. In that preceding section Marx had, conversely, equated money with logic.

Money, since it has the property of purchasing everything, of appropriating objects to itself, is therefore the object par excellence. The universal character of this property corresponds to the omnipotence of money, which is regarded as an omnipotent being . . . money is the procurer between need and object, between human life and the means of subsistence. But that

which makes a match between my life and my means of subsistence turns also the existence of other men into my means of
subsistence. It is, for me, the other person, Marx, then, referring to a passage in Shakespeare's *Timon of Athens*, points to two
properties of money, particularly emphasized by Shakespeare.
First, money is the visible deity, the transformation of all human
and natural qualities into their opposites, the universal confusion and inversion of things; it brings incompatibles into a
fraternal relationship. Secondly, it is the universal whore, the
universal procurer between men and nations. The power to
confuse and invert all human and natural qualities, to bring
about a conjunction of incompatibles, the divine power of
money, resides in its character as the alienated and self-alienating essence of the human species. It is the alienated power of
humanity.

But, as this alienated form of power, money is a genuinely
creative power. The difference between effective demand, supported by money, and ineffective demand, based upon my
need, my passion, my desire, and so on, is the difference between being and thought, between the merely inner representation and the representation which exists outside myself as a
real object. Money is the external, universal means and power
(not derived from man as man or from human society as
society) to change representation into reality and reality into
mere representation. It transforms real human and natural
faculties into mere abstract representations, that is, into imperfections and excruciating chimeras; but on the other hand it
transforms real imperfections and fancies, faculties which are
really impotent and exist only in the individual's imagination,
into real faculties and powers. In this respect, therefore, money
is the general inversion of individualities, turning them into
their opposites and associating contradictory qualities with their
qualities. Money, then, appears as a perverting power for the
individual and for the social bonds which claim to be self-
subsistent entities. It is the universal confusion and transposition of all things, the perverted world, the confusion and
transposition of all natural and human qualities.

Though it is beyond the scope of our theme, the "critique of
heaven", to analyse the function of these reflections within the
framework of the *Economic and Philosophical Manuscripts,* a few

references are indispensable. The heart of the analogy between money and religion lies in the dependence of both upon the alienated capacities of man. The power of money is a product of the modern science of asceticism, the science of political economy. The more you are able to save, the greater will become your treasure which neither moth nor rust can corrupt—your capital. The less you are, the less you express your life, the more you have, the greater is your alienated life and the greater is the conservation of your alienated being. Everything which the economist takes from you in the way of life and humanity he restores to you in the form of money and wealth: and everything which you are unable to do your money can do for you.

Marx's reference to the accumulation of capital as the paradoxical fulfilment of Jesus' commandment, given in the Sermon on the Mount, should not be reduced to something like an ironic comment on Christian hypocrisy, but has to be taken literally. The power of money as the visible deity of modern society literally creates a "heaven" above the sphere of real human life, a "heaven" where neither moth nor rust consumes. The modern worker is an ascetic but productive slave. He is related to the product of his labour as to an alien object. The more the worker expends himself in work, the more powerful becomes the world of objects which he creates facing himself, the poorer he becomes in his inner life, and the less he belongs to himself. It is just the same with religion. The more of himself man attributes to God, the less he has left in himself. The worker puts his life into the object; and his life then belongs no longer to himself but to the object. The greater his activity, therefore, the less he possesses. What is embodied in the product of his labour is no longer his own. The greater his product is, therefore, the more he is diminished. The alienation of the worker in his product means not only that his labour becomes an object, assumes an external existence, but that it exists independently, outside himself, and alien to him, and that it stands opposed to him as an autonomous power. The life which he has given to the object sets itself up against him as an alien and hostile force.

These reflections read like an exegesis of Jesus' warning, "For where your treasure is, there will your heart be also", and they serve, in fact, as a literal interpretation. It is therefore not amazing that the economic theory of this alienated way of life, the science of political economy, is compared to theology. Marx's critique is, essentially, launched against the abstract procedure of modern economic science. Political economy begins with the fact of private property; it does not explain it. It conceives of the material process of private property, as this occurs in reality, in general and abstract formulas which then serve it as laws. It does not comprehend these laws; that is, it does not show how they arise out of the nature of private property. The only moving forces which political economy recognizes are avarice and the war between the avaricious, competition. It fails to grasp the real connection between this whole system of alienation and the system of money. The economist begins his explanation from a legendary, primordial condition. Such a primordial condition does not explain anything; it merely removes the question to a grey and nebulous distance. It asserts as a fact or event what it should deduce, namely the necessary relation between two things; for example, between the division of labour and exchange. In the same way, theology explains the origin of evil by the fall of man; that is, it asserts as a historical fact what it should explain.

This close analogy between the abstract methodology of economic science and theology is also illustrated with reference to the doctrine of the unity of labour and capital. Society, as it appears to the economist, is civil society, in which each individual is a totality of needs and only exists for another person, as another exists for him, in so far as each becomes a means for the other. The economist (like politics in its human rights) reduces everything to man, that is, to the individual, whom he deprives of all characteristics in order to classify him as a capitalist or a worker. Marx enumerates seven ways in which the economist establishes the unity of labour and capital, the final way being his postulating the original unity of capital and labour as the unity of capitalist and worker. "This," Marx concludes, "is the original paradisal condition."

Time and again Marx refers to this analogous methodology. Having demonstrated private property to be the basis and cause of alienated labour, he concludes that, in fact, the order is just the other way round: private property is, in reality, not the cause but the consequence of alienated labour, just as the gods are fundamentally not the cause but the product of confusions of human reason. At a later stage, however, there is a reciprocal influence.

Finally, I would point to the parallel drawn between Luther and Adam Smith. The comparison is derived from Friedrich Engels, who in his draft of a critique of political economy, published not long before in the *Deutsch-Französische Jahrbücher*, had called Adam Smith "the Luther of political economy". The analogy is taken up by Marx and further elaborated by him. Just as Luther recognized religion and faith as the essence of the real world, and for that reason took up a position against Catholic paganism; just as he annulled external religiosity while making religiosity the inner essence of man; just as he negated the distinction between priest and layman by transferring the priest into the heart of the layman; so wealth external to man and independent of him (and thus only to be acquired and conserved from outside) is annulled. That is to say, its external and mindless objectivity is annulled by the fact that private property is incorporated in man himself, and man himself is recognized as its essence. But as a result, man himself is placed in the determination of private property, just as, with Luther, he is placed in the determination of religion. Thus, in the view of this enlightened political economy which has discovered the subjective essence of wealth within the framework of private property, the partisans of the monetary system, and the mercantilist system, who consider private property as a purely objective being for man, are fetishists and Catholics.

This reference to fetishism is taken up once again in a later chapter. The nations which are still dazzled by the sensuous glitter of precious metals, and who thus remain fetishists of metallic money, are not yet fully developed monetary nations. The extent to which the solution of a theoretical problem is a task of practice, and is accomplished through practice, and the extent to which correct practice is the condition of a true and positive theory is shown, for example, in the case of fetishism. The sense perception of a fetishist differs from that of a Greek because his sensuous existence is different. The abstract hostility between sense and spirit is inevitable so long as the human sense of nature, or the human import of nature, and consequently the natural sense of man, has not been produced by man's own labour.

The parallelism is further complicated by the contrast between England as the fully developed monetary nation and France as a nation which has not yet overcome the fetishism of metallic money. The article by Friedrich Engels which served as a source of the parallel between Luther and Adam Smith may also serve as a source of interpretation, in that Engels explicitly refers to the progress engendered by the Protestant environment of Adam Smith, in contrast with Catholic countries which lagged behind.

It is interesting, though hardly surprising, to find these complications recurring in Marx's *Introduction to a critique of Hegel's Philosophy of Law*, which was published in the very period when he was writing the *Philosophical and Economic Manuscripts*. On the one hand, Luther's historical rôle is recognized as the carrying out of a theoretical revolution, namely, the Reformation. As the revolution then began in the mind of the monk, so now it begins in the mind of the philosopher. If Protestantism was not the true solution of the problem, it was at least the true posing of it. On the other hand, the deplorable backwardness of Germany, as compared with France and England, is likened to the stage of fetishism. Germany will one day find itself in the phase of European decadence before ever having been through that of European emancipation. It will be like a fetish worshipper pining away with the diseases of Christianity.

If these examples illustrate the key function of a metaphor like the term "fetishism" as the point of association between the religious, political and economic planes, one further—and final—example may serve to illustrate this multilateral symbolism from a different point of view. The metaphor in question relates to the term "procurer", which serves as a nodal point for various trends in Marx's thinking. We have just encountered this term in the above-mentioned passage from the *Philosophical and Economic Manuscripts*, which defines money as "the procurer between need and object, between human life and the means of subsistence", and again as "the universal whore, the universal procurer between men and nations", in short, as the visible deity, the universal inversion of things.

Before we consider the specific function of this term, "procurer", it should be noticed that in the same passage money is called both "the perverting power" and "the perverted world". Its divine power resides in its character as the alienated and self-alienating essence of the human species. These definitions remind one very strongly of parallel definitions in the *Introduction to the critique of Hegel's Philosophy of Law*, which describe religion as "a perverted world-consciousness", produced by "a perverted world", and as a phantasmal realization of the human essence.

A second noteworthy point is the definition with which this paragraph on money is introduced. It is pointed out that man's feelings, passions, and so forth, are not merely anthropological characteristics in the narrower sense, but true, ontological affirmations of being (nature), in a word, that they are only really affirmed in so far as their object exists as an object of sense. This ontological definition of man's nature must be understood in close connection with Marx's approach to the ontological proof of God's existence, which has already been discussed in an earlier lecture. Just as the Christian God and the pagan gods have a real existence, being the real objects and powerful products of man's creative imagination, so is money a visible deity, and so is the state a visible deity. Their divine power is not merely an anthropological characteristic, but is derived from the ontological character of human nature, of which it is the perverted realization.

With these definitions in mind, we turn now, at last, to the function of the term "procurer". In a passage of *The Holy Family* which has already been quoted in an earlier lecture, Marx refutes the contention that the state holds together the atoms of civil society, declaring that the members of that society are held together by the fact that they are atoms only in the imagination, in the heaven of their fantasy, whilst in reality they are vastly different from atoms, being not divine egoists, but egoistic human beings. This human egoism, which is the perverted and alienated form of man's real, sensible nature, is the force which pulls the members of civil society out of their imagined atomic essence into the reality of their human, earthly, sensible needs. In this way, Marx declares, be it only by his profane stomach which reminds him of a world outside himself, every individual is forced to become, so to speak, a procurer between his alien need and the object of his need.

To sum up, the members of civil society, living in a perverted self-consciousness which makes them believe in themselves as immortal, self-sufficient atoms, are forced by their profane dependence on the real world outside themselves to become procurers functioning as a perverted match-maker that restores the link between the real world and themselves, a link which their atomistic self-deception had tried to destroy. Of course, the perversion of a perversion is not the same thing as the restoration of true reality; but as counter to a perverted imagination, this procurer does an indispensable service.

In this context it is understandable that Marx should call this reciprocal procurer-function, which holds the members of civil society together, "a real bond". Its relative reality is the medium between two illusions. On the one side, the illusion that civil society resembles the world of eternal atoms. On the other, the political supposition that civil life must be held together by the state, whilst the truth is that the state is held together by civil life.

However, this "real bond" which holds the members of civil society together is only a relative reality, is the perversion of a perversion, is the sort of bond created by a procurer. The critique of this double perversion is the task of the critique of law, which is the necessary corollary and outcome of the critique of religion.

Thus his analysis of Epicurus' atomistic philosophy brought Marx to the very point where the critique of theology turns into the critique of politics. For as we have already pointed out, the contradictions which he discovered in Epicurus' philosophy are the very contradictions that dominate the political and economic philosophy of civil society. As it turns out, Epicurus' philosophy proves to be a prototype of the modern mind.

To be sure, Epicurus remained Marx's life-long companion, and in a sense, his double. Epicurus' career in this respect is a remarkable one. In the very earliest of Marx's writings we encounter Epicurus as an enemy of the Christian faith, in the defence of which Marx pens his religious composition for the finals of the high school, under the title *The Union of Believers with Christ*. The composition leads up to the conclusion that "union with Christ affords a joy which is sought in vain by the Epicurean in his superficial philosophy".

Next, at the outset of his academic studies in Berlin, Marx undergoes a radical conversion; the holy curtain has been rent in twain, the gods have descended into the very centre of the earth. Epicurus, the greatest Greek representative of Enlightenment, is now his hero. Although the dissertation was not written as a specifically anti-Christian treatise, one cannot ignore the vein of polemics running through it. The most explicit and direct attack is directed against a Father of the church, Clement of Alexandria, who re-interpreted St. Paul's warning against philosophy in general as an admonition against Epicurean philosophy in particular. Clement's re-interpretation is centred on Paul's exhortation (Colossians 2: 8): "See to it that no one makes a prey of you by philosophy and empty deceit, according to human tradition, according to the elemental spirits of the universe, and not according to Christ". Apart from the fact that Epicurean philosophers are mentioned in the Acts of the Apostles as having disputed with Paul in Athens (Acts 17: 18), Clement's basic argument centres on Paul's particular mention of the "elemental spirits of the universe"; which leads Clement to aver that in admonishing us against philosophy Paul must have had Epicurean philosophy especially in mind.

Against the background of our analysis of Marx's dissertation it is worthwhile, in conclusion, to take another look at this part of the argument. The term "elemental spirits of the universe" is a translation of the Greek *stoicheion*. This term indeed plays a rôle in Epicurus' philosophy. As I have already pointed out, Marx pays special attention to Epicurus' peculiar distinction between the atom as *arche* and as *stoicheion*—a distinction closely akin to that between form and matter, between essence and existence. It is the atom as *stoicheion* which comes into manifest existence, in contrast to the atom as *arche*, which remains concealed in the realm of pure, ideal essence. Whilst as *stoicheion*, that is, as having appeared in the world of material phenomena, the atom is alienated from its essence, it is only from this *stoicheion* that the world of appearance can proceed. Epicurus—so Marx concludes—in distinguishing between *arche* and *stoicheion*, has grasped the contradiction between essence and existence at its finest point.

As a matter of fact, this is precisely the same contradiction which we have just noted in Marx's peculiar use of the term "procurer". Just as the atom in its ideal, eternal essence, that is, as *arche*, is the product of self-idolizing imagination, fostered by the individual members of civil society, so the qualified atom, i.e., as *stoicheion*, the atom alienated from its eternal essence, constitutes the real world, where the repulsion between the individual atoms of civil society creates the sensible, material life of society. However, this contradiction, being the perverted consciousness of a perverted world, can be overcome only in a perverted and perverting manner, i.e., by a procurer.

St. Paul's warning is directed against idolization of the *stoicheia*, which are deified as elemental spirits of the universe, instead of Christ in whom the fullness of deity dwells bodily. Clement's comment interprets this apostolic warning as being directed against Epicurean or any other philosophy which "does not imagine the Creator". The verb "to imagine", in Greek, *phantazein*, which is used by Clement to denote the spiritual, creative power of faith, is interpreted by Marx in an opposite sense. Ironically, he praises Clement for rejecting those philosophers who did not invent phantasies about God. This ironic reversal of the meaning of the term conceals, however, a deeper issue. Against the background of the question of human imagination which, as I have explained, is a basic one in Marx's critique of heaven, his irony discloses a fundamental critique.

Marx's next comment on Clement's re-interpretation is to the effect that we in our time have a more adequate understanding of Paul's admonition, since we know that it applies, in fact, to all philosophers. This comment appears in a fresh light, when related to the fundamental critique aimed at the philosophers by Marx himself. We may recall the parallel, drawn in an earlier lecture, between the stories respectively of St. Paul's and of Karl Marx's conversion. To sum up the implications of what I have just been saying, there would seem to be good reasons for suggesting that paradoxically, Marx's conversion has something to do with St. Paul's warning against philosophy.

However that may be, Epicurus is the central actor in this drama. The next stage of his career is his apparent disappearance. In Marx's work subsequent to his dissertation, Epicurus seems to have vanished completely. In fact, he had simply gone beneath the surface. For Marx's critique of civil society, his critique of law, in a word, the critique of political economy which preoccupied him for the rest of his life, is to be understood as a struggle with the very contradictions which Epicurus had laid bare, without being able to overcome them.

Epicurus had disappeared from view, from the surface, in Marx's public writings, but not in his more intimate, private life. The day after Marx's death, which occurred on March 14, 1883, his friend Friedrich Engels brought Epicurus once more on to the stage and paid him, vicariously, a posthumous homage. Writing to a friend with an account of Marx's final hours, Engels rejoices that Marx had not been condemned to drag out the life of a helpless invalid. "With Epicurus, he was wont to say that death was no misfortune for him who died, but for those who survived. And to see this great genius lingering on as a physical wreck, to the greater glory of medicine and the mockery of the Philistines whom he so often flayed in the prime of his life, no, a thousand times better as it is, a thousand times better that we carry him to the grave where his wife lies."

Thus it was that as Epicurus had been the hero of his youth, so now he accompanied him to his grave. The grave is the place where we return to the earth that gave us birth. It is also the place of resurrection.